NEW COLLEGE

NEW COLLEGE

Edited by
Christopher Tyerman

THIRD MILLENNIUM
PUBLISHING, LONDON

©2010 New College, Oxford and Third Millennium Publishing Limited

First published in 2010 by Third Millennium Publishing Limited,
a subsidiary of Third Millennium Information Limited.

2–5 Benjamin Street
London
United Kingdom
ECIM 5QL
www.tmiltd.com

ISBN 978 1 906507 21 3

British Library Cataloguing in Publication Data:
A CIP catalogue record for this book is available from the British Library.

Edited by Chistopher Tyerman
Designed by Matthew Wilson
Production by Bonnie Murray
Reprographics by Studio Fasoli, Italy
Printed by Printer Trento, Italy

Dust jacket reverse main: *New College as viewed by David Loggan, c.1670.*

Dust jacket reverse inset: *The New College Jewel, also known as the Annunciation Jewel, or the 'M' Jewel, late 14th century.*

Endpapers: *New College from a vantage point between Mansfield and Parks Roads, by Philip Le Cave, c.1790.*

Above: *One of the New College gargoyles, carved during the 1950s and 1960s by Michael Groser as replacements for the worn medieval sculptures.*

Opposite (top right) and throughout the book: *detail from the study for the nave windows on the chapel, by Biaggio Rebecca, c.1774.*

CONTENTS

Foreword   6

PART 1 / **COLLEGE BUILDINGS**   8
A walk through William of Wykeham's Foundation 10

PART 2 / **COLLEGE HISTORY**   24
The Founder 26 / The Foundation and the Medieval College 30 /
The Reformation to Reform *c.*1530–1850 38 / The Modern
College since 1850 46 / College and University 54

PART 3 / **COLLEGE LIFE**   58
Religion 60 / Learning 64 / Teaching 72 / Music 76 / Gardens 82 /
College Estates 90 / Art 94 / Archives 98 / Books 102 /
The Life of a Don 104 / Sport 108 / The College at War 114

PART 4 / **COLLEGE PEOPLE**   126
Wardens 128 / College Servants 140 / College Leaders 146 /
Rogues and Eccentrics 152 / Public Figures – Church 158 /
Public Figures – State 166 / Authors 176 / Contemporary
New College Writing 182

Endword   188
Wardens of New College   189
List of Contributors and Reading List   190
List of Subscribers   191
Index   196
Acknowledgements   200

FOREWORD

The landscape of English culture is littered with
venerable institutions, deceptive witnesses to
apparent social stability and historical continuity. Oxford
and its university houses more than its share of such
monuments to adaptability, none more luminous or
remarkable than New College; and none more teasingly
misleading. Although novel in its fourteenth-century
concept, form and substance, from the start it was called
new only because it shared a dedication to the Virgin
Mary with an existing college, also known by its nickname,
Oriel. Physically, New College appears medieval; yet most
of its buildings have either been subsequently tampered
with, some almost out of recognition, or actually date
from much later periods. Proud of its Founder, whose
image inescapably peeps down from stone, glass and
painting, its modern constitution is almost exclusively a
product of nineteenth century earnestness and modern
inclusiveness, not of the original stern medieval piety
of William of Wykeham. Like other mature creations,
New College is a palimpsest of a varied, uneven past, yet
animated by a current vivacity.

The nature of all institutions, particularly those
in part dedicated to educating youth, is determined by
their people. Consequently the experience of such places
remains at once abiding and evanescent. There is no fixed
essence for historians, observers or even members to
capture, only patterns and relics, lasting monuments and
personal memories. This book seeks to express in words
and pictures something of the richness of the college's
past and present, the variety, contingency, tradition and
transience, the fleeting and the marmoreal, set in its

physical frame of such indelible beauty. This is not a
formal academic history and does not attempt to replace or
subvert the history published in 1979, *New College, Oxford
1379 to 1979*, edited by John Buxton and Penry Williams.
However, that appeared over thirty years ago to coincide
with the six hundredth anniversary and the admission of
women as junior members, a moment of completion and
beginning. There is always more to be said.

I am more than grateful to those colleagues and old members who have been so generous of their time, skills, imaginations and intellects to say it. The initiative of Richard Compton Miller prompted the idea for such a book. Without the co-operation and tolerance of the college community it could not have been brought to fruition. Especial mention and tribute must be made to Jennifer Thorp, the College Archivist, indefatigably patient, helpful and resourceful in meeting contributors' demands and amending their deficiencies. Successive wardens have lent their support both generally and specifically: Alan Ryan as contributor; Curtis Price as constructive reader of the draft typescript. Without the labours of Maggie Davies, in particular on collating the images, it is hard to imagine how the work could have been put together. As will be apparent from his contributions, Will Poole is a living college lexicon, his massive yet lightly-worn erudition only matched by his selfless enthusiasm which energised the scheme at an early stage. The task of editing has been rendered both a pleasure and a possibility by the patience and professionalism of Chris Fagg and his team at Third Millennium who have coped with academics' amateurism and idiosyncratic sense of time with exemplary understanding and patience. Without Michael Burden's Herculean efforts in suggesting, collecting, assessing and collating the pictures, this would not have been an illustrated volume, or, indeed, any volume at all. His high standards, taste, expertise and unrivalled knowledge of the college's chattels, pictures and artefacts are evident on every page; the value of his contribution throughout has been incalculable. To all who have helped to produce this book, and who have made the process and my part in it so painlessly enjoyable, I offer deep thanks.

Christopher Tyerman
Oxford, June 2010

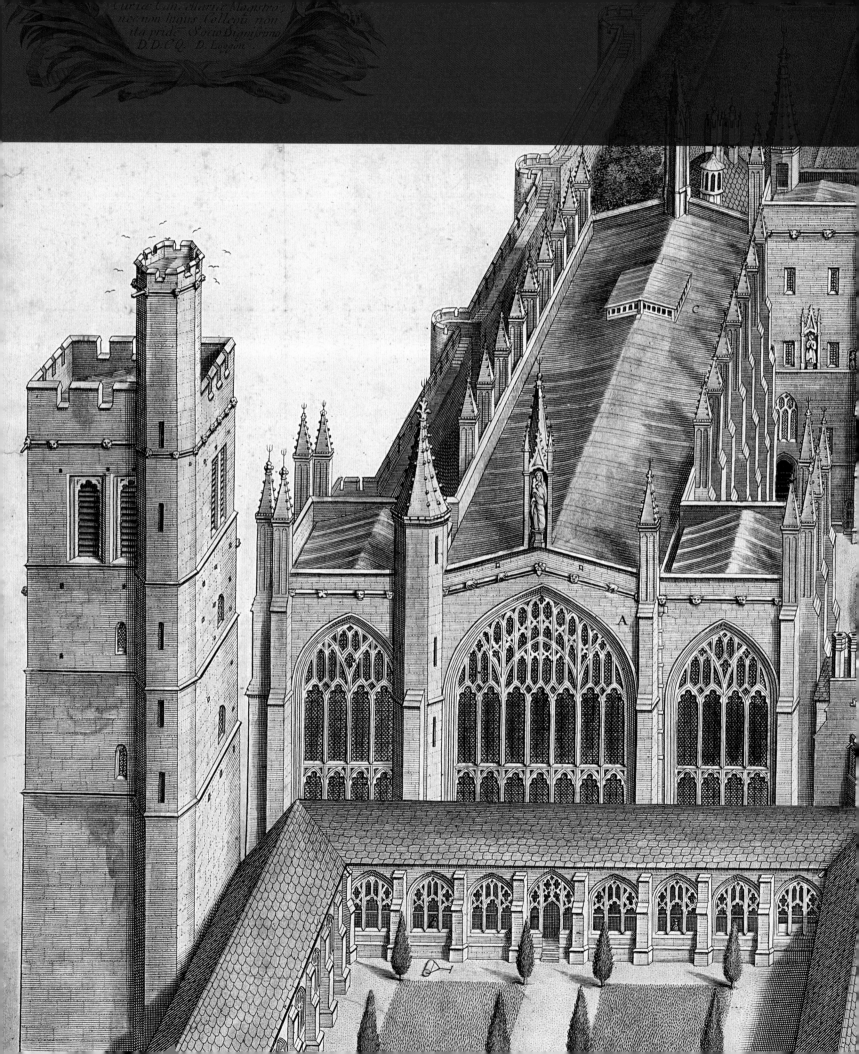

A. *Capella*
B. *Bibliotheca*
C. *Refectorium*
D. *Custodis Hospitiū*

A Walk through William of Wykeham's Foundation

MICHAEL BURDEN

Coming down New College Lane to the original entrance of William of Wykeham's foundation, leads the flâneur under Hertford College's Bridge of Sighs, past a small group of eighteenth-century houses, then between the walls of the New College Warden's Barn to the right, and the Cloisters to the left, to the tower of the New College Lane gateway. This is the first of the college's four towers – the New College Lane gateway, the Bell Tower, the Muniment Tower and the Robinson Tower – all offering different perspectives on the college and its purpose. Looming over New College Lane, the tower of the New College gateway is the work of William Wynford, a stonemason, working closely with Hugh Herland and perhaps Henry Yevele, and has always been part of the Warden's Lodgings. Its panelled Tower Room looks, Janus-like, into New College Lane to the west, and into Front Quad to the east. When this was the only entrance to the foundation, any warden could thus monitor the comings and goings of college members. Wykeham did not leave surveillance there either; there was – and is – still provision for the warden to see from the Lodgings' oratory into the Ante-chapel to see who was – and who was not – attending the routine of services in the chapel, then celebrated as a full office.

The tower served as the college's front entrance until 1983, when the Lodge was finally given up, and the focus of arrival moved to Holywell Street, and to the Robinson Tower, a late nineteenth-century Gothic revival tower by

Basil Champneys, an architect of some competence. While often regretted, the move was inevitable; the medieval charm of New College Lane that has made it a beloved film location, has also made it impractical to any visitors other than those on foot or bicycle. The process was in fact

ELEVATION

Left: *The windows designed by R. Fielding Dodd in 1947 for the New College gateway, and inserted in the Tower Room on the New College Lane side only.*

Opposite: *New College Lane gate, with Warden Fisher's hatchment, by Randolph Schwabe, 1940.*

started in the eighteenth century. To allow for the building of the final two pavilions of Garden Quad in 1700 and 1707, the entrance to the college from Queen's Lane was closed. The college then built a causeway across the dry moat linking the Slype to Holywell Street, and demolished part of the bastion in the kitchen yard to construct the gateway there that we know today. As a final touch, the college added the still-extant pair of substantial gates with a wicket, for this was still the outside boundary of the college.

The nineteenth-century buildings of Holywell Street – New Buildings and the Pandy – were not, of course, yet a glimmer in the college's eye. When they were, it was part of New Buildings that appeared first, constructed along Holywell Street on the far side of the dry moat, using land acquired from Merton. As designed by George Gilbert Scott, they were, in their original form, a sensible and low-rise group of gothic-revival staircases; as built, they were, after the intervention of the college, of monolithic appearance and lumpen aspect. Indeed, the design was described by one fellow as being 'the most trumpery office work'. Built in two stages – the first phase, next to the present Lodge, was begun in 1872,

Above: *Robinson Tower, 2010.*

Left: *The first and unrealised design by George Gilbert Scott for New Buildings, c.1870.*

New College. Old City Walls from the "Slipe" July 10 - 1906 Oxford.

Above: The Bell Tower, Hall, and city walls from the Robinson Tower entrance, in a postcard dated 1906.

the second completed in 1877 – they are partly shorn of Scott's detailing and a storey too tall, and, as a group of buildings, are only made acceptable through age and sentimentality. The second phase was less disastrous than the first – although it did attract the critical notice of the daughter of Bishop Lloyd, who noted '6 old Houses demolished by greedy New Coll: to make way for a useless *married* Tutor's House' – being saved from complete banality by a more varied facade and exterior ornamentation. By the time it came to build the Pandy, the college's connections with the Scott family – father George Gilbert Scott, and son John Oldrid Scott – had come to an end. In any case, Scott senior was by this time dead, and the foundation turned to Basil Champneys, who developed a sensitive and attractive design for staircases and a tutor's house, a building so well-mannered that its large size is not immediately apparent. The style – described as 'Tudor domestic' with touches of Arts and Crafts – was, at the college's request, in deliberate contrast to Scott's Gothic revival. These two ranges – the

plain, oversized New Buildings, and the well-detailed Pandy – formed a grotesque architectural mis-match, and the later Robinson Tower (plus two staircases which connected to Champneys' first building) is a neat, if not entirely elegant, solution to the problem that confronted the architect. The move to build the tower came, in fact, from a desire to honour Bursar Arthur Robinson, who had in effect run the college during the latter years of Warden Sewell's long incumbency.

Despite their superficial differences, both Wynford's and Champneys' lodges have much in common; they are both vaulted passage ways, and they are both fronted by large gates with wickets. And in contrast to say Trinity College and Christ Church where everything is laid out before the visitor, or the Turl Street colleges which offer only short views from their gates, the views into New College promise the traveller hidden architectural glories. From the Robinson Tower gate, the view is short, but before the visitor is the expanse of the City Wall, and behind it, the still-used, pitched-roofed, medieval kitchen, the chapel, Hall and Bell Tower, an impressive sweep only (but constantly) spoiled by the college's parking arrangements. From New College Lane gate, the view stretches across Front Quad down to the fabulous 1711 black and gilded screen by Thomas Robinson, through its gate, and on up to the sixteenth-century Mound.

The Mound, which closes the eastward view from the Garden Quad, was begun in 1529, and was finally 'perfected with stepps of Stone and setts for ye Hedges about ye Walke' in 1649. As Loggan's engraving shows, not only was the Mound itself formalised, but had laid out before it a formal Baroque garden, the outline of which can still be seen at the end of extended periods of dry weather. Like many Baroque gardens, some of its elements are in doubtful taste; the seventeenth-century floral sundial would, for example, be unlikely to be considered desirable today. The more recent steps up the Mound take the traveller to a point above the city wall, and its function as a viewing platform is still efficiently demonstrated, despite offering only short views through large trees. The view back towards Garden Quad exposes one of Oxford's great optical tricks; no side of the Quad is quite parallel, no line focussed on a single central point, and the whole illusion is topped off by Thomas Robinson's screen of 1711, the curves of which are adjusted to disguise the asymmetry of the architecture in such a way as to disguise its own asymmetry.

The New College Lane entrance also looks across Front Quad to the Hall stairs that draw the eye to the Muniment Tower, one of the most fascinating structures in the New College group. The tower's impact was somewhat reduced in 1674–5 when the Front Quad's third storey and crenellated parapet were added, probably to the design of William Byrd with the work being carried out by Richard Frogley; some of its visual consequence was returned when a version of the seventeenth-century sundial was restored to its south face in 2000. The appearance of Front Quad – and indeed, the first section of Garden Quad – after these additions and alterations was (as is now) slightly overbearing, but was at least homogenous; the medieval fenestration and the stone mullions were continued on the new third floor, and the crenellations were carried through to the new buildings in Garden Quad. But by the end of the eighteenth century, the windows in Front Quad had been largely sashed, and today it sports a wide range of sash styles; indeed, it has been said by architectural geeks that the history of the English glazing bar is written in New College.

The Muniment Tower was intended by the Founder to house the college's plate and the college records, and its four levels are stone vaulted and floored with contemporary glazed tiles with patterns that include English roses and the college's arms. The tower today still fulfills precisely its original functions, even if those functions take place on different floors to those specified by Wykeham.. The lowest floor contains the college's medieval and Renaissance plate, objects which include the Founder's ring and mitre, the College Seal and the

annunciation jewel. The first floor holds a large collection of post-Restoration plate, housed in a large Strawberry Hill-style gothic cabinet. Entering the upper floors via the internal stone spiral staircase is a rather *Name of the Rose* experience; old (if not original) presses and chests still contain the college plans, rent rolls, and the College Statutes.

Emerging from the top of the Muniment Tower staircase onto the roof of the Hall is an exhilarating experience. Close by is the top of the tower itself, decorated with a number of gargoyles sculpted – as are most of the rest of the college's – by Michael Groser. Two of those are among the most beguiling of the whole collection. One of these is a mermaid holding out a mirror and combing her hair. The other is the sculptor, sculpting his own face, his hands, hammer and chisel permanently suspended in completing his own visage, suggesting that the gargoyles, like the college buildings, will never be finished. In front, is the Hall's large low-rise lead roof, now sporting a newly reconstructed lantern, one of the

Below: The Muniment Tower, during the Gaude, by Clifford Bayly, 2003.

Right: *The Hall as Samuel Wyatt left it, by Joseph Nash, 1858.*

Below right: *The Hall (as proposed by George Gilbert Scott c.1858) with Wyatt's alterations swept away, realised by 1865.*

results of the Hall's restoration in 2003; this saw the nineteenth-century windows re-leaded and double-glazed, the sixteenth-century panelling rehung, and the installation of a hot water under-floor heating system. George Gilbert Scott was responsible for the fabulous reconstruction of the medieval Hall roof in the early 1860s; in fact, in 1857 the Junior Members had offered £1,000 (if the college would match it) to do the job. The college refused, but when the offer was renewed in 1859, it was accepted. The timber, felled from 1859, was grown on college land, the last tree being the king oak felled at Akeley in the presence of the Senior Fellow on 8 May 1862. Scott also specified the stained glass windows, removed the eighteenth-century fireplace (and replaced it with a gas burner and stove) and, a particular detail close to Scott's heart, reconstructed the medieval window embrasures. Some work was done on the panelling at this time; John Chapman added some coats of arms to those already set in the linen fold, and an emblazoner, improbably named 'Buggins', was paid £132 to spruce up some of the others, but it was not until the end of the nineteenth century that the tan-coloured paint was removed. The panelling was

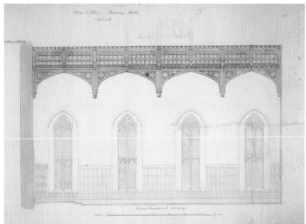

a gift to the college from Archbishop Warham in about 1520, but the recent work suggests that some of it is earlier, possibly dating back to 1490, and originally hung in a venue other than New College.

Across the Hall roof can be seen the much steeper pitched roof of the chapel, an architectural faux pas committed by the college a few years later. Indeed, it is hard to believe that the designer of the Hall as we know it today was also responsible; he not only introduced the

Above: *The Ante-chapel during the Regency, with Reynolds's window in its original form, by Thomas Malton, 1803.*

Left: *As recorded by J.M.W. Turner in 1798–1800: Wyatt's case with Samuel Green's organ, showing the design that allowed the Reynolds window to be viewed from the nave.*

Right: *The door to the roof of the Bell Tower, by Hort New, 1907.*

ahistorical hammer-beam roof, but destroyed the original roof line with its dramatic double row of crocketed pinnacles that, until then, had stood in unbroken silhouette against the sky. But as in the case of Scott's New Buildings, it was, however, the interference of the college in the architect's designs that produced the result. Scott presented three different designs to the college, and the vote led to the selection of the pitched design. The interior of the chapel had been thoroughly overhauled by Wyatt in the eighteenth century, when plaster vaulting, a plaster reconstruction of the reredos, and the marble floor were installed. Wyatt's plaster fantasies were swept away by Scott, who then constructed an interior of natural materials – wood and stone – while retaining the medieval and eighteenth-century glass, monuments and ante-chapel stalls. But the interior is, perhaps fortunately, not quite as Scott would have had it; had the college not run out of money, much of the panelling and the statues of the reredos would have appeared as a polychrome nod to the pre-Reformation Church in England.

The chapel abuts the cloisters, one of the greatest outdoor spaces in the whole of Oxford. Begun in 1397, the land they occupy was a 1389 purchase by William of Wykeham, and their building involved the diversion of New College Lane into its current dog-leg form. The land was – and remains – a burial ground, constructed under the papal bull of 1389, which also included the right to erect a bell tower. Entering the cloisters with its soaring beams and stone-slated roof, is to see the history of the college writ in stone, with tablets to members whose roles include those of warden, archivist, and organist, and professions, those of journalist, author, and teacher. The larger-than-life medieval (and later) sculptures from the University Church, transferred to the college after they were removed from the building in the nineteenth century, provide a sense of

scale to what is in fact an extremely large space. The fact that the cloisters are not a thoroughfare gives them a peace that might otherwise be lacking. The huge oak tree, of apparent antiquity but in fact only planted in the nineteenth century, can be seen in all stages of growth in photographs and postcards, and is now known to a generation of school children as 'Harry Potter's tree'; in the movie version of *Harry Potter and the Goblet of Fire*, Draco Malfoy climbed it to taunt Potter and was transformed into a bouncing ferret by Mad-Eye Moody.

The building of the bell tower, which opens from the cloisters, also involves another first, one of the earliest documented references to a crane used in its construction: 'a great wheel… and a large cable to run over a wheel for elevating the stone and timber'. Completed in 1403, it has been a feature of Oxford's skyline ever since. It is built on one of the bastions of the City Wall (after extended and probably tedious negotiations with the town), and now houses part of the library collections, as well as the clock and the college's peal. As recorded variously by Loggan in his 1675 engraving and by Dorothy Sayers in her 1935 novel *Gaudy Night*, it was for much of its existence also the home of a storytelling of rooks. Like the Muniment Tower, the ascent to the top (past the ringing, clock and peal chambers) is an exhilarating experience, and the views of the college from the top breathtaking. To the north, almost at one's feet, is the Memorial Library, started in 1938 to a design by Hubert Worthington, an example of a slightly affected 1930s Baroque, but with an attractive interior kitted out by Heals. Next to that is the row of largely eighteenth-century lath-and-plaster cottages, known collectively as the 'Holywell Cottages', but used as student residences and guest rooms. Mostly of uncertain origin, one pair was demolished to enable the construction of the library, and was rebuilt in a much sturdier fashion when the work was done.

Left: *Building the Memorial Library; the Bell Tower from Holywell Street, by Bernard Gotch, 1939.*

Further to the north are the more distant Warham and Savile Houses, both built by fellows on college land, the former by Dr John Moyle in or before 1922, and the latter by Professor Gilbert Bourne in 1896. Bourne's is particularly interesting, incorporating as it does various college emblems and mottos, and, in one room, a sixteenth-century stone fireplace. Behind are the buildings of New College School which fronts Savile Road; the school's well-mannered early twentieth-century building replaced their cramped quarters in New College Lane in 1903. Slightly to the east can be seen the Sportsground, which came into the college's possession through a purchase from Merton College in 1891, and forms part of the eleventh-century Holywell Manor estate acquired by Merton in 1294. Along one side run the two blocks of the Weston Buildings, built at the end of the twentieth century with a benefaction from Garry Weston, book-ending the new Brian Johnston Pavilion which replaced the college's earlier and much-loved (but by then precarious) sports building.

On the south side of the Bell Tower is a view directly into the warden's private garden, created partly during Warden Nicholas's short tenure from 1675 to 1679. By 1732, it was divided into an upper garden with crinkle crankle walls designed for fruit trees, and a lower garden with a lawn quartered by paths and a small summerhouse, built probably to the design of William Townesend. The walls and the summerhouse still survive, as does the bridge across New College Lane, built in 1675 by Nicholas to the design of William Byrd, which links the garden to the Warden's Lodgings. To the east, the view takes in the length of the Slype, at the far end of which can be seen the Morris Garages and the Sacher Building, both twentieth-century additions to the college's buildings of very different kind. The Morris Garages preserves to the street the original Morris works, an Edwardian confection of Queen Anne design, while on the college side a discreet façade fronts modern student accommodation. Nearby, with its roof-line just to be seen over the City Wall, is the prize-winning Sacher Building, designed by David Roberts as the first building devoted to graduate accommodation in Oxford.

Warden Smith's Windows

Si monumentum requiris, circumspice

Probably it was the death-watch beetle that started it all. When the time came after 1945 to convert the Founder's Library and the Wyatt Library (now known as the McGregor–Matthews Library) to purposes other than the housing of books, the timber of both rooms was found to be infested with these creatures. In the process of stripping the plaster three windows on the northeast wall were revealed. These were the original traceried windows of the Founder, two of them in excellent condition. Elsewhere in the college such windows had been removed in 1718 to make way for the sash windows that we see today. Warden Smith saw the discovery as an invitation to restore the Front Quad to its original state.

His plan was to replace the existing eighteenth-century windows in the Founder's Library with traceried windows and to provide mullions and transoms for the Wyatt Library above. His dissatisfaction with the existing windows arose not from a dogmatic preference for Gothic over Georgian but from a belief that the 1718 windows spoiled the internal proportions of the Founder's Library and failed to give the eastern side of the Front Quad the splendour that the Founder had intended. He was immensely knowledgeable about architecture, sensitive to its aesthetics and almost obsessively devoted to the buildings of New College, especially those of the Founder. The arguments for his proposals are to be found in great detail in his book *New College, Oxford, and its Buildings* (OUP, 1952), especially in appendix iii. He was almost certainly better informed about architecture in general and the history of the college buildings in particular than anyone else then on the Governing Body. That does not, of course, mean that he was right: his proposal might well not have achieved in the twentieth century the splendour of the fourteenth.

However, I am concerned here with the political struggles within the college rather than with the architectural niceties. The warden quickly gained the support of the college architect, Fielding Dodd, and of two architectural heavyweights, Sir Hubert Worthington, architect of the college's new library, and Sir Albert Richardson, president, surprisingly, of the Georgian Group. The latter contemptuously described the Georgian sash windows as 'subordinate furnishings'. The first round went to the warden. On 23 June 1949 the Governing Body agreed that a single traceried window be reproduced in stone in the Founder's Library and an oak window with mullions and transoms be installed in the Wyatt Library.

Action followed swiftly. First, a cardboard cut-out with Gothic windows was placed against one of the first-floor windows, rather like the scenery for a pageant. Then, over the summer, a stone window was substituted for the sash window in the northwest corner of the library. The

story, still current, that the warden had it built during the vacation, when the fellows were absent, is sadly false: his political skills were well up to the task of securing a favourable vote at that stage.

However, the political chemistry changed with the return from America of Isaiah Berlin, then a fellow in philosophy and for the year 1949–50 sub-warden. In December he wrote to Rowland Burdon-Muller lamenting 'a vast college intrigue … about my warden's desire to alter all our pretty Queen Anne and Regency windows in the front Quad … into some sort of sham Gothic'. He described the specimen window as 'very hideous and vulgar and discreditable too'. He told, with characteristic exaggeration, how the college 'was converted into a madhouse of jangling nerves. The warden, that nice, remote, but very strong character, suddenly emerged as a ruthless Napoleon, possessed, moreover, like all tyrants, with a passion to build and to leave a physical mark upon his world'. The college, Berlin claimed, was 'divided into

implacably opposed camps', and as sub-warden he had the task of reclaiming their lost democratic rights.

In the summer of 1951 matters were set to be decided at the Stated General Meeting on 21 June. This was adjourned until 10.00am on 10 July and then adjourned again until 6.30 that evening. John Buxton, an habitual conservative, proposed that sash windows be retained in the Founder's Library. His motion was defeated by 13 votes to 12. A counter-motion that traceried windows be installed was then carried by 12 votes to 10. Unfortunately, there was no recorded vote and it is impossible to know for certain how the college divided. I was, however, told at the time by a member of the Governing Body that the professorial fellows supported the warden and the tutorial fellows voted against him. However that may be, the warden seemed finally to have triumphed, and Sir Albert Richardson wrote to congratulate him on 16 July.

He wrote too soon. At the next Stated General Meeting, on 10 October, the matter of the windows was

Right: *As imagined: what the front Quad might have looked like, had Smith's proposal been accepted.*

raised again, this time with estimated costings from the bursar. Since a great deal of repair to the sash windows would anyway be needed, the extra cost of inserting new windows in the Upper and Lower Libraries would be only £1,000 (a sum that would need to be increased by a factor of at least 15 to give current values). Whether or not these estimates were crucial to explaining what then happened we cannot know. The Buxton motion for a halt to change was put to the vote and lost once more, by 13 votes to 12. The meeting was then adjourned until 2.15pm on 7 November when the warden's proposal to install traceried windows in the Founder's Library was defeated by 11 votes to 9. What had happened? Some fellows were obviously absent from the adjourned meeting. Of the 27 present on 10 October only 20 were present and voting on 7 November. I was told by my previous informant that one professorial fellow, confused by the contradictory motions, voted the wrong way. It may be, also, that the tutorial fellows, more intimately

concerned with the appearance of the college, had greater staying power.

At any rate, that was the end of the warden's grand scheme. He himself became vice-chancellor and turned his reforming energies to the business of the university and city of Oxford. After a respite from controversy for a few years, New College led the way into the crusade for the admission of women. Again, John Buxton fought a prolonged rearguard action, but this time he was in the end defeated. The single Gothic window in the Front Quad remains as a monument to Warden Smith.

Penry Williams

(*I am most grateful to Jennifer Thorp, New College Archivist, for help in the preparation of this article, and also to Henry Hardy for drawing Isaiah Berlin's letter to the attention of the college. See* Isaiah Berlin, Enlightening: Letters, 1946–1960, *ed. Henry Hardy and Jennifer Holmes (Chatto & Windus, 2009), pp.156–8.*)

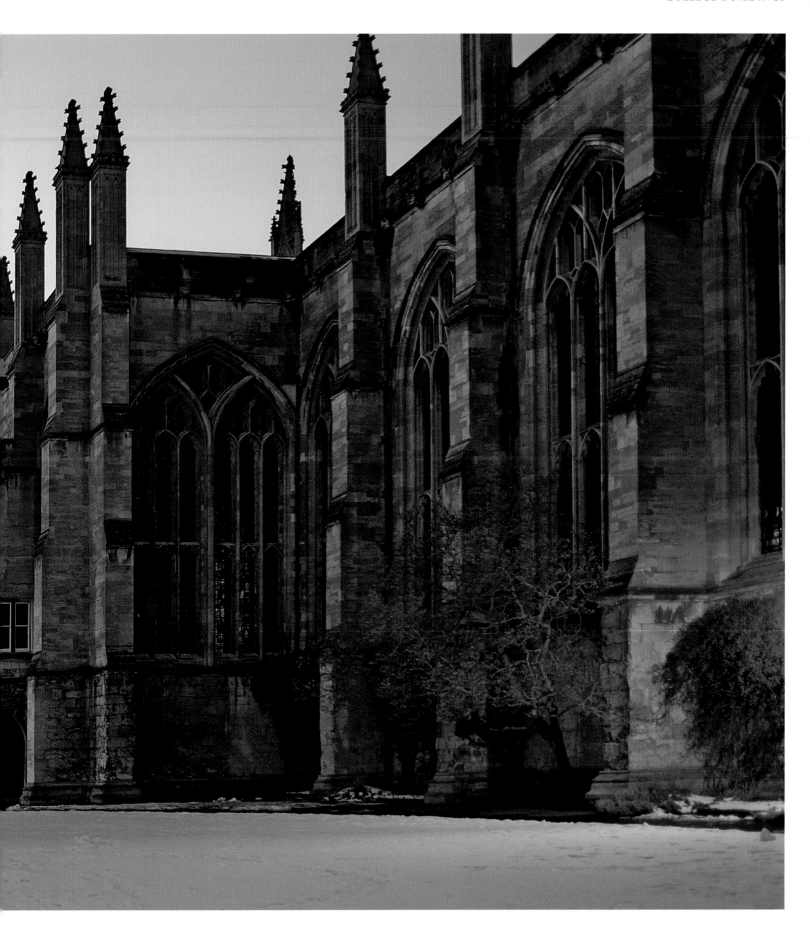

THE FOUNDER

CHRISTOPHER TYERMAN

William of Wykeham, the Founder of New College, was born in the summer of 1324 in the Hampshire village of Wickham into what would later be known as yeoman stock. His father, John 'le Longe' (William was reputedly a tall man too), was a free tenant; his mother, Sybil, had propertied connections. William received his early education at the grammar school attached to the priory of St Swithun's in nearby Winchester. There he acquired the rudiments of Latin and, it seems, a lifelong devotion to the cult of the Virgin Mary, to whom his two colleges are dedicated. Unusually for a future bishop in fourteenth-century England, William did not proceed to university. Instead he began his career working for William Edington, bishop of Winchester (1346–66), treasurer and later chancellor to Edward III, through whose patronage he steadily rose into royal service by the mid-1350s, after a variety of freelance administrative and quasi-legal jobs. In 1356 William was appointed Clerk of Works for two favourite royal manors and justice for labourers and then Clerk of Works at Windsor Castle. By 1359 William had established himself as the leading administrator of the King's Works in southern England outside London.

His role as a royal clerk soon expanded. In 1360 he witnessed the Treaty of Bretigny with France; by the end of 1361 he had risen to a leading position in the king's private office, the Chamber, where he acted as his principal secretary and from 1363 as keeper of the Privy Seal, holding a brief across all royal government. To match his rise in authority, William got himself ordained and made a priest (1361–2), giving him access to a new seam of lucrative preferment. By 1366 William had become the wealthiest and most egregious pluralist in the realm. Politically, Jean Froissart noted, 'everything was done by him, and nothing was done without him'. His reward came in 1367 on his elevation to the chancellorship and the bishopric of Winchester, one of the richest sees in Christendom.

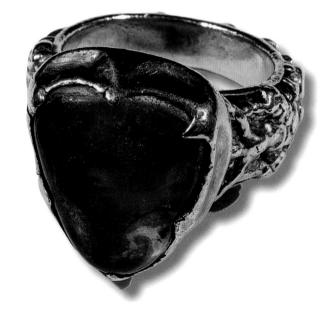

Right: *The Founder's gold ring with a foil-backed rock crystal, late fourteenth century.*

Left: *The Founder's crozier, which incorporates a set of earlier enamel plaques of angels playing musical instruments, late fourteenth century.*

Below: *William of Wykeham's mitre, restored in the nineteenth century, and again in 1929.*

William's ministry attracted jealousy from political rivals and criticism from reformers such as John Wyclif. It was also marred by failure. Renewed plague, economic malaise and military defeat invited charges of sleaze and maladministration, and in 1371 William was forced to resign the chancellorship. However, although out of office, he remained close to the court and the king's council. In 1376 his fortunes suffered their only genuinely threatening reverse. After having helped lead parliamentary criticism of the management of government (like 'Satan rebuking sin' in Bruce McFarlane's memorable phrase) in the so-called Good Parliament, William found himself caught in the political backlash. Arraigned for incompetence and corruption during his chancellorship, he was stripped of his temporalities, banished from court and put on trial. He was only pardoned in the summer of 1377. One fruit of his restoration to court favour and membership of the royal council was the 1379 royal patent for his college at Oxford, where he had been supporting scholars since 1371 at the latest.

Over the next 25 years, William remained at the centre of public affairs, active in parliament and the royal council and on numerous commissions of enquiry. He tiptoed with skill and a bit of luck through the turbulent and increasingly bloody politics of Richard II's reign, and he was even appointed chancellor again between 1389 and 1391, this time as a retrenching reformer. He survived the crises of 1386–8 and the deposition of Richard II in 1399. As late as 1401 he was appointing temporary suffragans for his diocese because he was 'so occupied with the affairs of the king and kingdom'. In fact, William, for all the distractions of government, was an assiduous diocesan, conducting visitations and overseeing ordinations. Despite his rapacious and energetic pursuit of lands and possessions, often with a view to secure the future of his two collegiate foundations at Oxford and Winchester, William appears conventionally pious, his statutes for New College showing a tinge of monastic rigour.

He was a generous nepotist, establishing his extended family as prosperous gentry. Opinion varies as to whether his effigy in Winchester Cathedral shows him as ascetic or sleek. Humility may have been personal rather than institutional – his carved image appears three times in New College and his cult was soon established in his colleges possibly even before his death in 1404. William's crozier in New College and his grand chantry tomb at Winchester speak of public luxury, while his accounts suggest private frugality. Remarkable for his rise from provincial obscurity without the benefit of birth or university education, living witness to his borrowed motto that 'Manners Makyth Man', William compensated for his own academic and professional struggle by leaving a revolutionary and indelible mark on Oxford and on the world of learning that has long outlasted memories of his spectacular career.

Above: *The Founder's tomb in Winchester Cathedral, drawn by R. Essex, engraving published 1828.*

Opposite: *The Founder as imagined in the sixteenth century, with New College, top left, and Winchester College, top right. After Samson Strong, 1596.*

ANNERS MAKETH
MAN

THE FOUNDATION
AND THE MEDIEVAL COLLEGE

CHRISTOPHER TYERMAN

In its Founder New College was provided with one parent and two midwives. The whole conception, in outline and detail, was that of William of Wykeham. However, its existence derived from his private interest, while its material substance depended on his public status. Without all three, Wykeham's creation risked being stunted, disabled or even still-born.

By the late fourteenth century there were only a few colleges in Oxford. Most undergraduates resided in digs or private halls, often little more than boarding houses presided over by a master. The non-monastic colleges that did exist by 1350 (Balliol, University, Merton, Exeter, Oriel, Queen's) were small fellowships, reserved for graduates or masters. Some were financially exiguous, such as Exeter; others, such as Queen's, failed to match the grandiose aspirations of their founders through inadequate endowment. Wykeham was determined to avoid both the model and the pitfalls. His college was to be lavishly endowed and devised, constructed on a grand scale and the largest both in size and membership in Oxford. He would provide the most extensive academic buildings in the whole university and double the number of college fellows. As well as supplying the college's site and the necessary

properted assets to build and maintain his foundation, Wykeham secured official authority for tax exemption and composed the most meticulous statutes in Oxford regulating his college's nature, purpose, membership, conduct, curriculum, culture and lifestyle. He even, in his joint foundation of a feeder school, Winchester College, provided its intake.

Contrary to modern misconceptions, New College was not founded as a nursery or staff college for mandarins. Wykeham's purpose was three-fold: to provide an eternal chantry for his soul and those of his patrons and college benefactors; to promote learning for the defence and enhancement of the faith; and to provide an educated secular clergy. The statutes emphasized the primacy of theology, not civil or canon (Roman) law, as a higher degree, insisting on a maximum of 20 out of the 70 fellows being permitted to read law. That many of his fellows quickly found legal training more lucrative may not have surprised the worldly bishop, but it was not his prime or stated objective. Except for his close relative Nicholas Wykeham (1379–89), all wardens were theologians until the election of the loathsome John London, a doctor of civil law, in 1526. If his statutes are to be believed, revised during a quarter

Left: *The college seal matrix, gift of the Founder, fourteenth century.*

Opposite: *The illuminated first page of Founder's college statutes, c.1398.*

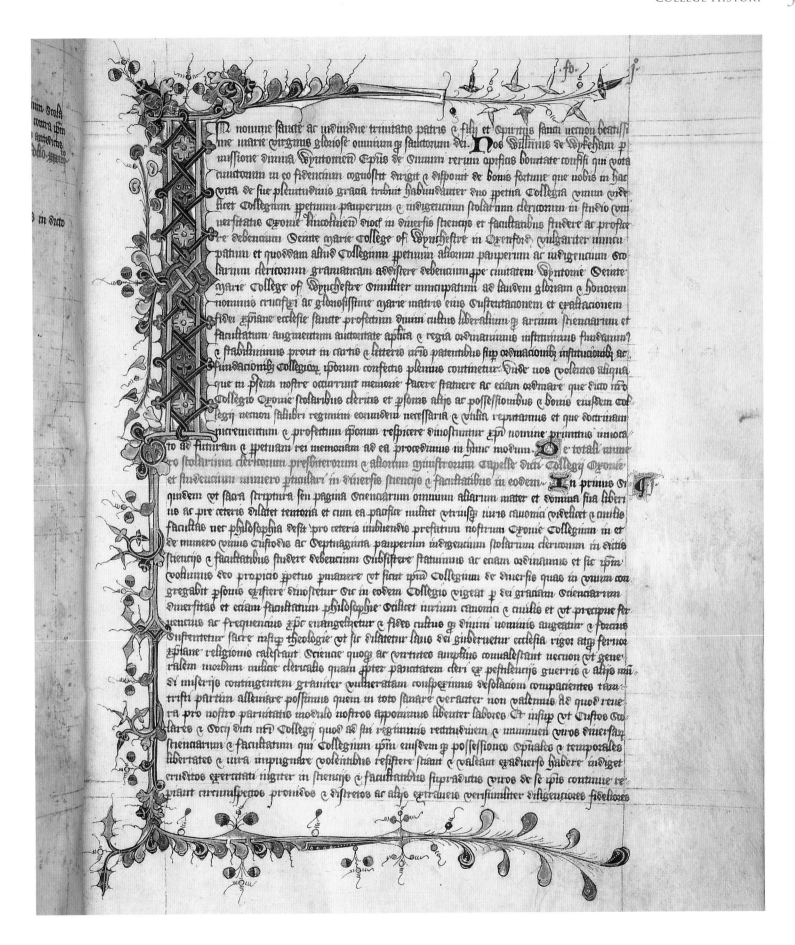

Above: *The chest which held the seal matrix; to avoid the forging of college documents, the chest required three different key holders to open it, and it was kept in the lower Muniment Tower behind a door which could only be opened with three more key holders present.*

Opposite: *Wykeham's ideal college: a warden surrounded by the members, from the manuscript compiled by Thomas Chaundler, between c.1461 and 1465.*

of a century before their final, explicitly unalterable redaction in 1400, Wykeham wished to create a sober, learned community solemnly directed towards its higher educational and commemorative purposes to the praise of God and the Virgin Mary. The statutes made clear the priority of the college's chantry function: the lavish provision of 10 chaplains, three clerks and 16 choristers were the last to remain if the endowment failed and the fellowship had to be disbanded.

Wykeham had begun plans for his colleges almost as soon as he had become bishop of Winchester, starting to buy property in Oxford in 1369. By 1371 he had established a community of scholars in accommodation towards the western end of what is now New College Lane; they survived his temporary political eclipse in 1376–7. From 1378 property outside Oxford began to be assigned to the college. Determined to provide a secure financial basis, Wykeham used his public position to amass a substantial estate, to secure the college's legal title to it and, vitally, to obtain tax exemption in 1395. By 1397 New College's

endowment brought in over £627 a year. In addition, Wykeham left the college a vast treasure of £2,000 to be kept secretly in hand in case of major emergency capital expenses. This lasted less than a century, looted after a former fellow probably first let slip its existence to a hard-up and rapacious Edward IV in the 1460s.

The original royal letters patent and the Founder's charter of 26 November 1379 confirmed both Wykeham's intentions and the college's site. This was a derelict rubbish dump in the northeast corner of Oxford, described by a city jury set up to investigate Wykeham's plans as 'full of filth, dirt and stinking carcasses … often a concourse of malefactors, murderers, whores and thieves'. The foundation stone was laid in March 1380, and the main quadrangle was completed for occupation in 1386. In 1389 land west of the chapel was purchased, New College Lane was diverted, and the cloisters (finished 1400) and bell tower (1403) were constructed. Significant of the importance and complexity of college finances and the changing tastes of the fellows, in 1450 the Bursary was extended towards the garden into what is still called the Chequer and in 1480 a law library was built above it, now the Panelled Room. In 1500 the original garden was extended by the purchase of the plot behind St Peter's in the East, later the fellows' bowling green. Along with its kitchen, Warden's Barn and Long Room, New College formed the largest group of university buildings in Oxford. As early as 1392 the Oxford foundation, called in the 1379 Charter 'St Mary's College commonly the college of St Mary of Winchester', was being known as New College, to distinguish it from Oriel College, founded in 1326 and also dedicated to the Virgin Mary.

The physical and institutional design of New College was harmonious, comprehensive and novel. In a unique fashion, the college realized its founder's stated commitment to the need for Christians to care for 'the beauty of the house in which the true and living sacrifice is offered on the altar'. The design and building work were placed in the hands of the master mason William Wynford and his team, who had been working with Wykeham ever since the Founder's time as Clerk of Works at Windsor in the 1350s. The extensive carpentry – as survives in roof timbers of the kitchen roof and Long Room – was entrusted to the master carpenter Hugh Herland. The statutes paid minute attention to the physical and social as well as to the intellectual and spiritual space in the college, with details of the fellows' chambers and arrangements for commons and accommodation. Nothing in Oxford or Cambridge matched New College in size or thoroughness of physical, educational, financial or domestic design. The Front Quad was the first example of a closed quadrangle in Oxford. The statutes provided for 70 fellows, graduates, as in other colleges and, for the first time, undergraduates; for their first probationary two years, fellows were called 'scholars'. This combination produced the first regular tutorial system in the university. By 1398 the older fellows were paid 9d a term for each scholar they taught (perhaps under £16 in modern money, low pay even by today's modest tutorial rates). The administration of business was in the hands of the warden, from 1396 elected by the fellows, and three bursars, given financial oversight from 1389, and, increasingly, the senior fellows, 'the Thirteen', as they became known.

Wykeham's statutes display an extraordinary wholeness and completeness, from the arrangement of the fellows' chambers, to the purpose-built library and Muniment Tower, to the rigorous round of religious services and to the ban on ball games in Hall for fear of damaging the chapel reredos next door. No detail appeared too trivial for the Founder, from the times of closing the college gate, to the injunction to fellows in first-floor chambers not to spill water, wine or beer lest it splash on those in lower rooms, to prescribing what entertainments were to be allowed at Gaudes (13 feast days were celebrated), including songs, poems, chronicles of kings and stories of 'wonders of the world'. The prescribed humble behaviour, simple attire, liturgical observance, firm discipline, strict obedience to the statutes

and modest commons lent a distinctly monastic idealism to this secular college. Its rigours may have been too much even for the earliest members: the first mention of infringement of the statutes came just as the fellows were taking possession of their grand new premises. Given the youth of most of the fellows, adolescent high spirits were clearly a constant concern.

Equally, the regulated order of the statutes may conceal a more complex officially sanctioned reality. Before the college was built Wykeham had leased tenements at the end of New College Lane, including Hart Hall, held from its landlord, Exeter College. Richard Tonworth, presumably then head of Wykeham's Oxford scholars, appears as principal of Hart Hall in 1378–80, when he died, succeeded at Hart Hall by the first incumbent warden, Nicholas Wykeham. In 1384, as completion of the college buildings neared, he was followed at Hart Hall by Thomas Cranley, later second warden of New College. But even after the opening of the college in 1386, Hart Hall was kept on, perhaps as an overflow hostel or surplus accommodation for scholars, servants or builders. At least three more fellows acted as principals of Hart Hall in the 1380s and 1390s until the original lease ran out. It is entirely feasible that they charged residents for board and lodging. If the principals or the college made profits on the venture – and fellows were statutorily allowed private incomes of up to 5 marks a year (£3 6s 8d) or benefices worth up to 10 marks a year (£6 13s 4d) – or whether or not Hart Hall acted as a lucrative annexe after 1386, none of this appears in the college plan. Along with the Founder's own stated anxiety about the integrity of his statutes, this arouses suspicion that more may have been going on in northeast Oxford in the late fourteenth century than now meets the eye.

The academic life of the college was no less regulated by the Founder, although it, too, suffered modification in practice. To ensure his fellows'

competence in Latin (something that, possibly unfairly, he was accused of lacking himself) entry to New College was restricted to scholars at his foundation at Winchester, with preference going to 'Founder's Kin'. Although only 11 fellows were 'Founder's Kin' between 1379 and 1500, the institutional and consequent geographical restriction in entry, coupled with the novel admission of undergraduates, exerted a marked effect in reducing the proportion of fellows who went on to distinguished later careers as compared with other colleges.

The object was for all the scholars/fellows to progress to BAs and MAs. Thereafter, a maximum of 20 were permitted to study civil (Roman) or canon law, two medicine and two astronomy (a mixture of mathematics and astrology), oddly as the university had no faculty in the subject (and only one medieval fellow is recorded as having followed this path). The rest were expected to proceed to study theology. This ideal was compromised in a variety of ways. Between 1386 and 1540 just over 10 per cent died within four years, before they were 20 and without taking any degree. Another 8 per cent died in college, all but five under the age of 40. The graves of the young filled the cloisters; their seniors' the ante-chapel. Others just left 'having no mind to study' – over 14 per cent in their first 2 years, and another 14 per cent in the following two years. The consequent turnover was great, an average of 10 new fellows a year. This produced an overwhelmingly young fellowship, with an average age of just 25. The oldest fellow to die in the medieval college was only 48, and he had been a fellow for 30 years. The longest serving fellow notched up 32 years. Warden Hill, who died in 1494 aged about 62, was unique in having spent such a long life and career entirely in college. The oldest medieval fellow was William Packett, resident fellow in 1428–50 then rector of the college living at Redclive until his death in 1496, who was probably in his mid-80s.

Those who survived and stayed were soon found to be ignoring Wykeham's scheme. Between 1380 and 1400

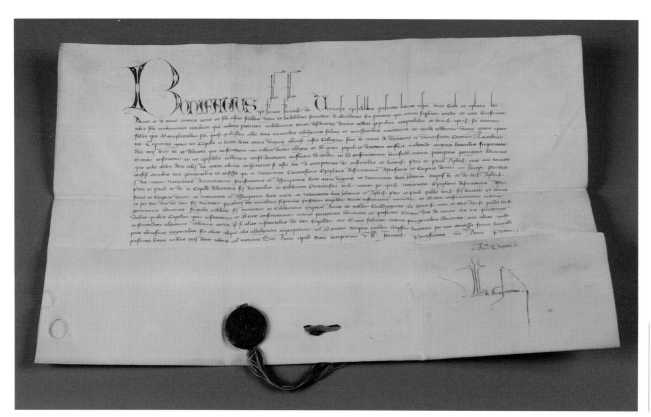

Left: *The indulgence for a hundred days knocked off hell granted by Pope Boniface IX for pilgrims visiting the chapel on certain feast days, 28 December 1389.*

less than a fifth of the fellows enrolled in higher faculties studied theology. In the fifteenth century the next most common degree after the MA was the BCL, which fitted a fellow for work in church and royal prerogative courts, government administration and diplomacy. As government increasingly became the preserve of laymen, so fellows like Ralph Greenhurst (1389–1401) pursued a lay career, in his case in Chancery. University lawyers, too, sought instead the common law by leaving Oxford for the Inns of Court. John Kingsmill swapped the law schools of Oxford for the common law to become a Justice of Common Pleas (1504–9). Many others ignored or delayed the statutory encouragement and financial inducement to take full holy orders.

Although in the fifteenth century perhaps half the fellowship received parish livings (some in absentia), after 1494 never more than 12 fellows were priests at any one time. Religious vocation as opposed to the Church as a career was conspicuously absent. By the early 16th century fellows were leaving to get married – at least one after having done so. Learning was another matter. Fellows left to teach in the growing number of grammar schools. The importance of teaching within the college grew, and in over half the years between 1480 and 1529 over half the fellows in residence were undergraduates. Just as clerics had to

bend to a secular wind in law and government, so scholars adapted to new trends. Thomas Beckington, who rose to be Henry VI's secretary and bishop of Bath and Wells (1443–65), Thomas Chaundler, later warden (1454–75) and chancellor of the university, and William Warham, archbishop of Canterbury (1504–32), were all active patrons of new humanist classical studies. Among other fellows, John Farley (died 1464), a rare unordained theologian, may have been the first Oxford graduate to study Greek in this period; another, William Grocyn (fellow 1465–81), one of the leading English humanist scholars of his day, was the first to give lectures on Greek in Oxford, although only after he had left New College and had studied in Florence.

The social backgrounds of medieval fellows were generally modest, like that of the Founder. This provided an incentive to accept Wykeham's regime and a spur to self-advancement beyond. Usually this meant an obscure parish, frequently a college living. For some, however, the heights of Church and state beckoned. Henry Chichele, a member from before 1386, rose through diplomatic service to be archbishop of Canterbury (1414–43). In 1438 he founded All Souls College in direct imitation of his alma mater, except that he planned for two-thirds of his fellows to be lawyers like him. There was a fair sprinkling of New College men in royal service, mostly in

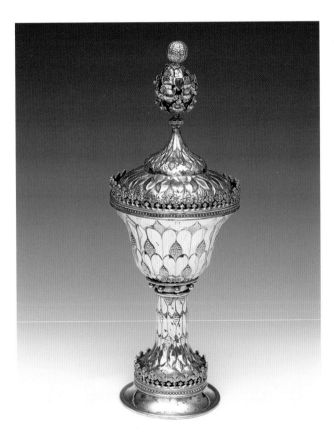

Right: *The Warden's Grace Cup, c.1480.*

John Russell, a lavish donor of books to the college, even adopted Wykeham's coat of arms on his elevation to the see of Rochester in 1476.

Apart from its effect on the lives of its members, the most lasting impact of medieval New College was as a model of education, both in its teaching scheme and its buildings. All Souls (1438) and Magdalen (1458) in Oxford and King's, Cambridge (1441), with its feeder school at Eton, were all created with New College in mind. The link with Henry VI's foundations was formalized by the *Amicabilis Concordia* between all four of them in 1444, a suitable recognition for the colleges of a man who had waxed rich in the service of three kings. More generally, the classic closed quadrangle pioneered in Oxford by Wykeham became the university's most instantly recognizable institutional as well as architectural signature.

Wykeham intended his college to be an unchanging monument to him and his vision of a secure Church and an educated clergy. Although before the 1520s and Warden London's murder of the Protestant fellow John Quinbey through incarceration, starvation and hyperthermia in the Bell Tower, New College's orthodoxy was hardly in question, its members, corporately and individually, reflected the changing temper of the times: economic vicissitudes, political instability, high mortality rates, the slow erosion of clerical monopoly in government administration, the rise of the common lawyers, the emergence of new humanist learning, the stubborn traditions of parochial preferment and the tenacity of the liturgical round. In 1385 Wykeham had worried lest his new vineyard receive corruption from wild vines. Yet for all his care and scrupulous insistence on the maintenance of his statutes, neither he nor the most conservative of the fellows of his college could, or saw much need to, exclude the little foxes of change. Although historically untypical in its production of numerous leaders of Church and state, the medieval college was in one way at least in tune with its future: private diversity and change beneath a carapace of what seemed and was for the next 300 years a seemingly immutable façade of tradition.

law, government and administration. Some, like Richard Hankford (1414–15), who very likely fought at Agincourt, or his contemporary, Nicholas Upton, author of a major treatise on warfare, even went to the French wars. Regionally and socially from a restricted constituency, the highly regulated, possibly stifling institutional environment of college life nonetheless witnessed an eclectic and possibly serendipitous comprehensiveness: early death, the abandonment of academic life and/or the Church, a quiet parish, serious scholarship, government service, a public career or the pinnacles of the establishment. In the higher circles of learning, Church and state, strands of an old college network are discernible. Equally, the sustained affection of some old members for their college is reflected in donations of property, objects and books. One New College bishop,

THE REFORMATION TO REFORM
c.1530–1850

DAVID PARROTT

The last decades of the fifteenth century were a high point of New College's influence in Church and state. John Russell rose through the bishoprics of Rochester and Lincoln, becoming chancellor of Oxford in 1483 and being made Lord Chancellor of England by Richard III in the same year. Richard Mayhew became first President of Magdalen College, ambassador to Spain, chancellor of Oxford in 1502 and bishop of Hereford in 1504. William Warham rose to the bishopric of London and was made Lord Chancellor in 1504 and archbishop of Canterbury in 1505. Perhaps because of this success, New College changed less in the course of the sixteenth century than many colleges with smaller fellowships. Whereas many of the latter responded to rising demand for a university education by increasing the numbers of undergraduate scholars and commoners and making new tutorial provisions, New College held to its Founder's statutes and maintained the fellowship fixed at 70, including the probationaries. A handful of gentlemen commoners were accepted, but they were expected to live outside the college.

Though there had been strong demand from fellows throughout the later fifteenth century to read civil and canon law rather than theology (a clear departure from the Founder's intentions), the only evidence that this might imply pressure for change in the college was the 1526 election of the lawyer John London as warden. The college fellowship remained for the most part intellectually conservative. There was some interest in humanist ideas and writings among the fellows and a handful of early enthusiasts for reformist theology, but the close ties with Church and state encouraged conformity, especially given the generous patronage offered the university by a succession of powerful and wealthy public figures, from William Waynflete, Lord Chancellor and bishop of Winchester, to Cardinal Wolsey.

The changes that were initiated by Henry VIII's break with Rome provoked responses among the fellows of New College typical of the ambivalence of the wider political nation. Historians have come to understand the early Reformation not as a straightforward clash of distinct theological principles but as a much more opaque process, where 'reformist' ideas, not initially

Left: Episcopal gloves worn by William Warham, Archbishop of Canterbury, late fifteenth or early sixteenth century.

Above: *The Ape Salt, a gift of William Warham, Archbishop of Canterbury, c.1500.*

understood or condemned as Protestant, combined with extreme political and social pressures to conform with government diktats – whether in directions that were radical or conservative. Warden London, doubtless like many of the fellows, appears to have had little difficulty in accommodating himself to the elimination of papal authority over the English Church and to the oath of Royal Supremacy. Moreover, as one of Cromwell's Visitors to the Monasteries after 1535, he appears to have seen no incompatibility between suppressing the monasteries but asserting elsewhere a theological conservatism that was sufficiently uncompromising to get him into trouble

with Thomas Cromwell. Though he survived the fall of Cromwell, his ill-judged involvement in a conspiracy against Archbishop Thomas Cranmer led to London's disgrace and imprisonment and his enforced resignation from the wardenship in 1542.

In fact, Henry VIII's reforms represented an ambiguous and partial attack on Catholic doctrine, which conservative fellows could for the most part reconcile with an obligation to royal obedience. In contrast, the first royal visitation of Edward VI's reign in 1549 began a much more uncompromising assertion of explicitly Protestant doctrine and practice on the university. In the face of this, the fellows of New College employed a blend of outward compliance and some carefully modulated resistance. Both the 1549 and 1552 Protestant Books of Common Prayer were purchased for the chapel, but the fellows warded off the Visitors' demands for the destruction of the stained glass, using what was to become the time-honoured excuse: pleading that the college could not at present afford their replacement with plain glass. Despite this resistance, the blurred lines that allowed theological and doctrinal conservatives to continue within their college fellowships were gradually becoming more difficult to maintain.

Yet if the hostility of the conservatives became less muted, the changes also established for the first time a faction of college fellows fully committed to Protestantism, and in 1551 they were able to elect Ralph Skinner as an active Protestant and the first married warden of the college. But though the Edwardian reformation had made these theological divisions explicit, the rival factions continued in situ during his reign, and there was no systematic attempt to eliminate religious conservatives. This changed when Mary came to the throne in 1553 and began a Catholic reaction under which New College not merely became a powerhouse of Catholic theologians, apologists and teachers, but Protestants were purged from the fellowship. The brothers John and Nicholas Harpsfield became leading literary and administrative exponents of the Catholic revival, while Thomas Harding, professor of

Hebrew, was to prove a vociferous Catholic opponent of the Elizabethan Settlement, matched as a polemicist by the Catholic writer and lecturer in canon law, Nicholas Saunders. The restoration of Stephen Gardiner as bishop of Winchester and therefore Visitor of New College in 1553 encouraged the development of this militantly Catholic intellectual life and facilitated in the first year of the reign the removal of seven Protestant fellows, which was accompanied by the resignation of Warden Skinner. Fifteen new appointments gave an even more overtly Catholic character to the college by the end of Mary's reign, while such changes in the religious life of the college that had taken place under Edward were quickly reversed. Had Mary survived there is little doubt that New College and its fellows would have played a major role in providing intellectual and polemical support for a Catholic revival.

With Elizabeth's accession in 1558, however, and her emphatic repudiation of her sister's Catholic restoration, the theological stance of New College's fellowship could expect to attract hostile attention. Some of those most associated with the Marian regime fled to the Continent, including Saunders, Thomas Stapleton and John Fowler. Others, including the warden, Thomas Whyte, who had been appointed in 1553, waited on events and showed an outward willingness to comply with the new government. A few initial expulsions were followed by an extensive series of visitations and enquiries from 1561, which aimed to enforce conformity with the Elizabethan settlement, to root out residual Catholic sympathies and to investigate the general academic and disciplinary state of the college. Ultimately, 33 fellows were removed as a result of these investigations in the first decade of Elizabeth's reign, and five more were expelled after 1568. The losses seem extremely heavy in a college of 70 fellows, although some colleges with a much smaller fellowship suffered proportionately an even higher level of expulsions.

More importantly perhaps, was that in losing its distinct identity as a seedbed of the Marian Catholic revival and the key intellectual figures associated with

Whereas by the intent of the founders of Colleges… elections of Scholars are to be had and made of the fittest and most meet persons…yet notwithstanding, the fittest persons to be elected are seldom or not at all preferred.

For remedy whereof be it enacted…that if any persons…which have election…take any money fee reward or any other profit…in electing,…the place of such persons in the said Colleges shall be void, and any other person may be elected in the room of such persons so offending, as if they were naturally dead.

Above: *A calligraphic version of the extracts from the statute of Queen Elizabeth I still read on the election of a fellow.*

that role, New College lost a sense of academic direction and discipline in the first decades of Elizabeth's reign. Successive visitations uncovered disquieting evidence not just of subversion and open contempt for the Anglican settlement but of widespread disciplinary lapses and abuses and a general level of disorder and indifference by the fellows to the rules of college life. Despite his protestations of loyalty to the new regime, the authority of Warden Whyte seemed entirely lacking: this was a choral foundation in which many of the choristers had never been taught, nor were expected to sing, the daily services; chaplains were regularly absent from the performance of the chapel offices; and fellows ignored the religious requirements of college life with impunity. The first round of investigations culminated in 1566 with 62 injunctions from the Visitor, prescribing religious, moral and pedagogic conduct. Significantly, when the second major visitation took place in 1576 evidence of Catholic recalcitrance and foot-dragging adherence to an Anglican settlement was far less in evidence. In this respect the expulsions and replacements of fellows had evidently succeeded.

However, standards of general conduct were still considered highly problematic, with fellows maintaining a lifestyle and behaving in ways that fell considerably short of the Founder's austere ideals. A particular problem identified by the second visitation concerned corruption in the elections to fellowships, a problem exacerbated by the statutory limit of 70 on the total number of fellows. Given that fellowships at New College would be awarded only to Winchester scholars as places were vacated, the practice grew up of deals made between scholars and existing fellows, who would resign their fellowship to a candidate for a financial consideration. In an attempt to curtail this practice, widespread well beyond New College, of allocating fellowships in return for underhand payments, an Act of Parliament was promulgated in 1588 'Against abuses in Election of Scollers' (31 Elizabeth, cap. vi), the key paragraphs of which are still read out in New College Governing Body meetings before any new fellow is proposed for election.

Despite this apparently forceful attempt to impose external regulation on college appointments, practice continued to be shaped by the comfortable financial realities of the situation. The Founder's requirement that a fellow should remain resident in the college had been tacitly abandoned, and it was now easy to hold the benefits of a fellowship while also occupying a curacy or a more profitable Church post. This was combined with a substantial improvement in the college's overall financial position, as its income from the endowment grew from around £900 a year during the reign of Edward VI to an average of £1,100 a year during the first five years of Elizabeth's reign. From there it was to climb steadily to around £3,330 by the second half of the 1630s. From the 1590s the surplus of income over expenditure was shared among the fellows, and the originally frugal stipends fixed by the Founder were increasingly transformed into attractive and sought-after benefits. If attempts to restrict 'corrupt resignations' failed to change behaviour, equally unsurprisingly the considerable improvement in the financial benefits of holding a fellowship encouraged the proliferation of claims made by Founder's Kin: demands for preferential access to fellowships in accordance with the statutes of the college for those who could claim (often tenuous) connections with Wykeham's family. The Fiennes family in particular managed to establish a foothold in the college on the basis of a dubious claim to kinship, which was upheld by the powerful royal favourite Christopher Hatton.

Below: *Robert Pincke, warden 1617–47, after 1647.*

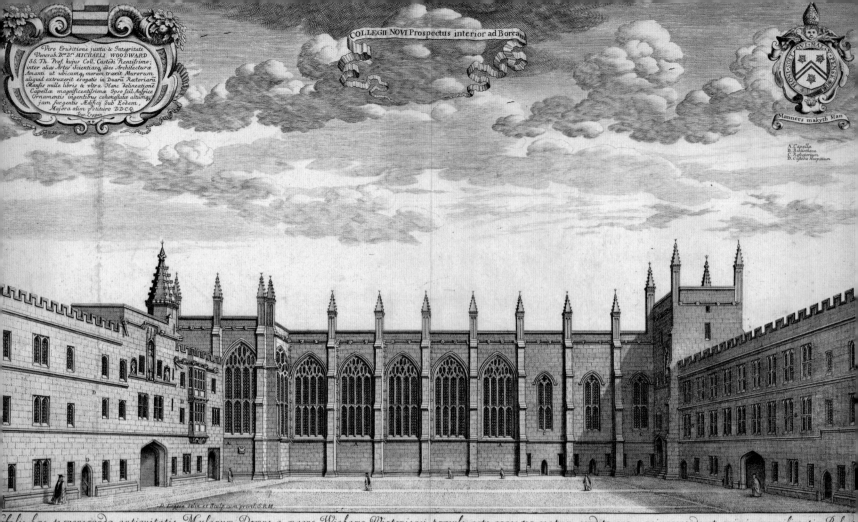

Nobilis hac & veneranda antiquitatis Musarum Domus, a magno Wickamo Wintoniensi præsule ante annos ter centum condita, quo magis responderet eximiæ magnificentiæ Refect.
Capellæ, latus septentrionale areæ Majoris implentium; hoc ipso anno, nimirum 1674 sumptibus Custodis & sociorum, tertiâ contignatione additâ quasi iuventâ postliminio acceptâ, desider.
... decus, atq. augmentum feliciter consecuta est

The subsequent attempt to contain the practice specified that there should be no more than eight Founder's Kin holding fellowships at New College at any one time, but by 1651 this had been raised to 20, and the numbers continued to be substantial into the mid-nineteenth century. Indeed it was probably the vow of celibacy, a survival from the pre-Reformation Church, which continued to be imposed until the nineteenth century (though not upon the warden) that probably did more than anything else to encourage resignations and some degree of mobility in the fellowship.

Fellowships became more lucrative and their scholarly and pedagogic obligations less demanding into the first decades of the seventeenth century. The mediocre achievements of the fellowship in the 1630s were noted by Archbishop William Laud, who perhaps tactfully attributed it to an excessive study of Calvin's *Institutes*, imposed on the scholars in their first years of study by the senior fellows. The reasons for under-attainment seem more prosaic, and indeed there seems evidence, both in the embellishment of the chapel and the later reputation of the college after Oxford's surrender to the parliamentarian forces in 1646, that a significant number of the fellows of New College were enthusiastic Laudians, for whom study of the original wellspring of Calvinist theology may not have been a high priority.

From 1617 the college was under the wardenship of Robert Pincke, a capable administrator and an unusually impressive scholar, who had the confidence of the king and Archbishop Laud and whose assertion of discipline over the fellows contributed to reviving the college's flagging academic fortunes in the 1630s. It fell to Pincke as pro-vice-chancellor to organize the defence of the university in 1642 after the vice-chancellor, the bishop of Worcester, had abandoned Oxford. Pincke supervised the mustering and drill of the university-trained bands and encouraged the first attempts to fortify the town. None of this prevented the arrival of a troop of parliamentary cavalry under the command of Lord Saye and Sele, an old member of New College, who nonetheless had Pincke arrested and his study searched for incriminating papers. Withdrawing before the battle of Edgehill, the

Above: *Front Quad as depicted by David Loggan in 1675; Warden Smith's scheme was based on the Quadrangle as it appeared in this state.*

Right: *Michael Woodward, warden 1658–75, bust after 1675.*

military and political presence of the king imposed further financial burdens on the colleges. Although the fellows of New College do not seem to have 'lent' their silver to the king when the first royal request was made in 1642, they would appear to have succumbed to the king's demands in the worsening situation of 1644 and given over a large proportion of their plate. In addition, Oxford was directly involved in the fighting of the Civil War and subjected to two substantial military blockades, which brought parliamentary forces within cannon shot in 1644 and 1645. In 1644 combined forces under Essex and Waller forced the king to withdraw a large part of the royalist forces from Oxford to avoid the danger of being bottled up in the city with limited supplies. In 1645 the army of Thomas Fairfax blockaded the city and again forced the king to withdraw with most of his troops, Fairfax using the opportunity to lift the siege and pursue the royal army. Finally, in 1646 Oxford faced the prospect of a full-scale siege, with all the risk of artillery bombardment, storming and looting by the besieging troops, a grim prospect, which was forestalled by the decision to surrender to Fairfax's army in June 1646. The royalist troops withdrew from the city under the terms of the treaty and were replaced by three parliamentarian regiments billeted at the expense of the inhabitants.

The trials of the colleges did not end with the cessation of fighting. In 1647 a board of Visitors was set up directly answerable to a parliamentary committee to purge royalist supporters from the governing bodies of colleges. Unsurprisingly, New College was seen as especially culpable, both for its royalist and Laudian traditions, and it compounded its insubordinate reputation in November 1647 by moving to the election of a new warden following the death of Robert Pincke, defying the Visitors' demand that they should approve the choice before election. The fellows' candidate, Robert Stringer, Regius Professor of Greek, was removed by the Visitors in August 1648. Asked whether they would submit to the authority of the visitation, the vast majority of fellows and

parliamentarians were replaced by the royalists forces, who established Oxford as the king's administrative and military capital until the end of the first phase of the Civil War. Pincke was restored to the wardenship, but New College became part of the royal arsenal, with weapons and munitions stored in the cloisters and bell tower and a breach made in the cloister walls to allow direct access to New College Lane.

Academic life withered over the next four years of war, as university matriculations overall fell from a high point of 786 in 1634 to 21 in 1644. In common with the other colleges, New College's revenues fell by over two-thirds to a low point of £1,059 in 1643–4. Meanwhile, the college employees refused to do so. Over the next few years at least 50 fellows, four chaplains, 12 choristers and 13 servants were removed by the Visitors under threat of force, and about 55 new fellows were appointed.

With their authority strengthened by this process, the Visitors proceeded to impose a new warden, George Marshall, an MA from St John's College, Cambridge, who had served as a chaplain to the parliamentary armies during the war. This was directly contrary to the statutes of the college, which prescribed that only a fellow or ex-fellow of the college was eligible for election to the wardenship. However, there were other reasons why Marshall had a hard time imposing his own authority within the college, more obviously connected with the appointment of a large number of new, junior fellows, who did not share the warden's enthusiasm for Puritanical habits of prayer and academic austerity. As had now become customary, visitations that began in order to impose religious and political conformity became half-hearted attempts to impose greater disciplinary and moral restraint on the fellowship.

The Restoration of the monarchy was followed by the restoration of choral services in the chapel from December 1660 and the expulsion of some of the more uncompromisingly Puritan fellows imposed by the Visitors. The wardenship had already changed hands in 1658, with the free election of Michael Woodward, who had little interest in the politics or religious practices of Puritanism and adjusted easily to the royalist and Anglican reaction of the 1660s. Woodward was an outstanding college administrator, under whom the rents of the college recovered from the disastrous lows of the Civil War years and by the early 1660s had once again reached the peaks of the 1630s – £3,300–3,400 a year. The Restoration reinforced the tendencies towards a prosperous and privileged fellowship, with a comfortable lifestyle measured in terms of dining, drinking and the quality of their accommodation and unburdened by any need for academic achievement or commitment to teaching.

The additional storey in the front quadrangle was constructed in these decades to provide more spacious living quarters for the fellows, while in 1677 the first wings of the Garden Quadrangle were completed to house 16 noble and gentlemen commoners who would pay fees for their residence, a sharp break from previous practice when commoners were only permitted to live outside the college. The success of this financial initiative led to its being repeated in the first years of the eighteenth century, when the still larger and more luxurious additional wings were added to the Garden Quad to expand provision for gentlemen commoners. In fact though, overall numbers of students at Oxford fell in the decades after the Restoration, as the costs of attending the university restricted the experience either to wealthy aristocrats or scholars training for the Church. Insofar as fellows taught their charges – and much of the teaching took place outside the college – it was to provide a basic clerical education for scholars who would in many cases come to hold the various and frequently profitable college benefices.

New College fellows had ceased to compete for or occupy high office in the state and only occasionally

Below: An unrealised proposal for Garden Quad, by William Byrd, c.1678–81.

Right: *Philip Shuttleworth, warden 1822–40, by Thomas Phillips, 1842.*

managed to achieve it within the Church, but this did not prevent political factions continuing to take a strong interest in Oxford. Whig and Tory interests recognized the patronage offered by college fellowships, and the potential political influence enjoyed by heads of college. In 1703 the rivalry of Thomas Braithwaite and Charles Trimnel for the wardenship was fought out as a struggle between Tory and Whig partisans in Oxford, and the quarrel reached as far as Trimnel's strongest supporter, the archbishop of Canterbury. Braithwaite was appointed warden on appeal to the Visitor, and the majority of eighteenth-century wardens were elected as Tories, though without strong party allegiance. Although the New College fellowship remained preponderantly Tory through the first half of the eighteenth century, this was leavened with a strong and often vocal minority of Whigs.

The mid-eighteenth century also saw the final disappearance of a tradition by which the wardens of New College since the 1670s had subsequently been appointed to the wardenship of Winchester, by the later seventeenth century a considerably more lucrative post. In 1757 the election of Warden John Purnell to Winchester was vetoed by the Visitor, who not only made his own appointment

but also ensured that the tradition of successive wardens' appointments was never resumed. Throughout the eighteenth century the primary destination for fellows of New College remained parochial livings within the Church, and this was not to change until the gradual growth in student numbers from the 1820s onwards.

New College initially played little part in the plans for teaching reforms, the introduction of examinations and the broadening of the syllabus to prepare undergraduates for a wider range of careers. But the downward spiral in college revenues through the first half of the nineteenth century started to make the holding of a fellowship less attractive and certainly stimulated the more activist fellows to consider reforms that would bring the college more into line with other Oxford institutions in which the pool of scholars was larger and selection more competitive. In 1814 Augustus Hare unsuccessfully proposed that New College should agree to abandon its right to present fellows for degrees without taking university examinations, arguing that the stimulus of public examinations would be beneficial for the academic life of the college. If Hare failed to persuade his colleagues of the benefits of integration within the wider university, the election of Nicholas Shuttleworth as warden in 1822 provided critical support for a reformist faction. Shuttleworth's attempts to reduce the numbers of Founder's Kin within the college were defeated, but in 1834 he finally persuaded and cajoled the fellowship to surrender the right to conduct examinations independently of the university and in 1838 established the principle that probationer fellows could be transferred to senior status only with the permission of the warden. Though in 1850 New College still distanced itself from the larger university, there was evidence of willingness, at least among some of the fellowship, to make changes and to respond to the wider forces that were already transforming many Oxford colleges in a manner that marked a radical break with the university's medieval and early-modern past.

THE MODERN COLLEGE SINCE 1850

ALAN RYAN

A little guidebook of 1906 observed that a New College undergraduate arriving that year would have found the college of 1856 a much stranger place than the college's Founder would have done, while the situation would have been reversed if they had visited the college of 1880. Three periods in the college's history since 1850 made it the college it is now and transformed it from its almost fossilized condition in 1850 into a large, lively and outgoing academic – and not only academic – community. The first and most important was the 20 years that followed the college's adoption of the statutes proposed by the royal commission of 1854. The commission had been set up to examine the universities of Oxford and Cambridge with powers to give them new statutes, preferably by agreement or, if not, by imposition. The second is hard to date but is the transformation of the college from the 1960s onwards from an essentially undergraduate college into one in which graduates and young research fellows play an increasingly active role. The third is easy to date: the arrival of women undergraduates in the autumn of 1979.

The successive royal commissions on Oxford and Cambridge were an inevitable result of the reforming zeal of Victorian England. All endowed institutions had been under scrutiny since the 1830s, and Oxford in particular had been under attack since early in the century for its stuffiness, its low intellectual standards, its inaccessibility to all but confirmed members of the Church of England and the cost of attendance. It was not obvious that the

endowments given for the education of poor scholars and the advancement of religion and learning were being spent as they should be. Luckily for Oxford, the German research university was too associated with infidelity in the

Below: *William Spooner, warden 1903–25, and the fellows, 1921.*

form of the historical criticism of the Bible to provide an alternative model. Otherwise the nationalization of college assets and the installation of a professorial tyranny would have been on the cards.

Under the old statutes, intended by the Founder to be perpetual, and, if alteration was essential, only to be altered by the bishop of Winchester, the college must always have 70 fellows, both undergraduate and graduate; they must come from the college at Winchester; they must take orders within seven years of graduation; the choir and the 10 singing chaplains were inviolable. Some provisions were impossible to fulfil – nobody could study for a higher degree

in canon law that had been unavailable for three centuries; others were fulfilled only nominally – of 70 fellows, few were in residence. Rarely were even 20 undergraduates on the premises; most graduate fellows were working as curates in the countryside and hoping for a college living so that they could marry and have a decent income. The college's academic standards were not high. The right to claim a degree without submitting to examination had been given up only in 1834; scholarships to Winchester were given on patronage not merit, and the priority given to Founder's Kin was a notorious scandal. As to scholarships from Winchester, they were awarded on seniority.

Below right: *Arthur Cooke, warden 1976–85, and the fellows, 1981.*

Above: *H.A.L. Fisher, warden 1925–40, and the Junior Members, 1926.*

The statutes agreed in 1857 swept all this away. Fellows had to be graduates; their number was first reduced to 40 and almost immediately to 30; Founder's Kin was abolished; and the requirement to take orders was abolished – New College was unusual in abolishing it for everyone other than the chaplain. The college was opened to commoners – formerly, a handful of gentleman commoners had been on the books, but otherwise, it was a society of fellows. Undergraduate fellows were replaced by scholars, half from Winchester and half not. Astonishingly, the college embraced these changes without visible conflict, perhaps because the fellows who might have resisted had resigned in larger than usual numbers as soon as the first royal commission had been appointed in 1850. Fellows such as E.C. Wickham, Hereford George, Alfred Robinson and W.A. Spooner began to create a modern college. After 1868 fellows could marry, and the college gave itself powers to elect as a fellow anyone it needed as a tutor. The modern academic career had been created.

Then, as today, there was a good deal of anxiety that reforming commissions might look askance at the expense of the choir and chapel. The college was uneasily aware that, on the evidence of the accounts at least, New College spent almost four-fifths as much on maintaining a choir and a chapel as Christ Church spent on maintaining a choir and a cathedral. Nothing happened. The only misfortune the chapel suffered was to be restored against the good advice of Sir George Gilbert Scott, with alterations to pews and roof that did nothing for the internal appearance of the chapel and less for the symmetry of the front quad. The new buildings in Holywell Street had at least the justification that an expanded undergraduate population had to live somewhere, but they, too, were graceless.

The population of the college grew slowly at first, then swiftly. By 1873 there were 75 undergraduates, far fewer than the 145 at Balliol, but already five times more than in 1856; but in 1884 there were 225, on their way to 300 by the 1914 war. The college's character changed, too. The old fellowship may have been undistinguished, but there was no sharp distinction between juniors and seniors. Hereford George recalled that it would have been unthinkable for an undergraduate to call his tutor 'Sir'. They were equally fellows, and as fellows they were equals. In becoming more like other colleges, New College acquired their hierarchies and patterns of deference. It also acquired their taste for sports. In one realm, this was to great effect – between 1885 and 1906 the First Eight was never out of the first three places in Eights Week – but the college never became a sporting college in the pejorative sense. Hastings Rashdall in particular was an avid mountain walker, but a thoroughgoing enemy to the public school cult of games.

Below: The clean and elegant lines of the Sacher Building designed by David Roberts in 1961, soon after completion.

It is not wholly true that the college implied by the statutes it received from the second royal commission in 1883 is the same college as today's, even though the college ran on those statutes until 2006. The 'ordinary' fellowships of those statutes were prize fellowships of the sort to which All Souls still elects. They were for seven years, forfeited on marriage, and assumed to be a stepping stone to a career in the outside world. It came as a surprise that so many fellows were happy to go on to become tutors and university lecturers. They eventually fell victim to the financial stringency of the twentieth century on the one hand and the demands of the university on college resources on the other. Their modern equivalent, more demanding and of shorter duration, is the junior research fellowship.

The modern college, divided between undergraduates and graduates, who today make up two-thirds and one-third of the whole student body, came into existence slowly. The first real acknowledgment of the new world was the creation of the Sacher Building in 1963 and more recently the creation of the Weston Buildings. The change reflected two things. The first was the postwar transformation of Oxford into a university that took science as seriously as Cambridge had done – although it is still true that 60 per cent of Cambridge students study science and only 40 per cent of Oxford students do so. The second was the growth of higher education and the demand that not only must would-be lecturers and future researchers get a higher degree of some sort, but students wanting to engage in anything

Left: *The plaque by Rod Kelly commemorating 25 years of women at New College, installed 2005.*

Opposite: *Anne Barton, the first woman fellow of the college, elected 1977, by James Lloyd, 2001.*

Opposite: *The college graduation, October 2009.*

Right: *An Oxford still-life, January 2009.*

from high finance to urology. With well over 300 graduate courses offered by the contemporary university, it is a long way from the choice between classics and mathematics offered in 1850.

One implication is that academic careers begin later than they used to. Fifty years ago many fellows and tutors started teaching immediately on graduation. Today, they take several years to get doctorates and several further years as post-doctoral fellows of one or other sort. At any given moment there are around 30 junior research fellows, 40 tutorial fellows and a dozen professorial fellows in college, a far cry from the four tutors of 1850; and some 650 students in total, an equally far cry from the fewer than 300 of the years between the wars.

The largest difference, perhaps, is that an entirely male institution is now almost evenly divided between men and women. The SCR has in the nature of things changed more slowly than the JCR and MCR. The college almost became co-educational in the early 1960s, when the historian Harry Bell persuaded his colleagues to make the change. Dame Lucy Sutherland, then the Principal of Lady Margaret Hall, resisted the idea, fearing that clever girls would prefer New College to the women's colleges and that lively and intelligent women tutors would do so, too. Since advocates of change were sensitive to the feelings of women academics, they abandoned the idea. Younger fellows returned to the charge in 1969, when several other colleges also embarked on the necessary changes to their statutes. New College meant to admit women in 1974 but missed the deadline before the university decided that only five colleges should start the ball rolling. The first woman fellow – Professor Anne Barton – was elected in 1974, but the first women undergraduates arrived in 1979, a suitable start to the second 600 years of the college. It made, as many observers said, both an enormous difference and none. Academic, musical, sporting and other activities continued unabated and much as they had, but the tone of life was very much changed for the better. The college

became gentler, friendlier, more cohesive. As successive editions of the undergraduates' *Alternative Prospectus* had it, when you entered New College, 'great waves of niceness washed over you'.

COLLEGE AND UNIVERSITY

Oxford is a collegiate university and has been since the thirteenth century, at first to a small, then greater and later overwhelming degree. The creation of New College in 1379, of itself and as a model for later foundations, greatly encouraged the collegiate system. However, the relationship of Oxford colleges to the university has consistently baffled outsiders and not a few insiders. Currently, the university matriculates and awards degrees to students, but only to those who are presented by colleges or permanent private halls.

Colleges are independent charitable corporations, established by law. Each has its own statutes, autonomous Governing Body and endowment. Although constituted within the university of Oxford, colleges are not directly controlled by the university. Since the reforms of the nineteenth century, the university has organised and run examinations for degrees, while colleges prepared the undergraduates through teaching. This last pedagogic function has become increasingly shared between colleges and academic departments of the university that provide lectures open to members of all colleges, a system developed from the inter-collegiate lectures pioneered by New College and Balliol in 1868. College-based teaching suited the traditional academic fare of classics and other arts subjects, although the university played a fructifying role in its maintenance of the Bodleian Library. When, after the First World War, the future warden, H.A.L. Fisher, as President of the Board of Education, asked Oxford and Cambridge how they would like to receive public

funding to offset the previous half century of declining income from agricultural land, Oxford plumped for aid to college teaching posts, while Cambridge chose assistance to faculties, a recognition of their then respective balances between arts and sciences. The necessary provision of laboratories for scientists militates towards more centralised university departmental structures, as has the recent emphasis on postgraduate degrees. Yet the colleges remain the defining institutions within the university, places where academics study and teach, and where students live, learn, play and socialise, even if in ways far less enclosed than before the abolition of gating hours and the arrival of co-education in the 1970s. Memories of Oxford habitually privilege college over university.

However, the links between the two run deeper and wider than simply organising lectures and exams and giving out degrees. The majority of tenured college fellows also hold university funded posts, mainly lectureships and professorships, with consequent university duties, such as lecturing, examining and faculty administration. All fellows are members of Congregation, the parliament of resident academics that is in theory constitutionally sovereign within the university, even though most powers are devolved to the university administration under the Vice-Chancellor. Originally, the chief official of the university was the Chancellor, some, like Warden Chaundler (1457–61, 1472–9), from New College. However, since 1483 and the appointment of a former New College fellow, John Russell, bishop of Lincoln, Chancellors have been absentees, the business of the university being left to Vice-Chancellors.

Above: *The High Table lunch for the election of Martin Williams as Proctor, March 2009.*

As a sign of the dominance of the colleges in the politics of a now federal university, these tended to be selected from amongst college heads and fellows until, under the new Laudian statutes of the 1630s, Vice-Chancellors were chosen solely from among the heads of colleges, wardens of New College included, a system that prevailed until the 1980s. The most recent New College Vice-Chancellor was Warden Smith (1954–7). The other ancient university office is that of Proctor, historically concerned with discipline but increasingly representing the ordinary senior members across a whole range of university committees and business. To them has been added the post of Assessor, originally designed to

care for the interests of women's colleges, now especially linked to student welfare. These posts are still chosen on a college rota system, each holder elected by the fellows of his or her college to hold office for one year. In such ways, colleges and their fellows, by membership of faculties, Congregation and by electing one of their number as Proctor or Assessor, are directly involved in running the university, notionally still an institution run by its academics. The first New College Proctor was Robert Thurbarn in 1399 (later a Doctor of Medicine and warden of Winchester). The most recent has been Professor Martin Williams, fellow in Engineering, installed with the usual colourful flummery in 2008.

RELIGION

WILLIAM POOLE

Religion, specifically and exclusively the Christian religion of the western European tradition, was once the heart of college life. Wykeham's foundation was ostensibly a clerical production-line: excepting 20 lawyers, two physicians and two astronomers, the remainder of the 70 fellows were supposed to proceed from their arts degrees on to theology. Although Wykehamists achieved fame later in life as administrators or lawyers, Wykeham's statutes were designed both to cajole (cash hand-outs) and coerce (expulsion after a fixed term of probation) the young fellows into holy orders and then ministry. The medieval and early-modern college, for most of its occupants, was a waiting-room until a college-controlled benefice became vacant. This ethos persisted until the nineteenth-century reforms.

The physical manifestation of the centrality of religion was the chapel. This was and is the most impressive component of the built environment. It was designed to seat all the fellows other than the probationers, who stood, as did the choir. Uniquely for the time, the nave (the ante-chapel) was shortened to two bays in length towards the west, and the bays to the north and south are not really set back deep enough to be called transepts. The result is that the chapel complex functions as two distinct spaces: a short but tall ante-chapel, set transverse to a long, impressive choir, reaching down to the altar, backed by the imposing reredos. This reredos (and most of the other carvings and sculptures in the chapel) would initially have been painted in bright colours, and when the original was

Above: *The only surviving English pre-Reformation pax, silver and gilt, c.1520.*

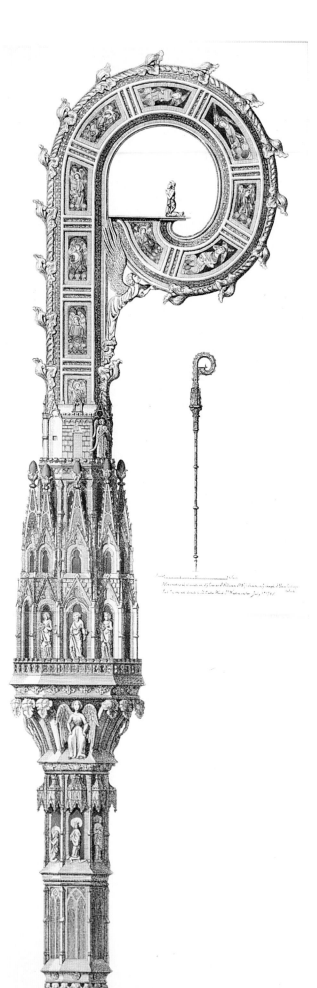

Right: The Founder's *crozier, as depicted in 1785.*

replaced in the eighteenth century traces of ultramarine paint were found in the niches. The chapel was staffed by 10 chaplains, three clerks, and 16 choristers. Mass was said seven times daily, but the academic fellows, who were, after all, supposed to be studying for degrees, were excused from full attendance, being required (merely) to sing the hours and attend High Mass with procession on Sundays, saints' days and 46 specific feast days. On all other days fellows were supposed to attend one of the set masses whenever they had a convenient hour.

This two-space chapel was originally put to both ecclesiastical and academic use. High in the south wall of the ante-chapel a slit in the masonry allowed (and still allows) the warden to look down from his lodgings into the ante-chapel, presumably to make sure that the fellows were all present and correct. Academic disputations were held regularly in the ante-chapel for centuries; there, too, morals were inspected. Rubric 60 of the statutes concerned the thrice-yearly *scrutinia*, in which all fellows were summoned to the ante-chapel for the original version of what today have become the more private and academic 'Warden's Collections'. The statutes were then read out, and offenders against them – or indeed any other suitably wicked 'surfeit, crime, or illicit pleasure' – were publicly upbraided and fined without right of appeal. The interlocking of the religious and the moral life of the fellows was thereby consolidated.

The Reformation changed the religious character of the college, although New College was long regarded, right into the seventeenth century, as a hive of closet papists. Seeming conformity under Edward VI turned with suspicious ease into seeming conformity under Mary I, with only a couple of fellows pushed out for their Protestantism. But the Elizabethan settlement shook up the fellowship considerably, with successive waves of purges, with almost 40 fellows ejected throughout the reign. A significant number became prominent scholars abroad, the Anglico-Lovanienses. The fellowship was outwardly conformist by the Jacobean period and was even starting to produce luminaries, notably Thomas

Bilson, bishop of Winchester, and Arthur Lake, warden and subsequently bishop of Bath and Wells. The Civil War saw further upsets and furnish us too with a story of iconoclasm visited on a window we would not otherwise know had ever existed. In the interregnum, as John Aubrey later recalled, the one stained glass window in the original college library, a representation of the Trinity placed in the east range, was smashed or removed.

Religion, of course, was not confined to the chapel. The teaching fellows oversaw the spiritual as well as intellectual habits of the undergraduate fellows and organized prayers and catechism. Even meal times in the early centuries of the college were rather austere affairs, with a chapel clerk or junior fellow required to read aloud while the rest of the college ate in silence, without 'verbosities, tall tales, shoutings, sniggerings, murmurings, or other unruly tumults', as the statutes admonish. Games were forbidden in both Hall and chapel, with a particular note that football was not to be played against the west wall of Hall, specifically in case the reredos above the altar on the other side of the wall was damaged by the shock waves. Religion meant decorum and respect for the college fabric. Private devotion, too, must have taken place in the residential chambers, both that supervised by the teaching fellows and that undertaken by individuals. Surviving book lists suggest that fellows supplemented their curricular reading with devotional material and sermons.

Chapel life continued unremarkably in the eighteenth century, but the mid-nineteenth century reforms cut the number of chaplains to three (and allowed tutorial fellows to wed). The fabric of the chapel itself was transformed later in the century when the architect Gilbert Scott adjusted the roof and pews and reconstructed the reredos into its imposing modern form. The college also became home to a number of distinguished scholar-priests. Here we might recall Hastings Rashdall, the philosopher and theologian, who transferred in 1895 from Balliol, where he was the chaplain, to New College, where he became fellow and tutor in philosophy. In the mid-twentieth century the college chaplain, R.H. Lightfoot, was a biblical critic of some boldness and distinction. Borrowing from the conclusions of the German 'higher criticism', Lightfoot argued that the Gospel of Mark originally ended intentionally halfway through what is now chapter 16, a conclusion accepted by scholars today, but a bold

Above: Arthur Lake, warden 1613–17, by Richard Greenbury, 1626–7, new version c.1700.

Above: *St James of Compostela, by El Greco (1541–1614), gift of Alfred Allnatt, 1963.*

to a college fellowship, and divine service is said or sung on an almost daily basis throughout full term. Sermons are preached, and the spot attracts major contemporary figures. The practice of academic debate in the chapel is currently undergoing an experimental revival.

The artistic life of the chapel continues, too. Most strikingly, the chapel is home to the sculptor Jacob Epstein's *Lazarus*, installed before the west door of the chapel in 1952, while on the north wall close to the altar is a St James by El Greco, gifted in 1963. More recently, the York Glaziers Trust has (since 2000) undertaken an ambitious restoration programme of the medieval stained glass in the ante-chapel. The original Tree of Jesse glass that had stood in the west window has, since the eighteenth century, been in the south wall of the nave of the Minster Church of St Peter in York, but a new Tree of Jesse window has just been installed in the vestry in 2006 by Rachel Thomas. Some 610 years after Wykeham's original statutes were ratified, his choral foundation has become arguably the most famous of its type in the world, as the twentieth settles into the twenty-first century, gradually tugging the palm away from the college's Cambridge counterpart, King's College. Indeed, New College is currently the only college in both Oxford and Cambridge in which both the dean of divinity and the choir director are practising academics and Governing Body fellows, a distinguished and distinguishing feature of the college. The chapel also still supplies certain ceremonial functions to assist the continuity of Wykeham's original design. In 2008 the fellows met as a body in the chapel to seal formally the election of the current warden by declaring aloud, one by one and in decreasing order of seniority, assent to the outcome of the secret ballot held earlier in the day. At the end, the fellows left the pews to walk directly into the cloisters through the great west door, specially opened for the occasion. It was an unusually sunny day, and as we turned west, there was Lazarus, raised from the dead, a dark shape streaming with light.

statement in the 1930s. He was also once reputedly pegged down by students with croquet hoops. One of his successors, G.V. Bennett, was a noted post-Restoration Church historian.

The modern religious life of the college is both more diverse and less central than it has been in the college's past. The college no longer offers theology as an undergraduate degree, and there are now no formal theologians among the tutorial fellows, something that would have horrified the Founder. Even worse from his point of view, mass is not said daily for the soul of William of Wykeham. The chapel is no longer used for formal lectures, examinations or the quarterly inspection of modern morals. Religious life, however, continues, although chapel attendance is no longer compulsory and the college no longer inquires into the religious beliefs of its members. The chaplaincy is a permanent post attached

LEARNING

WILLIAM POOLE

New College has not been uniformly celebrated for its scholarship. As the antiquary Anthony Wood protested in 1682, the fellows were 'much given to drinking and gaming, and vaine brutish pleasure. They degenerat in learning.' Wood damningly described the intellectual *cursus honorum* provided by New College: 'Golden Scholars, silver Bachelors, leaden Masters, wooden Doctors.'

To some extent this is so. Wykeham was an administrator and a churchman, and although he made sure his college was endowed with a sizeable collection of manuscript books, 'pure' scholarship as such was a low priority for Wykeham. Nevertheless, his utilitarianism can be exaggerated. Wykeham is to be commended, for example, for stipulating in his statutes designated fellowships in astronomy and medicine, two apiece, a very unusual move at the time. In the college's earliest days these fellowships prompted the creation of a special 'astronomy desk' in the library.

The first scholar of New College for whom any work survives was John Walter (died 1412?), an astronomer who was a fellow by 1386, and who has left only two works, both on how to calculate horoscopes. He also presented the college with one manuscript, a commentary on Revelations. Another early scholar was Robert Heete (died 1433), legal writer, donor of books and the first biographer of Wykeham. But the first college writer of any substance was Nicholas Upton (*c*.1400–57, matriculated 1413), author of *De studio militari*, a work on heraldry and war-craft written in 1447 and dedicated to Humfrey, duke of Gloucester. The famous name from the early centuries of the college, however, is William Grocyn (1449?–1519, matriculated 1465). As a student of Greek, he was preceded in the college by John Farley, the first man to have attempted Greek in Oxford, but Farley died young. Grocyn, on the other hand, has achieved permanent fame as the first Oxford public lecturer on Greek, having left England for Italy in 1488 to better himself in the language, before returning to Oxford three years later to commence his lectures on the Pauline Epistles and on Dionysius the Areopagite. Two of his Greek manuscripts remain in the library.

The next college scholars of note were the grammarians William Horman (1457–1535, matriculated 1475) and John Stanbridge (1463–1510, matriculated 1480). Horman became headmaster of Eton and then Winchester and published humanistic textbooks, notably the *Vulgaria*, a large collection of English sentences with model Latin translations, first published in 1519. Stanbridge, who published similar textbooks, opened the free school in Banbury.

Opposite: Book of St John's Apocalypse, *fourteenth century, donated by William of Wykeham.*

Below: *Ptolomey's Almagest, fourteenth century, donated by John Farley.*

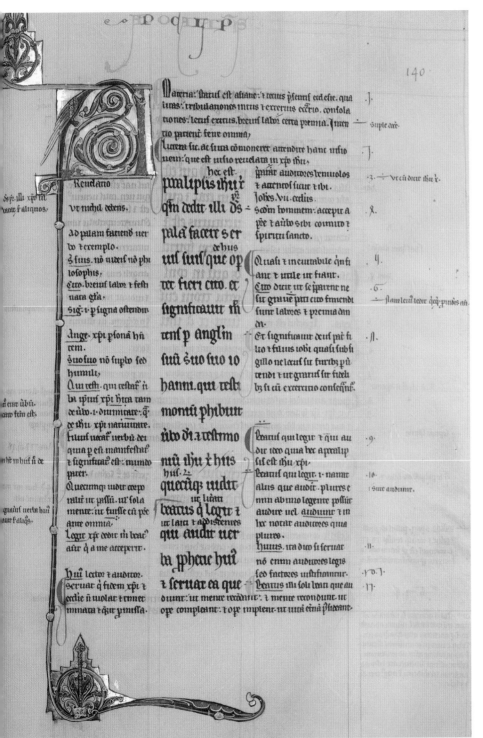

The dominant, if now largely unreadable, phase in New College scholarship was implemented by Roman Catholic scholars in an increasingly Protestant world: the antiquaries Robert Talbot (1505/6–58, matriculated 1521) who wrote on the Antonine Itinerary, and Richard White, who wrote a history of Britain; the scholarly brothers John and Nicholas Harpsfield; the long string of controversialists, Thomas Harding, Nicholas Saunders, Thomas Dorman, John Rastall, Robert Poyntz, John Martiall, Thomas Stapleton, Thomas Hide and Thomas Darrell; the translator William Blandy; the geographer and poet Richard Willes; and the early Hebraist Thomas Neal. After the death of Mary most of these men fled to Louvain and picked up their pens to attack the nascent Elizabethan Church. But the Protestants can claim a Marian martyr from among the scholars: John Philpot, who wrote on language, was burned at Smithfield in 1555.

In the visitation of 1566–7, in a backlash against widespread recusancy in the college, the bishop of Winchester banned the fellows from reading the works of the earlier popish fellows, especially Harding, Saunders, Martiall and Dorman. Nicholas Harpsfield, however, composed a notorious manuscript tract on the divorce of Henry VIII, and although this was not published until 1878, New College owns two later seventeenth-century manuscript copies of it, probably commissioned by the college in around 1670. The tract was subsequently much handed about by the fellows of that time, an interesting example of the clandestine circulation within college of an indigenous work at least a century after its initial composition.

The late sixteenth and seventeenth centuries saw a welcome change in emphasis from religious controversy. There were still theologians, of course, most famously Thomas James, first librarian of the Bodleian Library and patristic polemicist, and most voluminously the dour Calvinist William Twisse, probably the reason why Archbishop Laud could later make the otherwise bizarre complaint that New College men spent too

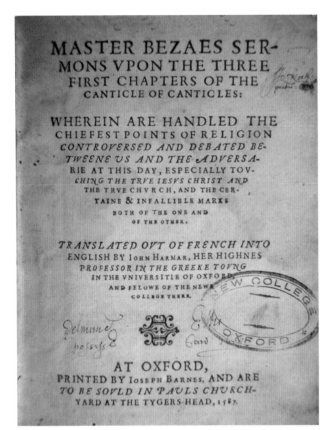

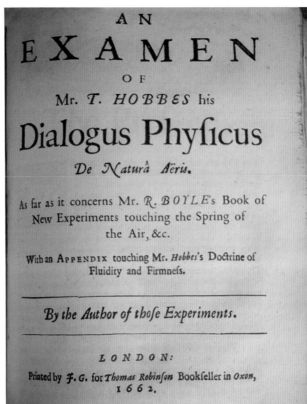

much time reading Calvin's *Institutes*. Twisse, a flaming predestinarian, later sat on the Westminster Assembly. But less partisan scholarship was flowering. Earlier, Cyprian Lucar (1544–1611?, matriculated 1561) had published works on artillery and surveying, arts that depended on a decent training in practical mathematics. John Harmar, the Regius Professor of Greek, was responsible for the first book entirely in Greek printed in Oxford, a little set of sermons by Chrysostom taken from New College manuscripts. Harmar was one of the translators of the Authorized Version, as was the Regius Professor of Hebrew, William Thorne of New College, who published in 1592 an interesting rhetoric textbook in which he divided classical rhetoric up following logical categories. Harmar's nephew, also John, also of New College, also became Regius Professor of Greek and was responsible for the etymological appendix to the standard Greek–Latin dictionary of the seventeenth century, Scapula's *Lexicon*. The greatest English technical chronologer of the period, Thomas Lydiat, locked horns with Scaliger and Kepler, and he also wrote on astronomy, proposing the elliptical orbits of the planets before Kepler himself. He was careful to donate a set of his books to the library of his old college, where they still reside.

The most important legal scholar of his time was Richard Zouche, one of the founders of international law and an architect of the Laudian Code for Oxford. As Anthony Wood wrote of him: 'An exact artist, a subtile logician, expert historian, and for the knowledge in, and practice of, the civil law, the chief person of his time; as his works, much esteemed beyond the seas (where several of them are reprinted), partly testify.' Zouche, as we shall later see, was also a playwright in his youthful days.

In the Restoration natural philosophy became the dominant scholarly output of college. The records of book borrowing and purchasing in this period show that the college was increasingly keen on acquiring the works of the 'new philosophy', and fellows themselves were now gifting the texts of Bacon, Galileo, Kepler, Descartes, Gassendi, Digby, White, Hobbes and eventually Robert Boyle – the modern college holds at least 140 separate Boyle titles published before 1700, most acquired in the seventeenth and eighteenth centuries. We know there were celestial and terrestrial globes in the college from at least the sixteenth century, and a mathematical lecture had been established in 1616 by Warden Lake, three years before the university's Savilian chairs in astronomy and geometry were established. At the end of the seventeenth

Above: *Halley's Observatory and* (below) *telescope, atop 7 New College Lane, 2010.*

century the Savilian Professor of Geometry John Wallis leased 'Stable Hall' from the college in what is now New College Lane, and after his death the lease was passed to the university on behalf of the Savilian Professor of Astronomy. Hence the famous turret, still there today, at the top of what is now an undergraduate residence, but which was once Edmond Halley's observatory. (Another famous astronomer, James Bradley, succeeded Halley to

the chair and hence to the observatory.) In New College the significant figures working in the new sciences were the librarian Robert Sharrock, friend and translator of Robert Boyle and an important writer on plant sciences; Ralph Bohun, tutor to the Evelyn family and a pioneer meteorologist; Walter Harris, physician, chemist and pediatrist; and William Musgrave, the first New College FRS, also FRCP, antiquary, Secretary to the Royal Society and therefore editor for a time of the *Philosophical Transactions*. In 1683 the Oxford Philosophical Society was founded, and among its first members were New College men: Sharrock himself, and Francis Turner, later the non-juring bishop of Ely.

In the eighteenth century New College was littered with future bishops, but its achievements in scholarship were noticeably thinner than in the previous centuries, and the number of (remembered) poets also went down too. The high Tory writer William Pittis (1673/4–1724) might grudgingly be recalled, although we can certainly regret his 1701 edition of Chaucer, in simplified verse ('Written by no Body'). The great figure of this century is probably Robert Lowth the grammarian, biblical critic, antiquary and eventually bishop of London (1710–87, matriculated 1730). Lowth was elected Professor of Poetry in 1741, and from his second term, commencing in 1746, he delivered the lectures that were to be published as *Praelectiones de sacra poesi Hebraeorum* (1753). Lowth argued that Hebrew poetry was structured not on classical but oriental principles, in which parallelism replaced western ideas of strict metre or rhyme. Lowth thereby popularized an understanding of ancient Hebrew poetry as a form with an authority and power both more ancient than, and formally distinct from, the kinds of poetry hitherto attempted in the western vernaculars. Lowth's lectures are credited with having inspired the experimental poetry of Christopher Smart, notably his *Jubilate agno*, written from 1757 in the madhouse. It is pleasant to think that the most famous hymn to a cat in English – 'For I praise my cat Jeffrey' – may have been written under the influence of Lowth's notions of Old Testament poetry. Lowth also wrote an English grammar and an important life of the Founder. William Smith (1711–87, matriculated 1728) was Lowth's contemporary and also a classical scholar. He published on Longinus, Thucydides and Xenophon.

The remainder of the eighteenth and nineteenth centuries are dotted with figures of interest in the college, but none of them pointing to a definitive college trend in any given area. Charles Abbot (matriculated 1779, DD 1802) became a prominent botanist and entomologist, arranging Bedfordshire flora along Linnaean lines. John Walker (fellow 1797–1820) was an important antiquary of the university itself. Bulkeley Bandinel (BA 1805, DD 1823), the well-known Bodley's Librarian of his time, clung to his post for almost half a century. But it was the nineteenth-century reforms of the college that heralded a wider renewal in scholarship in the college. Warden Shuttleworth, at the beginning of the process, was also an admired anti-Tractarian preacher and writer. Hereford Brooke George, one of the first new men and a fellow from 1856 until his death in 1910, was a tutor, reformer, alpinist and writer on military and imperial history. His *Historical Geography of the British Empire* (1904) appeared in many editions, including a posthumous revision. The

Wykeham Professors of Logic form an imposing line right into the present day, of which the most famous of the early incumbents is John Cooke Wilson and, in the twentieth century, A.J. Ayer, whose *Language, Truth, and Logic* (1936) is still an influential work, especially upon modern historiographical method. The two Savilian chairs in geometry and astronomy also tied academic brilliance to the college. Of the many incumbents, we might recall in particular the mathematician G.H. Hardy, Savilian Professor of Geometry and the 'discoverer' of the legendary Indian mathematician Srinivasa Ramanujan. Hardy wrote a fine autobiography, *A Mathematician's Apology* (1940).

The physiological sciences came of age with the arrival of John Scott Haldane as a fellow in 1901. Haldane was a physiologist of a philosophical bent, who believed in the teleology of biological life, but he also insisted on the practical applications of research and was consistently interested in improving the conditions of miners, for instance. His son, John Burdon Sanderson Haldane, received his degrees at New College just before the war and returned as a fellow just after it. The younger Haldane was to become a famous geneticist, but he left for Cambridge in 1923. He also became a communist, later

Opposite: *Robert Lowth, fellow 1733, bishop of London, by Robert Edge Pine, c.1777.*

Inset: The Holy Bible containing the Old Testament and the New… *Oxford, 1717, presented by Robert Lowth.*

Far left: *G.H. Hardy, Savilian Professor of Geometry from 1920.*

Middle: *J.S. Haldane, fellow 1902–36, by Tom Van Oss, 1930.*

Left: *A.J. Ayer, fellow and Wykeham Professor of Logic, 1959–78, by Don Bachardy, 1959.*

leaving the party in protest against Stalin's interference with scientific research. The Wykeham chair in Physics attracted a succession of outstanding scholars, none more so that the Nobel Laureate of 1955, the Californian Willis Lamb (1956–62). Domestically, perhaps Lamb's most lasting contribution was his donation to the SCR of its first TV set. (Warden Fisher had had one in the 1930s.)

Work in the humanities was also growing stronger over the decades crossing the turn of the century. There had always been a decent tradition of Hebrew in the college stretching back to the sixteenth century, and Samuel Rolles Driver's *A Treatise on the Use of the Tenses in Hebrew* (1874) proved a landmark in the study of Hebrew syntax. He is the 'Driver' of the still standard 'Brown, Driver and Briggs' lexicon of Old Testament Hebrew. Hastings Rashdall, elected fellow and tutor in philosophy in 1895, was a philosopher, theologian and legendary tutor, but he is probably best remembered for his *The Universities of Europe in the Middle Ages* (1895), a work that was revised and reprinted for almost a century, the last reprint being 1997. D.S. Margoliouth (matriculated 1877) was a linguistic polymath of uncommon range. As a student he won almost all the prizes on offer, including those for Greek, Hebrew, Syriac and Sanskrit. He became

a fellow of the college and soon afterwards was elected to the Laudian chair of Arabic. He was prone to argue some curious theses, of which the most notorious was his contention that pre-Islamic Arabic poetry was, in fact, forged a few centuries later.

Quite different was Sir John Arthur Ransome Marriott, undergraduate and then lecturer in modern history from 1883. He left to become an educationalist and a Conservative MP, but he found time to write many historical works when not in public service, including *The Life and Times of Lucius Cary, Viscount Falkland'* (1907). H.L.A. Hart,

David Margoliouth (1858–1940)

David Margoliouth was a brilliant Orientalist educated at Winchester, and at New College, where his double first in Greats was accompanied by an unprecedented number of awards and prizes. His Jewish father converted to Anglicanism, as did his uncle Moses; the former worked as a missionary to the Jews in Bethnal Green. Margoliouth himself was also briefly a priest in the Church of England before becoming Oxford's Laudian Professor of Arabic, a post he held from 1889 to 1937. His volumes included *Mohammed and the Rise of Islam* (1905), *The Early Development of Mohammedanism* (1914), and *The Relations Between Arabs and Israelites Prior to the Rise of Islam* (1924). For much of his career he was a prominent member of the Royal Asiatic Society, serving as a member of its council, its director and then its president; he was awarded the Society's triennial gold medal in 1928.

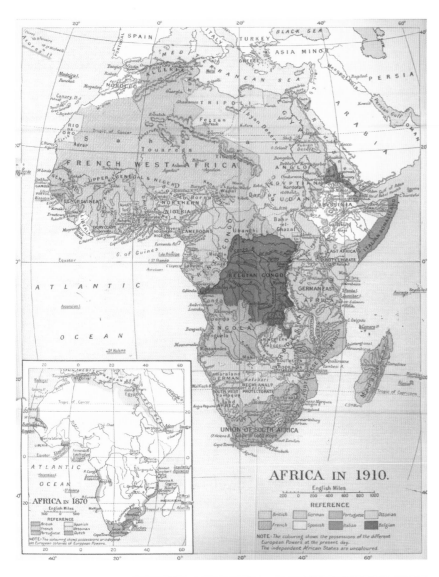

Above: *Africa as seen in 1910 from Fisher's monumental* History of Europe, *1935.*

Right: *Isaiah Berlin, fellow 1938–50, photographed probably by Christopher Cox, 1933.*

a scholar and fellow of the college, became one of the most influential legal philosophers of the twentieth century, progressing to the chair of jurisprudence in Oxford (1952–68) and the principalship of Brasenose (1973–8).

The expansion of the fellowship from its classical base came only slowly. Fellows in chemistry and biology had been elected before the First World War; one in physics in 1925. The introduction of PPE led to an appointment in economics in 1922 and a further strengthening of philosophy, long a staple of classical Greats. Apart from professorial fellows such as H. Price and A.J. Ayer, few colleges could improve on the succession of contrasting philosophy tutors in the twentieth century that included H.W.B. Joseph, Richard Crossman, Isaiah Berlin, Herbert Hart and Stuart Hampshire. Until after the Second World War undergraduates still overwhelmingly read Lit. Hum., law or history. In arts subjects no English fellow was elected until 1939 and no modern linguist until after 1945. Subjects not covered by the fellowship were taught by college lecturers or outside tutors. Despite an often gruelling load of tutorials, some of the arts fellows nonetheless managed to pursue research and even, a feature not that common in pre-1960s Oxford, publish books. Among the productive academic tutorial fellows was the distinguished line of historians: Fisher, on Napoleon (his famous *History of Europe* was written when he was warden), David Ogg on the seventeenth century and Alan Bullock on Hitler.

The intellectual life of the college since the mid-twentieth century has maintained and consolidated the standard provoked by the nineteenth-century reforms. It is perhaps indecorous to comment on the scholarship of the recent, but we might note that the Governing Body in 2010 includes about a dozen statutory chairs in the university (about a fifth of the total Governing Body), and that it is now only a matter of fine taste among the top three or four colleges in the university where New College stands.

TEACHING

WILLIAM POOLE

The original Oxford colleges were not teaching institutions; they were graduate colleges housing students for the higher degrees who received instruction outside the college itself. New College was rather different, however, for in tandem with Winchester College it purposively covered the entire educational cursus from the first steps in grammar to the attainment of the highest degrees. It therefore performed the functions of an undergraduate college without having any 'commoners' – that is to say, students supernumerary to the scholars on the 'foundation'. In short, all New College students were *socii* or 'fellows'; a 'scholar' was merely a new student from Winchester on probation for two years before his fellowship was confirmed.

Wykeham's college was geared towards teaching potential clergy. A number of the graduate fellows were appointed and paid as tutors to the undergraduate fellows, perhaps overseeing between six and ten undergraduates each. The original undergraduate fellows were also barred from applying for 'graces' or dispensations from the university, a mechanism by which Wykeham hoped he could enforce academic quality. (Over time this custom, it has been argued, was grossly distorted: as a 'grace' became the right to supplicate for a degree and not dispensation from certain of its requirements, the statute was interpreted as excusing New College scholars from the need to sit university exams, precisely the opposite of the spirit of the original statute.) Indeed, before New College scholars were allowed to dispute in the university for their degrees, they

had to rehearse before a board of senior fellows in order to prove that they were adequately prepared. This partial assumption of responsibility for undergraduate teaching has been seen as the germ of the tutorial system. The irony here is that Wykeham's giant foundation, with its internal academic watchdog, its injunctions of silence at meals and its continual round of sung and spoken devotions in the chapel, was semi-monastic in both organization and inspiration; yet this very emphasis on senior-to-junior teaching was the spring of the future, and to this day the tutorial system is what distinguishes not just New College, but all Oxford and Cambridge undergraduate colleges,

Below: *A medieval lecture or admonition, New College misericord, late fourteenth century.*

Right: *David Cecil,
fellow 1939–69, by
Cecil Beaton, c.1971.*

from other higher education institutes in this country. In
the context of the other Oxford colleges, this move was
also a radical innovation, because it assumed that a college
has a pedagogical as opposed to a merely pastoral or
proprietorial role in the lives of its members.

Nevertheless, we can easily exaggerate the initial
success of this model. As so often in New College history,
once again what had been a means of reform was in
time used as an excuse for stagnancy. For whereas the
other colleges throughout the sixteenth and seventeenth
centuries reformed their own structures in order to take
on undergraduate students, New College largely opted
out of reform. Indeed, apart from a few modifications,
until the nineteenth century the college remained by
Wykeham's statutes a community of a warden and 70
scholars who were in effect all fellows. As demand for
university education rose in the sixteenth century, other
colleges welcomed the new category of commoner – that
is, a student not on the foundation or, in New College
terms, a member not among the statutory 70, hence not
a fellow and hence not paid for by the revenue generated
from college estates. New College eventually made slight,
but only slight steps in this direction: in 1677 it agreed
to admit 16 noble and gentleman commoners, and the

Garden Quadrangle was built to accommodate them; the
names of all the donors for the extension are recorded
in John Ayliffe's chapter on New College in his *The
Ancient and Present State of the University of Oxford* (1714).
But while most other colleges expanded their scope of
operations, New College, content with its statutory 70
fellows and its sprinkling of gentleman commoners, was
slowly left behind. With it languished its daughter college
All Souls, the society in modern Oxford that today most
resembles early-modern New College.

Matters were not entirely moribund, however,
from the point of view of teaching and learning. A few
of the fellows, as we noted, were salaried separately as
what we would now term 'tutorial fellows', and some
internal strengthening took place in the early sixteenth
century, when the royal visitation of 1535 established
lectureships in Greek and Latin in the college. Early
in the next century Warden Lake added lectureships in
Hebrew and mathematics to these, and so apart from the
standard arts instruction in logic and rhetoric there were
now designated teachers in not only Latin but Greek
and Hebrew as well as mathematics. In 1677, as we saw,
resident non-foundation students were admitted, in small
quantities at first.

Nevertheless, the Restoration marked the
commencement of the decline in student numbers,
and New College remained a static society of generally
rather well-off fellows and certainly well-off gentleman
commoners, where few were disposed to do work. A
glimpse at what kind of instruction was received in the
early eighteenth century is provided by the commonplace
book of Edward Filmer of New College (Bodleian MS
Eng. e. 2312), commenced in 1700 and containing
conventional cribs for logic, spherical astronomy, geometry,
the use of the quadrant and historical and legal notes.
(This Filmer, afterwards 3rd baronet of that establishment,
later married the granddaughter of John Wallis, Savilian
Professor of Geometry and Oxford's most famous resident
mathematician at the time of Filmer's matriculation).

Left: *Horace W.B. Joseph, fellow 1891– 1943, by Kenneth Knowles, 1931.*

Later in the century we have the famous diary of James Woodforde, who rose up the college hierarchy between 1759 and 1776. His undergraduate years were almost entirely barren of work. He was taught, but by external tutors, and his diary is largely concerned with eating, drinking and gaming. To be sure, the indolence of Woodforde can be exaggerated – we learn too, for instance, of his early purchase of John Wallis's textbook on logic and of Commandinus' edition of Euclid, so it would seem that Warden Lake's earlier hopes for mathematics in the college were not in vain. As required, Woodforde now and then also declaimed in chapel on a set rhetorical theme, the chief public exercise of the *artista*. But these are only cameo entries; more representative was the evening in 1759 when Woodforde went to hear Handel's *Alexander's Feast* in the Holywell Music Room. Afterwards, he sat up with three friends from Magdalen until 2am while they worked through six bottles of wine. There is not a flicker of guilt in Woodforde's diary, not the slightest hint that there was any better way of living the academic life. Happy days!

Relative intellectual stagnation reigned, then, because fellows were happy with their lot; because the college remained set in its 'warden-and-70-scholars' mould, with only a few wealthy and similarly indolent additions; and because – an important consideration – anyone claiming 'Founder's Kin' (a supposed blood-relationship to Wykeham) could assume priority in election. New College was, in truth, suffocated by pseudo-Wykehams enjoying prosperity innocent of scholarship. This situation continued well into the nineteenth century.

Change came with Warden Shuttleworth, a man of anti-Tractarian resolve and inventor of the Port Railway. Shuttleworth persuaded the college to give up its right to award degrees without public examination, and he made it harder for probationer fellows to become full fellows. Under his more reluctant successor Warden Williams the university commission, appointed in 1850, initially met with resistance from the college, which refused to hand over a copy of the statutes. In the succeeding negotiations for

educational reform the college gradually conceded that it had limited options in the face of a government commission with executive powers. By 1857, among other educational reforms, the original configuration of a fellowship of 70 was replaced by a dual community of 30 scholars and 30 fellows, the latter class now appointed by examination, with half the fellowships, for the first time, open to men with no connection to either Winchester or New College. (The loss of 10 fellows was to free up money to pay for the new system.) In a move that in the long term has done much to enhance the academic status of the college, the Savilian chairs were attached to the foundation. The stifling privilege of Founder's Kin was abolished, as was the necessity of proceeding to holy orders.

In the next generation three fellows in particular, E.C. Wickham, Alfred Robinson and Hereford George, pushed for further educational reforms. In 1868 intercollegiate lectures were set up, shared between Balliol and New College. In 1877 came the royal commission and with it a new set of statutes for the college, after almost five centuries of the originals. Even the warden, now, was encouraged to be a scholar. The fellows were divided into professorial, official, emeritus, research and supernumerary fellowship categories, more or less the division still current. The two Savilian and three Wykeham chairs were permanently tied to the foundation. A Tuition Fund was established for the payment of tutors and lecturers, and statute XIII.2 insisted that tutorial teaching be provided all year round: 'The warden and fellows shall provide courses of instruction for the Undergraduate members of the College during at least 24 weeks in the Academical year.' Those elected to teaching fellowships were required to be vetted by a board that

Right: *A tutorial essay in progress…*

was supposed both to appraise the teaching needs of the college and to consult the appropriate faculty concerning the candidate's suitability as an instructor. The modern tutorial system had arrived.

The modern tutorial is now the core of college life and is not just something a few recently graduated fellows are pressed into providing. With the shifting of the tutorial system towards the centre of the college's activities, undergraduate numbers inevitably increased. Perhaps surprisingly, undergraduate numbers today have not changed greatly since the Second World War. Indeed, in the immediate aftermath of the war undergraduate numbers peaked, rising to well over 400, and the modern community of taught undergraduates fluctuates around that number. Many receive instruction from their faculties in the form of lectures and classes, but all are taught in tutorials or classes (or both) within the college and usually by a teaching fellow on the Governing Body. Styles of tutorial of course differ from subject to subject, but increasingly in the humanities the culture of the read-out essay is giving way to longer pieces of work submitted in advance by both undergraduates in a tutorial pairing, who in an age of computers are also in danger of forgetting how to argue with a pen in hand. But the greatest change, of course, is that women now teach and learn in the college. Indeed, the first female teaching

fellow was appointed in 1974, well before the first female undergraduates, who arrived in 1979 and who now comprise nearly half the undergraduate body.

Another great change in recent years has been in the number of graduate students. Before the Second World War there were few research students; by the late 1970s there were perhaps one hundred or so; today, the MCR numbers around 200 students, comprising therefore roughly a third of the junior body. And within the graduate cohort, almost one-half are classed as 'freshers', an indication that one type of graduate degree has been very much on the rise: the taught, short-term masters' degree or similar qualification. It might be assumed that these new types of graduate have little to do with the college teaching effort because their instruction is provided for largely by their faculties. But increasingly the larger graduate body plays a part in the college teaching effort: today's graduates are encouraged to seek out teaching opportunities, and the fellows in turn are encouraged to find ways to enlist MCR support within the tutorial system. More people in the modern college are, therefore, involved in teaching than ever before, even as demands for research 'output' continue to rise. Going, but happily not quite gone, are the days of Woodforde, with his wine, his billiards and his bowls, and a bit of Euclid on the side.

Music

EDWARD HIGGINBOTTOM

What would William of Wykeham think of the musical enterprise he set in train? He would recognize its locus, the chapel, be rather pleased that we still maintain 'his' 16 choristers and be gratified that the clerks are now more in number. Setting aside his dismay at finding a reformed Church (less inclined to pray for his soul), he would – I hope – applaud the vigour and regularity of the choir's singing. But the chapel is no longer a medieval chantry, and it is more than a place of Christian worship. As for the secular music-making of undergraduates, a low form of entertainment in the fourteenth century, today's fellows are generally approving of their tutees' involvement in orchestral and chamber music, complaining only when it appears to take over. Certainly, now that the subject 'music' has been absorbed into the academic framework (though the degrees of BMus and DMus are centuries old), we can talk of a different ethos surrounding music-making within the university and of a greater range of activity.

New College's part in all this is not very different from the part played by any of the medieval foundations and, indeed, by those of later vintage. The relative grandeur of the college, and spectacularly its chapel, obviously helped sustain musical provision. Where other colleges lost their choir schools during the twentieth century, New College did not, and it is one of now three 'choral foundations' in the university, Oxford vying with London as the place where you encounter an *embarras de richesse* in the field of liturgical music.

What then has marked out New College during its six centuries? There is evidence as early as the fifteenth century of the use of the latest and most elaborate polyphony (fragments of which were recovered from college wallpaper), with concordances in the iconic collection of the time, the Eton Choirbook, but there is no evidence of an association with any leading English composer of either the fifteenth or early sixteenth century to compare with John Taverner's association with Christ Church or John Sheppard's with Magdalen College.

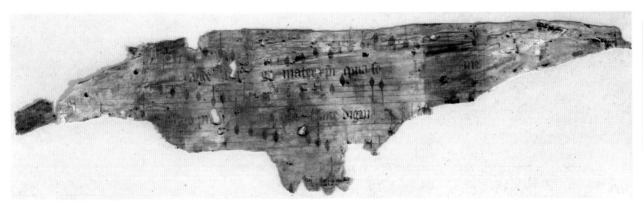

Left: *As found behind New College wallpaper; a fragment of* Gaude flore virginali *by Edmund Turges (b. c.1450). Turges was possibly employed as a chaplain at New College, Oxford, in 1507–8.*

Right: *Philip Hayes (1738–97), organist 1776–97, in his DMus gown, by John Hamilton Mortimer, 1777.*

Far right: *Hugh Allen, fellow 1908–46 and Heather Professor of Music, by John Singer Sargent, 1925.*

In fact, New College has to struggle to find an association that matches – the best we can do for this period is Thomas Weelkes, who took his BMus at the college – yet we know that New College was lavishly provided for its music and had at one time no fewer than three organs installed in its chapel. We also know that the fifteenth century was intellectually a high watermark for the college.

We have to move forward to the eighteenth century to see the college emerging on to the uplands of music achievement. Starting with John Weldon (organist 1694–1702, and a pupil of Henry Purcell) and moving on to Philip Hayes (organist 1776–97), New College enjoyed a period when its directors of music were musicians of high repute. Weldon moved from New College to the Royal Chapel. Philip Hayes became Heather Professor of Music and accumulated posts also at Magdalen and St John's. He had many connections with London musical life, often climbing into the eighteenth-century equivalent of the Oxford Tube (from which sprang the sobriquet 'Phil chaise' – his 20 stone left little room for company). The music books purchased by the college at this time show it fully abreast of new publications by William Croft, Maurice Greene and William Boyce, and the

surviving manuscript material contains among other things transcriptions from Handel's oratorios made as early as the 1740s. Hayes directed Oxford performances of Handel and secured much of Boyce's music library (later to find its way to the Bodleian). This was the period when the college was spending large sums of money on Wyatt's reconstruction of the chapel roof, new stained glass for the main body of the chapel and the Reynolds window. It was also the same period when a visitor commented somewhat unkindly that, attending evensong, he found it 'idly performed'. But whatever the eighteenth century was like for musical performance, the college was certainly in the swim of things, and it was ambitious for its liturgical practice.

The nineteenth century was marked perhaps more by its honest toil. Gilbert Heathcote and Stephen Elvey were clearly assiduous in their commitment to chapel music. Psalters were pointed and published. A New College hymnbook eventually saw the light of day in 1900. Performances were promoted in Hall, including Handel's *Samson* in 1847, and traces of the chorister activity surface in the programme for an 'Entertainment' provided by them for the college, consisting of madrigals, part-songs, a piano duet and recitations.

A different picture emerges in the first half of the twentieth century, when a succession of eminent musicians – Sir Hugh Allen (1901–19), Sir William Harris (1919–29), Sir John Dykes Bower (1929–33), Dr Sydney Watson (1933–8) and H.K. Andrews (1938–56) – held the post of organist. Once again the chapel reflected wider musical concerns and interests, visited by figures such as Jean Sibelius, Albert Schweitzer, Ralph Vaughan Williams and Leopold Stokowski. In Hugh Allen musical patronage lay in the hands of one of the most vigorous and determined musicians and administrators of the day, elected to the Heather Professorship in 1918 and appointed Principal of the Royal College of Music in 1919. He was a champion of the works of J.S. Bach, and ensured that the composer's works were often sung in New College chapel or performed in the Sheldonian with the Oxford Bach Choir. Allen also achieved recognition in the college in his election to a fellowship in 1908.

Allen's successor, H.K. Andrews, was the world's leading authority on the music of William Byrd, and the chapel was known, more or less affectionately, as 'The Byrd Sanctuary'. He took offence, however, at the jingle posted by an undergraduate:

Nothing could be cleaner
Than the style of Palestrina.
A thing in which Byrd
Sometimes erred.

During this period the chapel choir deservedly enjoyed a high reputation for the quality of its work. It was selected to broadcast regularly during the Second World War and began the tradition of making commercial recordings, the first in 1927 on the HMV label (these early recordings are available on a New College Choir Archive CD). The choir's recordings, which now number over a hundred, cover the whole range of sacred repertory from early sixteenth-century antiphons to music of our own time.

Another change was effected by David Lumsden (organist 1953–76) with the installation of a new organ in

1969, designed Grant, Degens and Bradbeer, with a screen by G.G. Pace. Lumsden went on to be Principal of the Royal Academy of Music.

All of this now, of course, forms a part of a wider practice of music within the college. The community at large supports regular orchestral and chamber music-making. The clerks are often heard as vocal soloists, and since the 1990s the New Chamber Opera has established itself as a small-scale Glyndebourne, having now staged over 40 productions, from Stradella to Maxwell Davies. Under the leadership of Michael Burden this initiative has transformed the provision of opera in the university. Its activity includes commissions and recordings, and its productions are accompanied by an in-house 'period' orchestra, the Band of Instruments. An opera studio has been established to provide undergraduate singers with operatic experience and to support the lectures given by the university's visiting professors of Opera.

The music course in the university, naturally enough, encourages the practice of music as well as its theory, composition, analysis and history, and a number of options in the syllabus allow undergraduates to offer their performance skills as part of their degree. Here the college acts as a catalyst, encouraging and promoting weekly musical performances by its highly motivated and talented students. It is a place where excellent opportunities lead

Above: *New College organ book, volume 1, open at Handel's 'O come let us worship', from* Messiah, *late eighteenth century.*

display, more or less lavish, of the college's musical activity is entirely in keeping with the medieval foundation, the first of its kind in England to provide so grandly for its music, and is in keeping with Wykeham's ambition to provide a solid benefit to society at large.

A CHORISTER'S WAR

William of Wykeham's statutes established a choir of sixteen choristers as an integral part of the scheme for his college. The choir has remained ever since despite changes in confessional allegiances, shifting liturgical fashions, altered religious habits and institutional reforms. **John Platts,** *who later came up as an undergraduate to read History at New College (1949), recalls his experience as a chorister (1938–44) during exceptional times.*

eventually to distinguished musical careers. Though these students are not restricted to a college experience and find outlets in the many university organizations dedicated to musical performance, New College is the base from which it all springs.

If a recent change in college manners has been the adoption of an 'access' policy, the music of the college pointed the way rather earlier: here was a richness in liturgical and musical practice to be shared. And the college continues to share it with the community, the choir reaching a worldwide public through its recordings, foreign tours and broadcasts (including webcasting). This

In June 1938, I was one of the candidates on trial for the choir waiting my turn in the cheerless vestry, crammed with nervous little boys and fussy mothers. The Practice Room next door was inhabited by a race of gentle pipe-smoking giants: Colin Baynes, who was Usher (ie Headmaster of the Choir School); Sydney Watson, who hovered benignly in the window recess; and H.K. Andrews (HKA), who put me through my paces – *How beautiful are the feet* and identification of 'the middle note'. This was to be the last year of peace. That Christmas, Mrs Fisher entertained us to a party in the Warden's Lodgings – Eton suits, smarmed-down hair, jelly, cake and charades. The following June, Sir Hugh Allen, HKA and A.H. Smith (later to become warden) took us on a picnic on the White Horse Hill. I sat in the horse's chalky eye, eating a hard-boiled egg. But these were the last such treats that we choristers were to enjoy.

At the beginning of the Michaelmas Term 1939 the Headmaster addressed us solemnly on the subject of the war and told us how we could all help by making sacrifices such as not wearing socks in the summer. I wondered how my going sockless was going to bring the Third Reich crashing to its knees, but was too timid to ask. To outward appearances the college changed little, apart from the removal of the more

Right: *Kevin Skelton (Polidoro) and Tim Armstrong-Taylor (Simone) in New Chamber Opera's* La finta semplice *by Mozart, photograph by Sasha Snow, 2005.*

Right: *The organ of 1969, by Grant, Degens and Bradbeer.*

Below: *The trebles at work, 2009.*

valuable fourteenth-century stained-glass windows in the ante-chapel. Other treasures, the Founder's crozier and the misericord seats in the chapel were stored 'in safe places'. Only the most urgent repairs were carried out on the buildings and city wall. The sacred turf in the Front Quad, originally laid in the eighteenth century, was desecrated by the installation of a static water tank. It was still there when I returned as an undergraduate in 1949. Most degree courses were suspended, except in vital subjects such as medicine. New College was host to victims of the misfortunes of war – a function of which the Founder would have approved.

What of the choir? HKA was determined that the singing of daily services and the quality of performance would not be affected. With characteristic single-mindedness, he believed that Hitler's sole objective was to disrupt the choral routine and he took it as a personal challenge. Of course, sacrifices had to be made. The choir dispensed with cassocks and eventually even Eton collars, except on Sundays. As the blacking out of the huge chapel windows was impractical, Evensong in the winter was moved to the afternoon. A far greater problem was the shortage of lay clerks. Clarrie Roberts (tenor) joined the RAF; Harold Cutbrush (alto) joined the army and later lost his life on active service. His name is recorded on a plaque

in the cloisters. There seemed also to be a shortage of chaplains. Some, like the kindly snowy-haired Rev. Blockley from Magdalen, were hauled out of retirement. One young priest suffered from terrible chapel fright before every service. While the men gathered in the Practice Room for a fag and a natter, the boys sat on the hard benches in the vestry in solemn silence to get in a suitably reverent frame of mind. This unfortunate fellow would stand perfectly still in the middle of the floor, fully robed, struggling to control hiccoughs. We laid surreptitious bets on the number of convulsions and the seconds between each one.

The outstanding cleric was the Rev. Dr Robert Henry Lightfoot, Dean of Divinity. Despite rationing, he occasionally entertained us to tea in his rooms, which were at the top of a staircase in the Garden Quad, chosen because he had easy access to the roof on which he kept a small pagoda. We watched him wrestle with an enormous kettle on a gas-ring and munched our way through fruit cake in embarrassed silence. We would then repair to his sitting-room to inspect his etchings. Everyone was immensely relieved when the time for Evensong arrived. Some choristers of this period will remember HKA's taking senior boys to bathe in Parsons' Pleasure and being greeted by Dr Lightfoot clad only in a panama hat.

What did we sing? As far as I can remember, HKA inherited a traditional cathedral repertoire, largely Victorian and Edwardian: the Wesleys, Wood, Stanford and Parry – supplemented by Byrd, Gibbons and Purcell. Gradually, HKA's preferences were phased in; far more Byrd, and huge dollops of unaccompanied Palestrina. Strangely, there was very little Bach and Handel and no Elgar. Mendelssohn emerged annually in Epiphany (*When Jesus our Lord*) and was then firmly put back in the cupboard. We were probably the only choir in England that did not yearn for the wings of a dove. Activities beyond the normal services were very restricted, but 'late musics' (ie motets, anthems) took place in the ante-chapel on summer evenings, and the Christmas Carol services attracted long queues along New College Lane. I remember one enjoyable Three

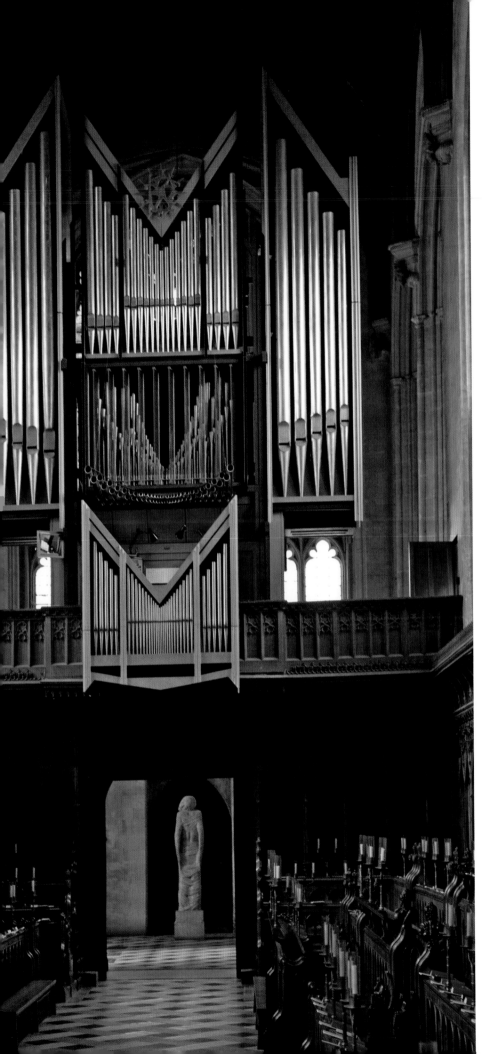

Choirs Concert (New College, Magdalen, Christ Church), ending with Wood's *Hail, gladdening light*, conducted by Sir Hugh Allen. He was obviously pleased as he left us to sing the closing bars on our own as he gazed at the ceiling, hands hanging at his sides. New College ('a college chapel somewhere in England') broadcast Choral Evensong regularly on Tuesday afternoons, alternating with our arch-rivals, King's, Cambridge. The BBC paid us in National Savings stamps and occasionally sent a large tin of toffees which HKA dispensed to those who deserved them. Fan mail arrived from people in all walks of life; one regular correspondent was a dustman, a critic as well as a devotee.

Wartime Oxford attracted interesting people. HKA played the organ at ceremonies in the Sheldonian and sometimes let us view the proceedings from the gallery. We saw the exiled King Haakon of Norway receive an Honorary Doctorate, as did Vaughan Williams whom HKA introduced to us afterwards. He glared at us from beneath beetling eyebrows. New College had its share of 'characters'. In moments of stress, Sydney Watson had an unfortunate stammer. During one Sunday evensong, when the chapel was packed, the choir waited for the organ to play the opening of Stanford in A, but nothing happened. After a minute of two of strange scuffling in the organ loft, the red curtain parted and Sydney peered down and said 'The w-w-w-w-wind's gone!' Once, when HKA was absent, Sir Hugh Allen agreed to conduct Evensong. The unaccompanied anthem was by Palestrina and began with a treble lead. We were used to HKA's flamboyant gestures and were taken aback when Sir Hugh marched into chapel, blew a cursory note in his pitch-pipe, and made a single downwards thump on a cantoris choir stall. Silence. He repeated the thump. Still silence. He went red in the face and snarled, 'Go on! Get on with it!' With typical *sang-froid*, Dick Greening (later organist at Lichfield Cathedral) started to sing and we all followed.

(This is an extract from an article first published by Choir News *in 1997, reproduced here with the author's kind permission.)*

GARDENS

ROBIN LANE FOX

When I took over responsibility for the Garden from my great predecessor, John Buxton, in 1980 the college was just emerging from the financial tremors of 1974–6. Nonetheless there were four full-time gardeners and one part-time, for some of whom the college provided houses or housing allowances. The Head Gardener, Bill Heron, had just retired after years of loyal service, characterized by ample plantings of tender bedding plants, raised in the college greenhouse. Every year a large professional firm of tree surgeons would come up from Sussex and submit a typed report, tree by tree, on the 'state of the college's trees'. It was amazing how many of them were alleged to need the expensive attention of cable-wiring or the axe each year. Only the two holm oaks on the Mound had escaped attention, like much of the Mound itself, then accessible only from the rear. Each of these items soon changed, on the whole quietly.

The first task was to interview for a new Head Gardener and after the most qualified candidates from horticultural colleges had described how they would prune the college's spring-flowering Clematis montana by cutting it down to the ground in spring, the panel appointed Bob Thompson, the existing second gardener, who showed more of a grasp of reality when asked what was the most bothersome problem confronting a Head Gardener. After some thought he answered that it was the undergraduates' habit of taking hot teacups and putting them unprotected on the lawn, where they killed the grass and made brown rings. Bob duly served as Head Gardener for more than twenty-five years and maintained the same combination of appreciation of the college residents and an easygoing realism about their needs.

Above: *The Mound in the early eighteenth century, fronted by a large formal Baroque garden, from William Williams,* Oxonia Depicta, *1732.*

Right: *One of the New College birch trees, by William Turner of Oxford, c.1810.*

Even under the just and kind chairmanship of Warden Cooke, reports on the garden to a college meeting could be slow and provoke barbs. One of my first problems was the freshly-converted Morris Garage building, which was felt to need a central tree in its gravel quad. Although the builders had left no more than a foot's depth of soil, there was nearly a vote imposing the choice of a miniature purple-leaved Japanese maple, a shrublet for acid, deep ground, best seen in Surrey. The supporters of this suggestion were not proposing it as an ironic comment on the architecture of the façade behind. Most of them had voted keenly for it. Nowadays the need is met by a developing Crataegus prunifolia which retains a pleasant glossiness on its leaves.

Matters became more waspish over the bed under the iron railings which close Garden Quad. It had long been planted with regimented rows of Lilli Marlene red-flowering roses, edged with a single straight line of grey-leaved Stachys lanata, or Lamb's Ear. I had marvelled at this planting's insensitivity, even when first coming across to New College as a migrant from Magdalen for Greek history tutorials with Geoffrey de Sainte Croix. I was unaware that this particular planting was the subject of the one picture postcard of New College garden then in circulation. In 1980 I went on a personally-funded research trip to consult the king of old-fashioned roses, Peter Beales, near Norwich and together we decided on pink Comte de Chambord and the excellent twice-flowering Jacques Cartier as mainstays with the lilac-rose

rugosa Belle Poitevine for the end nearest the exit to Queen's Lane, and the exquisitely shaped alba Felicite Parmentier for the centre of one half of the two beds. They are all still alive and very well. The foreground was planted with groups of laced pinks, a blue-grey Campanula Blue Moonlight, clumps of the good Agapanthus Bressingham Blue and in due course, spoils from the clearance sale of the remarkable Plantsman's Nursery in Dorset in 1983, including grey-leaved Teucrium fruticans, various parahebes in blue and white and the sprawling Salvia lavandulacea. All still survive. The effect of my work for the garden which I most cherish is that a history undergraduate, some years ago, recalled that memories of the flowers on the 'silvery shrubs below garden quad's outer façade', our Teucrium fruticans, had sustained him

during his months in a mental hospital and helped him to want to return to the college.

After a first summer in which Japanese tourists filmed the Campanula Blue Moonlight, a college meeting let off pent-up steam in the wake of a query from the medieval history tutor as to why the beds had been given over to 'ground cover'. Fellows then aired random alternatives, from bedded annual lobelia, which would not have relished full sun, to yellow floribunda roses, the proposal of a then weekending Law fellow who found a clique of gleeful support, although my mind's eye, even then, conjured up a bed beyond the windows of some Chambers in Lincoln's Inn, surrounding a circular fountain which splashed into a pool edged with artificial stone. My insistence that these suggestions were ignorant and inferior drew questions as to how I knew that, to which I answered that it was like asking the then widely-drunk wine Steward to serve sparkling Australian sauternes at the St Thomas Dinner. One modernizing voice even asked why that would be such a bad idea. I decided in future to imitate the example of Julius Caesar: keep discussion away from the little men in the ever-enlarging Senate and present them with *faits accomplis*, but only on request. Before long, the Politics tutor adapted to the new reality with the flexible labelling for which his subject is well known and explained in his officially-commissioned text for new fellows that the garden is run by *Führerprinzip*.

Left: *The old bowling green, with now 'informalised' Mound to the right, by John Nash, 1831.*

Above: *The Georgian border, with gardener, by William Delamotte, 1821.*

the gardeners could not do it and the greenhouse was broken, he bleakly commented that such money was best not spent. For another five years I let matters run as if, somehow, money was to be left untouched.

A change of warden was followed by a less controlled attitude to hoarding and spending. As part of a 'refurbishment' phase, which made most mark on the Warden's Lodgings, I was asked to do a little to brighten up Holywell Quad, after its prolonged cleaning and refacing by Saul Rose in the wake of a million-pound gain from the college's long-suffering City property in Fenchurch Street. I decided on hedges of roses beside the main paths, punctuated by squares of clipped box. After conferring with the expert rosarian David Austin, I chose pink rose Ispahan on the grounds that it would flower in time for undergraduates' Finals. It remains magnificent, brought forward by warmer seasons since 1990. It features as a cut flower with many a subfusc outfit but its companion, dark red Tuscany Superb, is less often picked. I chose it for the foot of my then staircase, 6 NB, as a tribute to all I had learned from the great garden at Sissinghurst and the writings of Vita Sackville West. In her gardens she and Virginia Woolf believed they had found this 'forgotten' rose in Sissinghurst's orchard. In a garden Rose Tuscany Superb is prone to black spot but I chose it for the college as one of many flowers I wanted to know but which I would not grow for myself. This licence is one of the rewards of the job.

A cowed SCR Senate did not wish to debate planting again but referred it tamely to the equivalent of a popular assembly, a special meeting of the JCR. Appropriately, few people came to this equivalent of the ancient Roman *comitia* and in true Roman style they were certainly not representative of the lowest class. There was only one opposing voice from the floor, proposing that I should plant something tall enough to obscure as much of New Buildings as possible. It was adopted as a provisional rider to my plan, to be borne in mind.

Parties are one necessary limit on intensive college flower-gardening. The regular triennial Balls

I was slow to think through an endemic oddity of the garden budget. Each year as the accounting year ended yet another new machine would appear in the gardeners' sheds, although the older machine remained beside it. I discovered that the Bursar, Saul Rose, who set and controlled the budget, provided for an annual Machinery Allowance, as if the gardens were a local authority park, and the personable reps from local garden machinery companies were adept at fixing 'meetings' to take the gardeners away from gardening to explain the latest machine which would fulfil some unnoticed need. However, when I explained to Rose that the gardens needed about £1000 for phased replanting, which would be perennial and eliminate the charade of supposedly growing all our own yearly bedding plants, although are a recurrent obstacle to a purely gardened garden and account for the areas of open space which are left regrettably blank. The Holywell quad has benefited nonetheless from two fruiting Malus Red Sentinel and more recently two Judas trees, each on either side of sets of steps. The Judas trees commemorate the subwardenship of the French fellow, not on the grounds that she should hang herself for treachery practised during it, but on the grounds that they were her suggestion, to my mind suitably French. To keep up with this new intake, the older Davidia, or Pocket Handkerchief Tree, has been stunning in flower and even fruit which spatters the tarmac and is

squashed by fellows' cars. Nearer the Porters' Lodge I have high hopes of a recent winter-flowering cherry, the one by the Sacher having died sadly of honey-fungus. The loss of the intrusive two sycamores which used to flank drivers' turning onto the Slype is not only a blessing for car-parkers. There were requests to truck in a mature tree, even from the prudent Maths tutor in 1999, but I chose to replant with a chestnut-leaved oak, Quercus castaneiifolia, from the south Caspian Sea. It has grown amazingly on the Sunken Lawn and is already a fine feature.

I continue to ponder the idea of the late Tony Nuttall that this Sunken Lawn could become a maze,

Below: *The border, by William Matthison, 1918.*

viewed from above. My present image is of a Fellow Minotaur, elected yearly, to stand in the Labyrinth's centre and have his way, disguised in a bull-mask, with all recipients of end-of-term Reports marked 'bad', who would be released into the Maze without directions to the exit. I have had a similar vision of such baddies ascending the recent staircase up the Mound for a pseudo-Aztec sacrificial punishment, while lines of fellows and virtuous scholars pelt them with flowers.

The history of so much of the planting now in the college is in part a detailed history of my life, in which I see levels invisible to other onlookers. I have been so lucky to have been allowed to go slowly and work bit by bit for changes, most of which have been for the best. My daily life has a Shakespearian dimension, as it breaks off from ancient history and its teaching and has to focus on the sudden irruption of gardeners and their problems, not 'dangling apricocks' as in *Richard II*, but events like swarms of bees in Garden Quad, or the day when a former head gardener sprayed part of the lawn with grasskiller, instead of a selective weedkiller as agreed. The lawn duly turned orange, just in time for the college scientists who were returning from a summer of research in US labs. They

congratulated me on the excellence of the Fall that year in the college, as they had never seen grass turn colour so well in America.

From so much history, I have to select, not only for the sake of others' feelings, but I must record a little about the changes on the Mound. In 1992 the Mound benefited from a magnificent benefaction by Kenneth Rose, old member and writer. Unasked, a Health and Safety Committee in college had simply removed the few big steps which gave the Mound its rear access. Since then the front of the Mound had declined into an uneasy combination of weeds, seedling periwinkle and such flowery oddities as geums which the gardeners surprised me by bedding out into the front row. My vision therefore ran to an architectural innovation, a grand full-frontal staircase, tapering to the summit. The then college advisory architect, much busied in the college, estimated that the vision would cost over £200,000. I doubted him and was lucky to be helped by the drawings and brilliant advice of the London architect, John Robbins. He found the stone for the steps in Doncaster and recommended the Oxfordshire small business of John Steptoe and David Gorrod who did a heroic job of building the entire stairway for only £18,000 in all. The cost would have been less if I had not interfered with the placing of the two bottom steps and relaid them further out. Luckily the then Clerk of the Works, David Rolfe, realised that I had thereby sabotaged the entire scale and angle of Robbins's drawings and rushed the architect to the site to counter the damage. The bottom step is still far forward as a cautionary tale.

The new front access caused no end of turbulence and malice. The City council first voted for it and then as a hung council sent a Liberal member to ask me if I could compromise and perhaps 'put it only a third of the way up'. Every conservation body protested on principle without reflecting that the Mound of 1990 was overgrown with conservation trees, totally unlike the Mound of 1690. Which phase of this moving target should we preserve and why? London newspapers carried articles claiming

that the college was being resented for clearing out traditional coverts for secret sexual activity, news to most, if not all, of the fellowship. After speeches and hours of patient consultation I arranged that development was to be conditional on a prior archaeological survey, though the City would not accept the credentials of the then Wykeham Professor of Ancient History as fit to conduct it. The dig uncovered a cache of 'unidentified ancient animal bones', dispatched for conservation to the City Museum. Only later, at a party in London, did the mother of an old member exclaim to me, 'My God, they found Lambsie'. In the late 1980s her undergraduate daughter had agreed to house one of her godfather's lambs for a night or two in her college rooms before the lamb was sent on to market in London. She kept him illegally in the bathroom but during her absence at a lecture her scout gave Lambsie a Mars bar on which he choked and died that afternoon. She buried him 'duly, at dead of night, The Mound with her mortarboard turning'. Ten years later the City archaeologists classed Lambsie as an ancient historic relic. My historian's suspicions about archaeologists' datings remain reinforced.

My vision had been for an epigraphic programme, whereby each fellow would contribute a short formula or quotation to be inscribed on each step of the staircase, so that visitors would ascend up a mental map of the SCR in 1993; this unfortunately foundered. However, when the Mound staircase was in place the then warden welcomed it with a remarkable ceremony in which he and a group of male undergraduates processed and distributed themselves up the steps before passing a Loving Cup along their ranks in a sort of open-air Summer Auld Lang Syne. Amazed members of the Press watched, on invitation. The next

night was Corpus Christi, so the chaplain processed again, this time during Evensong with the choirboys and the faithful, and among clouds of incense ascended the steps and reclaimed them as sacred space. I smile nowadays when I hear people asking how long ago the historic stairs were built. There is no feature at the top, a deliberate void, symbolizing the uncertainties of the modern age.

The architect's discrepant estimate of £200,000 left me thinking about the budget for running the gardens themselves. I began to think of the virtues of a new broom. Retirements, the death of our loyal Ervine Schoen, and a policy of non-replacement meant we reached the necessary state of a garden with no permanent staff for the new millennium. It is run now at my direction, with two teams of contractors working at top rates of pay for up to three days a week between mid-March and mid-December only. Marius Hardiman and his employees are the mainstays inside the college and Jim Marriott outside in several of the nine outlying gardens which I have to keep up. Everyone concerned realises that the maintenance goes more happily when time in one place is limited. I reckon that we save the college 65 per cent of what would be the cost of the Saul Rose system. I also like to think that the range and variety of the gardens are better and better each year. If you doubt me, go and look at Balliol's.

In brief, young Caesar has had his way. Under the new dictatorship, whatever is planted is grown, ordered or imported by himself only. He hires and runs the staff and decides on the new initiatives. There are no 'machinery budgets', no staff-employees. The lawns are revitalized by the part-time cutting and chemical planning of our Head Groundsman, Paul Roper, my Lawns Manager. The tree survey is done by me, with one verbal consultation of experts, and once we had freed the cloisters' holm oak from the damaging wiring of its 'professional' past it was so happy that Hollywood chose it as the tree to film for Harry Potter and paid us a sum enough to fund the garden for three years. Finally, the main border speaks for itself, I hope, as more than 35,000 paying visitors testified last year.

COLLEGE ESTATES

JENNIFER THORP

The Founder recognized the college's need for steady income from landed estates and emoluments (spiritual and secular) from lordships of the manor and the rights of patronage over college benefices. The early endowments of the college therefore were marked by the acquisition of entire manors as well as city tenements and rural smallholdings, and the college statutes made provision for the appointment of stewards and bailiffs, answerable to the college bursars, who were empowered to collect rents and other revenues due to the college and to supervise local expenditure on farm buildings and other manorial obligations. The Founder also laid upon the warden a duty, still maintained to this day, to conduct annual progresses round the college estates.

During his lifetime the Founder, invariably backed up by royal confirmation to protect the title, gave 22 manors, mainly in Oxfordshire, Buckinghamshire, Wiltshire and Essex, to the college. He also assigned to the college funds for the purchase of additional landed estates as and when opportunities should arise. Part of that monetary endowment was put to use in 1441, when the college purchased from the Crown the estates of the dissolved alien priory of Longville, thereby adding to its own properties eight more manors in Buckinghamshire, Berkshire and Norfolk. These included areas of woodland in the Buckinghamshire manors of Akeley and Great Horwood, and the management of such woodlands and sales of timber from them were to become significant

Above: *The charter and seal of Archbishop Anselm confirming to the alien priory of St Valery the manor of Takeley in Essex, in 1097. William of Wykeham acquired the estates of the priory when its English lands were seized by the Crown, and gave them to New College. The oldest estate document in college, this manor was sold by the college in 1910.*

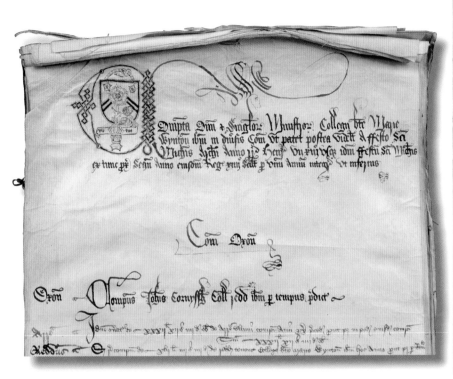

Above: *The elaborate heading of a New College bailiff's account roll, 1497.*

Above right: *Warden Woodward's memorandum on the parson's rights to collect firewood in the college living of Stanton St John since 1619.*

generators of income for the college until well into the nineteenth century.

The last great phase of expansion came during the sixteenth century, with the acquisition of six more manors in Oxfordshire, Gloucestershire, Bedfordshire and Essex and estates in Kent that had formerly belonged to medieval hospitals and religious houses suppressed at the Dissolution. By the end of the Tudor era the college had estates in, or income deriving from, properties in 15 counties as well as tenements in the cities of Oxford and London. Compared with all this energetic expansion since the Founder's day, the college's acquisitions of land since the seventeenth century became more sporadic, and since the late-nineteenth century was somewhat overshadowed by sales of properties intended not just to consolidate the college estates into fewer counties nearer to home but also to raise funds for the college to continue to function as revenues from agriculture fluctuated.

It was inevitable that there should have been great neglect and depreciation in value of the college's estates during times of plague, poor harvests and war. Spirited and

tenacious attempts on a large scale were made to remedy such depredations, from Michael Woodward (warden 1658–75) through to Samuel Gauntlett (warden 1794–1822) and beyond. Woodward's memoranda on the estates, written in his unmistakable handwriting and distinctive thick brown ink, fill innumerable notebooks on every aspect of estate management as he set himself to restore the lost revenues of the college by improving the efficiency of estates neglected during the Civil War and Protectorate. He did so by visiting the estates himself, most notably in a massive progress during August and September 1660 when he rode round, and took notes on, college properties in seven counties between Norfolk and Wiltshire.

Estate maps provide a rewarding visual record of the college's landed interests. One of the earliest maps at New College depicts a pedestrian's view of the properties either side of a disputed watercourse that formed the boundary between the Wiltshire manors of Alton Barnes (which belonged to New College) and Alton Priors. It perhaps dates from 1575 when the manorial court affirmed that

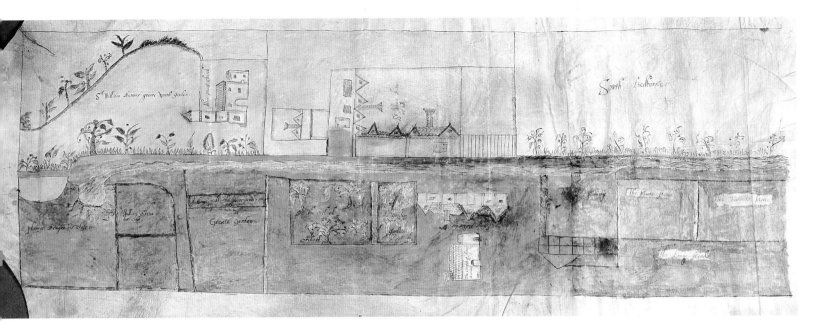

a local landowner, Sir William Button of Alton Priors, some 20 years previously had diverted the watercourse at Broadwell (an activity that seems to have been by way of family tradition, for Sir John Button had been ordered by the manorial court back in 1518 to put right his diversion of the same watercourse, and a later Sir William Button was to be challenged in Chancery on the same matter in 1660). The map shows the stream (which runs north to south, north being towards the left edge of the map), Button's fine house and great north garden next to the church of Alton Priors, the chapel of Alton Barnes and the house of Mr Anthony Malke, whose son would take the case to Chancery in 1660.

By the beginning of the seventeenth century the college was much concerned with its estates at Hornchurch, Essex, and in particular with the state of the flood defences. Richard Barnard was commissioned to draw up a map of the area in *c*.1600, but a decade later the college lost some of its land in Havering Marsh when an inset or protective dyke was swept away 'after a breach happening in the Thames wall there upon Tuesday the second day of November 1613'. Work on a new timber-lined inset, built on college land at Leeson Mead under the supervision of the tenant of Hornchurch Hall, started immediately and continued at every low tide for three months, reaching the huge total cost of £945 10s. All these efforts notwithstanding, the surveyor John Warner was to note in 1717, on his map of Sutton's manor in Hornchurch, that the college's marshlands could not be surveyed because the ground was flooded.

Similar attention to detail is also apparent in the great era of map-making for New College, which started in the 1760s and continued for almost a century. It began with the magnificent series of estate maps drawn up for the college and Warden Thomas Hayward by the London surveyor and cartographer Edward John Eyre between 1766 and 1768. Eleven of his maps still survive, and as a group they record in fine detail the college's estates in Essex and Wiltshire. Then followed a succession of some 50 or so estate maps drawn by local surveyors, who included James Collingridge (Buckinghamshire), Richard Randall (Hampshire), John Baker, James Jennings and Robert Weston (Oxfordshire), Joseph and Abraham Dymock (Berkshire and Wiltshire), William Browne and Robert Corby (Norfolk), together with many unnamed surveyors. Many of these maps were commissioned to record enclosures and exchanges of land, boundaries of glebe land and of tenant holdings. They were followed by yet another phase of concentrated map-making in the late 1850s, in connection with the Universities and Colleges Estates Act of 1856, which, for the first time, allowed endowed institutions to sell or exchange their lands under certain conditions and thereby made it imperative for the college to have up-to-date information about its estates. New College achieved this between 1854 and 1862 by drawing up some three dozen maps of its estates in Oxfordshire, Berkshire, Buckinghamshire, Wiltshire, Essex and Norfolk. Supplemented by surveys, rentals and all the documentation of manorial administration, the estate records of New College prior to the late nineteenth century are second to none.

Above: *The estate map showing the boundaries of the manors of Alton Barnes and Alton Priors, Wiltshire, c.1575.*

Opposite: *The map of Havering Marsh, Essex, by Richard Barnard, 1600.*

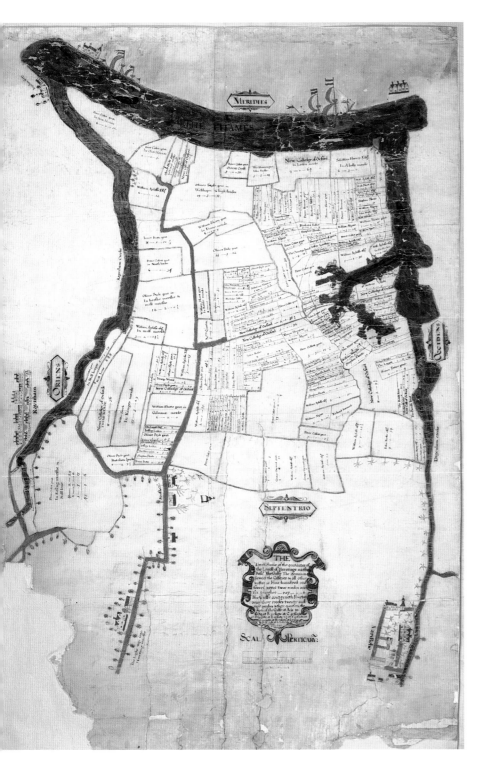

The human touch of estate management is discernible too, in the records of the warden's annual progresses, whether as the memorandum drawn up by one anxious notary concerning the provision of horses and other essentials for Warden Walter Hill's inspection of Newton Longville, Buckinghamshire, in 1481, or as the progress notes kept by later wardens. An incomplete series of notebooks exists for the four centuries since Warden Robert Pincke's day (his earliest notebook dates from 1638), but few of them make more entertaining reading than Warden Fisher's notes for the late 1920s, largely due to his propensity for including astonishingly candid verbal descriptions of the tenants he visited. At Harrow Weald, Middlesex, for example, he met 'Mr Goddard … a fat good-humoured shrewd old fellow, has been farming 105 acres under the college for 25 years … We find Goddard strolling about with a gun to keep the dogs from the cows. His conversation is a long dirge on the difficulty of keeping down trespassers. What with real rights of way and usurped rights of way, dogs, children, and loving couples, he finds it impossible to farm as he would like. The dogs also make it impossible for him to keep sheep.' When visiting Manor Farm in Upper Heyford, Oxfordshire, however, Fisher noticed not just the tenant but also the state of his barn: 'Croxhead is a young rather deaf and rather intelligent fellow. Nice manners, probably defective in drive. He farms 430 acres or so … We first visit the magnificent Tithe Barn, two holes in roof; otherwise farm buildings excellent. Then motor up the hill to view the arable.' And at another magnificent tithe barn, at Swalcliffe, Oxfordshire, Fisher noted: 'Our best farm. Gibson a Gentleman farmer … beautiful grey house, with vaulted dairy and superb grey stone tithe barn … [Gibson] was cashiered from the army for retaliating on his officer, separated from his wife owing to temper. He & his housekeeper gave us a beautiful tea. Rather a difficult customer but clear self-opinionated. About 67 years old.' It could never be said that New College's estates have been devoid of local colour.

ART

MICHAEL BURDEN

New College has its great artistic treasures: El Greco's image of St James of Compestella; one of the most important pieces of twentieth-century British sculpture in the shape of Jacob Epstein's Lazarus rising from the dead; and a number of portraits – by Richard Greenbury, Thomas Hill, George Romney, Von Herkomer, Reviere, Nicolson, Lloyd, Anderson and Richard Hamilton – that would not be out of place in a public collection, and others that would not be accepted by the most local of salerooms. There are also original cartoons by Max Beerbohm, Steve Bell, Landseer, Marc, David Parkin, Spy and Sambourne. It has one of the finest private holdings of medieval and Renaissance plate, and the stained glass ranges in date from 1390 to 2009. There are also some fine individual items, such as the celestial and terrestrial globes given to the college by Warden Oglander; the chest with its unique fourteenth-century carved illustration of the uprising and subsequent slaughter of the French cavalry by the artisans of Courtrai in 1302; and the college's two suits of armour purchased during the Civil War by Warden Pincke for the fellows to protect the college against the infidel. To a certain extent such holdings might be expected in an institution founded some 700 years ago – they represent the continuity of that institution, the generosity of the college's benefactors, and (in the case of the plate) the ability of the college's fellows to act decisively when the chips are down.

As a functioning educational foundation, the college's own collecting activities tend to be focused on objects relating to its own history and on the purchase of objects – furniture, silver – for everyday use. But like many small (and indeed, not so small) institutions, its holdings are best thought of as a collection of collections, discrete and yet interlinked within the larger grouping of objects. At New College there are both small and large collections, but three stand out. First, there is the Junior Common Room Art Collection, established with enviable foresight by the undergraduates themselves in the 1940s. Second, there are the college's holdings of works by the eighteenth-century caricaturist James Gillray. And lastly, the recent acquisition by benefaction of a collection of nineteenth-century papier mâché objects, all painted with views of Oxford.

Left: *Jacob Epstein, Lazarus, 1947–8.*

Left: *Wyndham Lewis*, Creation Myth, *1937, bequest of Professor and Mrs Russ in memory of Charles Russ, 1938, killed in action 1944.*

Below: *Michael Ayrton*, Minotaur Erect, *1975, purchased 2003.*

The Junior Common Room Art Collection was started after the war with what was essentially an undergraduate tax. Its holdings include works by such well-known artists as Patrick Proctor, Barbara Hepworth, William Gear, John Bratby, Antony Gormley and Damien Hirst. It also includes two fabulous paintings by the English vorticist painter Wyndham Lewis, the gift of Dr and Mrs Sydney Russ in memory of their son Charles Rupert Russ, who was shot down during the Second World War at the age of 24. These last two pictures have been borrowed frequently by organizers of exhibitions, and indeed, they both live the life of a starlet, rushing from one photo opportunity to the next. As I write, one, *Creation Myth*, is on loan to the Fundación Juan March in Madrid.

After some good early years the collection was managed somewhat haphazardly, the lack of anything that might be described as a purchasing policy saw the accession of a number of works of dubious taste and even more dubious artistic merit. However, a thorough overhaul by a knowledgeable member of the JCR and a similarly skilled member of the MCR, and with the assistance of the trustees, saw the refocusing of the collection on twentieth-century British art, with a particular emphasis on the years 1930 to 1990. This is a policy that both reflects the original

Left: *James Gillray,
'Tentanda via est
qua me quoque
possim Tollere humo',
Hannah Humphrey,
1810. 'There is a
path offered to me
through which I can
raise myself from
the ground.' The
print, published
on the installation
of Lord Grenville
as Chancellor of
Oxford, depicts him
in a hot-air balloon
in the shape of Lord
Temple, and ridicules
him for his enormous
backside and his
support for Catholic
Emancipation.*

purchasing patterns and plays to the collection's strengths. But the refocusing of the collection's holdings also saw a restatement of its original aim: to allow undergraduates to hang art works on the walls of their rooms during term. The collection now has significant holdings of loan items that include works on paper by David Hockney, Annish Kapoor, Keith Vaughan, Robert Colquhoun, Michael

Ayrton, Henry Moore, John Piper and Victor Passmore. And as part of the reorganization of the collection, a new two-roomed gallery was established on the JCR staircase in which to hang the larger and more valuable works so that they may be enjoyed by all undergraduates.

Like the paintings by Wyndham Lewis, items from the second collection, the F.W. Burger collection of works

Above: New College from the gardens, as depicted on a card case retailed by Spiers and Son of Oxford, c.1845.

on paper by Gillray, are frequently on loan. The collection was the gift of Dr Burger's widow, and its origins are somewhat obscure. It came to the college in 1974, and in recent years has come to occupy a more important position in the representation of Gillray's prints worldwide. Three Tate Britain exhibitions – 'Gothic Nightmares: Fuseli, Blake and the Romantic Imagination', 'Blake, Slavery and the Radical Mind' and 'Rude Britannia: British Comic Art' – have included New College items, an inclusion that reflects the superb state of the original colouring. A forthcoming exhibition will draw entirely on the college's holdings; that it will be curated by a former visiting fellow of the college is an indication of the interplay between the college's scholarly endeavours and its collections.

The engravings themselves are fascinating. Gillray himself seems to have been a madman. He was obsessed with his work and used to continue at the plates until his fingers bled. His early prints were mostly of social subjects, but by the mid-1780s he concentrated on political caricatures. His work from this period was sold mainly by William Humphrey and S.W. Forres. After 1791 he was published by Humphrey's sister, Hannah, in whose house he lived for many years and who nursed him through his final years – he died insane in June 1815. His take on life and politics was vicious, and his oeuvre includes works that would today never the see the light of day in a national newspaper – those of the royal family are particularly crude in subject and caption. Gillray's work, always popular, gained notoriety during the years of the French Revolution, and his depictions of the French and

of Napoleon so outraged the pint-sized despot that he demanded of French artists in general – and of Jacques-Louis David in particular – that they emulate the British product. They, of course, failed; it took a particular kind of warped genius to equal Gillray's achievement.

There is nothing warped about the college's collection of objects made out of papier mâché, presented to the college by Richard Compton Miller in 2005 in memory of his father Sir John Compton Miller (1919–2002), a quiet man of aesthetic tastes and interests who rose to be senior registrar of Probate, Divorce and Admiralty Division of the High Court. The collection is indicative of connections between objects and a donor's own enthusiasm. Compton Miller's interest in the material was sparked by visits to Antiquarius, then an antiques emporium in the King's Road, London. Consisting of some 23 objects, each is painted with a view of Oxford. The views, which include pictures of Brasenose, Queen's, Magdalen and Trinity Colleges, the High Street, Martyr's Memorial and Magdalen Bridge, were painted from engravings already in circulation. The papier mâché process was developed in the late eighteenth century, and by the Great Exhibition of 1851 was used for objects ranging from tables to wine coasters. The smaller items were manufactured by a number of firms – such as Alsager & Neville, and Jennens & Bettridge – and sold to local dealers, who bought them as blanks and then painted the views. Oxford's main outlet was through the firm of Spiers & Son. The finished products were essentially items for members of the university and for tourists. The Compton Miller pieces are now on show in the McGregor–Matthews Library, in cabinets that match those that house Warden Oglander's pair of globes.

These collections illustrate both the extraordinary generosity of the college's benefactors and the ability of the college, as an institution with long-term goals, to care for them. As an educational and research institution the college's mission is to lend, study and (in the nicest possible way) exploit these objects for the long-term benefit of all concerned.

ARCHIVES

JENNIFER THORP

The Founder's statutes gave very clear instructions for the secure storage of the college's 'evidences', the formal records of rights and obligations concerning the running of the college and its estates. These documents included the statutes themselves (both in draft and final, sealed, form), deeds of title (often with royal and papal confirmations as extra security), records of legal disputes, financial accounts, inventories of college goods and properties, and many manorial and estate papers. They were to be stored 'for ever' in the purpose-built Muniment Tower above the Hall, secured behind stout oaken doors, which to this day still require 11 keys to open all the locks, although they no longer require the presence of three bursars to operate them.

Below: *The Muniment Tower's North Press, made in the late eighteenth century by John Payne, to house the estate records.*

survives, as do the two presses themselves, still housing manorial court rolls, rentals, title deeds and legal papers. Less impressive furniture, in the form of cupboards and chests of drawers salvaged randomly from other parts of college, was added throughout the nineteenth and early twentieth centuries, and they look strangely at odds with their august surroundings. It is to be hoped that one day they will be replaced by something more pleasing.

It has to be said that, with a few exceptions, New College's idea of record-keeping prior to the second half of the twentieth century is best described as haphazard. The exceptions were the Founder himself (who also gave books to the college library, cannily recording one of the gifts in a chirograph, by which the details of the gift were written out twice on one piece of parchment which was then cut in two by a distinctive zigzag line to provide identical copies for both donor and recipient), Warden Culpeper (who, in the 1580s, helpfully sorted 3,500 of the medieval charters into their respective parishes, but then less helpfully sub-numbered them in no meaningful order), Wardens Woodward and Gauntlett (who both appreciated the necessity of accurate written records to run the college estates efficiently after the ravages of, respectively, the Civil War and the Napoleonic wars), and Warden Spooner (who was the first to call for the compilation of a systematic catalogue of the college archives and the first to be astonished by the Rev. John Wallis's assertion that the work could be completed within a few weeks). Others cared much less about the archives, however, and perhaps the prize for the most cavalier treatment might go to Spooner's predecessor, Warden Sewell, who had regarded the archive as his personal property and carried off much of it to the lodgings. As late as 1996 Warden Ryan discovered and returned one such document, recording the gift in 1402 of £100 to the college by the Founder's chaplain, John Knyght, to buy books for the library.

Indeed, that so much medieval material survives in remarkably good condition may be due more to luck or administrative torpor than to any deliberate policy over

Above: A detail of the medieval encaustic tiles from the 1380s, with which the four levels of the Muniment Tower are floored.

Time has apparently stood still inside the muniment rooms. The floors are still covered with fourteenth-century glazed tiles, and many of the parchment and paper documents amassed over the centuries are still kept inside furniture made for the tower from the sixteenth century onwards. The need for more storage space was clearly acute by the beginning of the nineteenth century, and the college commissioned two huge presses, over 12 feet long and 8 or 9 feet high, from a local carpenter named John Payne. The bill for his 'large oak piece of work' containing 84 drawers and six cupboards, and for 'turning two old oak chests into cupboards and shelves' in June 1797 still the centuries. Regrettably, that luck ran out for some of the more modern papers, and many from the eighteenth century onwards suffered from damp, rats and general grime. Francis Steer, the college's first professional archivist (from 1965 to 1978) noted, when he started work in the Muniment Tower, that 'nearly everything was covered with dust which had been undisturbed for a great many years'.

Steer provided a brief outline of the scope of the archives and also of the rather sad track record of the college's record-keeping in an article for *New College Record* in 1972, in which he noted that 'the types of archives are varied in the extreme. There are the title-deeds of the college site and of the properties which the Founder and others bought to provide an income; the court rolls and other manorial documents; accounts kept by the bursars and the local bailiffs; the progress books and the vast correspondence about the college estates; hundreds of leases of property; evidence registers; letters and other survivals of [New College] men like Parson Woodforde, Sydney Smith, Viscount Milner ... there are voluminous papers about the complex lawsuits in which the college was engaged ... the maintenance and administration of college and other buildings ... maps, tithe accounts, inventories of plate, registers of members, details of benefactions, literary miscellanea and so on.'

More detailed descriptions of over 14,000 documents or groups of documents appeared in Steer's published catalogue of the archives in 1974 and were also discussed in an essay published in the college's sixth centenary history in 1979. Since then, the archives have continued to take in a steady stream of administrative and legal papers, together with minutes, accounts, reminiscences and newsletters of the JCR, the MCR, the Choir Association and a few of the college clubs and societies. There are also collections of papers of some former wardens and fellows and a certain number of departmental files. Inevitably, the storage space they require has expanded beyond the Muniment Tower and, despite the advent of electronic

Below left: A detail from the confirmation of the college's foundation charter by Richard II, 1389.

Below: A page from the Registrum Protocollorum, the oath sworn by John Young as a new fellow in 1512.

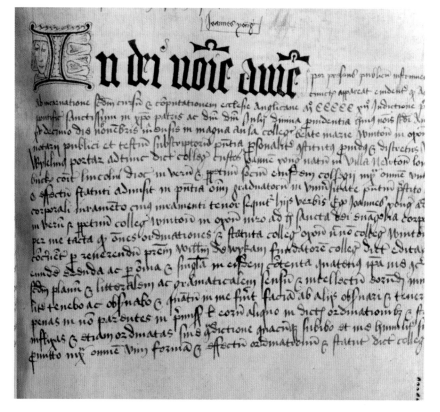

record-keeping, traditional forms of documents keep on arriving. Some acquisitions have been the result of gifts from former members of college, including the rewarding results of the appeal for photographs launched in 2005.

The oldest documents in the archives date from the eleventh century, over two hundred years before the college existed (and kept because they provided the written history of each endowment before it was transferred to New College and the legal steps by which it became a college property). The latest document in the archives dates from a few weeks ago. In between those two extremes are many thousands of documents, each one unique and informative. Without them and all that they represent and record, the college cannot function efficiently, cannot protect its rights adequately nor carry out its legal obligations. The archives also support research at many levels: college members may find in them a sense of how their own time here fits in with the college's past and who came here before their own day; visitors who consult the archives find that they can study unique collections of documentary evidence relating to people and places connected with this college over the centuries. When the three strands of the college's historic treasures – its chattels, its archives and its rare books – are brought together, they present an important and fascinating resource for study.

Above: *Programmes from the Commem Ball 1924, 1937, and 2010.*

Below: *The Commem Ball, 1937.*

BOOKS

WILLIAM POOLE

New College was the first college to have a library constructed as an integral part of the original college design. The Founder's Library in the east range of the Front Quad is situated farthest away from the noise of the street, and its deeply recessed windows provided its earliest readers with the maximum natural illumination. The Founder himself gave almost 250 manuscript volumes to his establishment, a huge number for the time. We may recall that Chaucer's contemporary Clerk 'of Oxenford' regarded a personal library of 20 books as suitably hyperbolic. Around a tenth of Wykeham's original books survive, and many can be derived from yet earlier libraries. In the first two centuries or so, the college's books were divided into two collections: one central collection chained to the desks in the library, and one unchained collection, distributed among the fellows at an annual *electio*. The earliest complete catalogue of this collection to survive was made by a young fellow of the college, Thomas James, and published in 1600 as part of his general union catalogue of Oxford and Cambridge manuscript libraries. James's competence is not in doubt: he was subsequently chosen by Sir Thomas Bodley as the first of Bodley's librarians. Yet the James list, which shows that the college owned over 300 manuscripts in his time – in addition to its burgeoning

printed collection – is worryingly different from the next surviving list, compiled only about three decades later. It is obvious that many manuscripts simply 'disappeared' at this time, and a few even mysteriously migrated to the new Bodleian Library.

The college started acquiring printed books early in the sixteenth century, and increasingly printed books replaced manuscripts as the purchase or gift of choice. (We do, however, possess one example of a transitional curiosity from the period – a manuscript copied out from an earlier printed book.) The Reformation saw many manuscript books destroyed, probably culled from the circulating collection; there is a famous letter of 1535 in which the Royal Visitor to the university reported with some satisfaction to Thomas Cromwell that 'we found all the gret Quadrant Court [of

Below: *Memorandum of William of Wykeham's gift of books to his foundation, 1402.*

Above: *Book of Hours, French, c.1500, Nicholson Bequest.*

New College] full of the leiffs of Dunce [the scholastic philosopher Duns Scotus], the wynde blowing them into evere corner'.

Nevertheless, manuscript donations continued even in the wake of the Reformation, the most important gift being a number of volumes from the library of the famous Cardinal Reginald Pole (1500–58). Pole's manuscripts were mainly in Greek, at a time when few Oxford colleges possessed extensive holdings in that language. Later still, manuscripts were donated to the library in increasingly exotic languages: by the end of the seventeenth century the college owned manuscripts not only in Latin and Greek, but also in English, French, Dutch, Hebrew, Arabic, Syriac and Armenian. There was even a fragment of printed Chinese listed as a manuscript by about 1700, and in the next century Burmese texts written on bark joined the collection. In 1693 the de Brailes Psalter, the most famous illuminated English manuscript in the collection, was donated by one Henry Howell, son of the bishop of Bristol. He also donated a sixteenth-century Flemish Book of Hours, a sign that the college collection was becoming a repository for collectable items, not just practical textbooks. In modern times the college has acquired through the generosity of benefactors several remarkable items, including eighteenth- and nineteenth-century works of literature, travel writing, numismatics, heraldry, photographic materials and the impressive series of diaries among the Woodforde Papers. Some early Dutch, Flemish and French Books of Hours have also been given to the college in recent decades, and in the late nineteenth century the college was presented with some important theological and historical manuscripts of Isaac Newton.

Printed books, however, dominate the antiquarian collections. Following the opening of the Bodleian Library, the college copied the Bodleian's device of instituting a deluxe Benefactors' Book, and retrospective entries back to the gifts of Wykeham himself were scribed into this ledger, which was then continued up to the twentieth century. But the library also purchased books using its own funds, and the college was only the second Oxford society to set aside a portion of its annual rental income for this purpose. But by the late seventeenth century the library had grown overcrowded and was infested with duplicates, and the Visitor was therefore petitioned to allow the fellows to break the statutes by selling off duplicates in order to broaden the college's holdings. Permission was so granted. The will of Warden Woodward, too, who died in 1675, settled an annuity on the library for book purchasing, and the register, running well into the eighteenth century, of new titles bought with Woodward's bequest is a fascinating barometer of the intellectual tastes and developments of the period, to some extent counteracting the usual story of New College as intellectually stagnant from Hanoverian times to the late Victorian period. The library itself expanded. It first spilled out into what is now the Panelled Room; it then colonized the attics, which were eventually converted into a third storey; and finally the whole collection was transferred to the New Library at the west end of the new buildings range, opened in 1941, where it stands today.

Today, students are encouraged to consult the rare books collections when pertinent to their work, and the college has also started acquiring the occasional choice item in order to keep the collection alive. Our historic holdings are indeed impressive. Among the many incunables we might note the rare Strasburg Virgil (1470); there is a first edition of Thomas More's *Utopia* (1516) with student verses on the college from 1633 scribed into the back; a copy of the Shakespeare Second Folio (1632); and there are many landmark scientific books, including first editions of both Hooke's *Micrographia* (1665), Newton's *Principia* (1687) and over a hundred original Robert Boyle imprints. The early-modern holdings are also particularly strong on medical works and on pamphlet literature. This combined collection of rare books and manuscripts is one of our greatest historical assets and responsibilities.

THE LIFE OF A DON

PENRY WILLIAMS

When C.S. Lewis was asked whether the combative medievalist J.H. Round (1854–1928) was a don, he is alleged to have replied, 'Good God, no! He was a learned man', which most certainly he was. In truth, some dons over the centuries have had a claim to learning, and others definitely have not. The one thing they had in common, until the middle of the nineteenth century, was being unmarried and in holy orders, but that did not necessarily lead to a life of bachelor scholarship.

A don can reasonably be defined as a fellow of an Oxford or Cambridge college engaged in the supervision and teaching of undergraduate or graduate students in college. Before 1379 students had generally lived in halls, while fellows alone lived in their colleges. Wykeham's achievement was to bring them together in the same community and thus to call the 'don' into being. Today, fellows of colleges are senior women and men mostly engaged in teaching, but for nearly five centuries a fellow could be a probationer aged 16 or a senior man entitled as a Master of Arts to lecture and teach. This can seem puzzling to members of the college today when undergraduates are known as scholars or commoners and only their seniors as fellows. However, for almost five centuries the term 'fellow' covered probationers and men with an MA, but the word 'don', if used at all, could properly refer only to the senior men.

Life was austere in the best Wykehamist tradition. The fellows shared accommodation in 20 sets in the old quadrangle, those on the ground floor taking four fellows each, the first floor taking three. In each set there was a single large room for sleeping and separate cubby-holes for study. Each set had a senior man to supervise the juniors and make sure they conformed to the statutes. In theory, time was spent either in study or in chapel, where the warden could supervise what went on through a spy-hole from the lodgings. Teaching was mainly conducted through university lectures in the Schools, but some sort of tutorial system emerged very early in the college's history. What dons did not do, by contrast with today, was to engage in 'original research' or write books as part of their job.

The most striking feature of tutorial responsibility, at least by the end of the sixteenth century, was the care expected of the tutor for the pupil's general conduct and financial affairs. Arthur Lake, who later became warden of the college and then bishop of Bath and Wells, acted as tutor to a well-to-do commoner, Robert Townshend, son of Lady Townshend of Rainham, Norfolk. Before Townshend came up Lake recorded that a payment of £3 3s 8d had been made for a straw-coloured canvas doublet and a green silk jerkin. At a time when a labourer earned £10 or £11 a year this was generous for a boy of 12. Lake then took control and promised to keep expenses within reasonable limits, insisting that Robert share a chamber with his cousin to save on fuel bills. But he also made sure that his charge's room was equipped with writing tables, paper, bookshelves, quill pens and globes. But academic progress was not neglected, and books like G. du Bartas' *La Semaine*, a famous Protestant poem, were bought.

By the seventeenth century the senior fellows, impatient at having to share a bedroom with younger men,

Far left: *An inventory of James Woodforde's 'Goods at New College' of 1774.*

Left: *James Woodforde, fellow 1759–76, in silhouette, 1773.*

From the moment he graduated as a BA until he left New College for the comfortable Norfolk living of Weston Longville in 1776, Woodforde played no visible role in teaching or supervising undergraduates. Although he was a member of the ruling council of the college, the 'Warden and Thirteen', he showed no interest in the intellectual life of the community. His interests lay in bowls, billiards, cricket, music, eating and drinking. 'I carried off my drinking exceedingly well indeed' was a typical entry in his diary. Matters had not much changed 50 years later when John Egerton recorded in his diary for 1823–5 a life of unbroken recreation: whist, billiards, boating, shooting, archery and music filled his days. The only difference between his daily routine and Woodforde's lay in Egerton's more moderate consumption of food and drink. Evidently, there were some fellows who taught the undergraduates, but most of them were simply using their fellowships as staging posts until they could obtain one of the many clerical benefices in the college's gift where they could marry and enjoy independent salaries.

Change came slowly with the election as warden in 1822 of Philip Shuttleworth, who made three important contributions to the life of the college: he introduced into the Senior Common Room a 'railway' for enabling its members to circulate the port without having to rise from the table; he persuaded the college to abandon its right of sitting separate degree examinations; and against some opposition he secured the appointment of three academic tutors. He commented sadly that 'the leaven of former times is not yet extinct' and that many still cherish 'the uninspiring indolence of their earlier life'.

However, change when it came was swift. The pressure of the royal commissions, combined with the reforming energy of dons like Hereford George, E.C. Wickham and Alfred Robinson and the subsequent professionalization of academic learning, transformed the life and purpose of the fellows. Freed from bonds of

started to build private lofts on the roof of the quad. After the Restoration in 1660 they went further and constructed the second storey on the south side of the quadrangle to get more privacy. When Celia Fiennes visited her nephew in 1694 she found that his tutor, Mr Gross, 'had a very pretty apartment of dining room, bed chamber and study, and provision for a servant'.

The liveliest picture of donnish life was given in the diaries of James Woodforde, fellow from 1759 to 1776.

Below: *The port railway ordered by Philip Shuttleworth, warden 1822–40, c.1810.*

celibacy and holy orders, they could now build careers in academic life, and the influx of undergraduate commoners established a need for teachers. By 1870 the college had become again the educational institution that the Founder had intended. Dons could now be married laymen, living out of college and devoting their energies to the business of tutoring, lecturing and running the affairs of the college.

In that respect they were like their successors in the twenty-first century, but their intellectual goals were different. In the humanities, but not in the sciences, an obligation to advance their discipline by research was largely unrecognized by them. However, in 1904 the distinguished historian of seventeenth-century England, C.H. Firth, became Regius Professor of Modern History and in his inaugural lecture argued for a programme of 'advanced training' for undergraduates in history to prepare them for undertaking historical research. The response of the dons was unequivocal: 23 of them issued a printed manifesto denouncing Firth's proposals. They insisted that their aim was the provision of a liberal education rather than a professional training. The quality required in a college tutor was that of 'getting on with the men', indispensable in that 'very intimate and personal form called the college system'. The dons won, and for half a century or so their views broadly prevailed against the ethos of German universities or, nearer home, the History Department of the University of Manchester, where research was dominant and the young lecturer was encouraged to 'get on with his own work'. For most dons, even the married ones, an Oxford college was a second home, a gentleman's club that cultivated the art of witty and competitive conversation.

In the end, however, Firth's cause triumphed. Even before the Second World War some dons in the humanities were engaged in writing and research: my own tutor David Ogg, author of distinguished books on Charles II and James II, is an example. By the 1950s nearly all the men and women appointed to Oxford tutorial fellowships were spending a good part of their time doing some form of writing and research. At New College the two fellows in history appointed after the war were H.E. Bell, whose apprenticeship had been in the archives of the Public Record Office, and A.L.C. Bullock, already engaged on his pioneering life of Adolf Hitler. The last of

Right: *Eric Yorke, fellow 1927–77, by Percy Horton, 1964.*

Far right: *David Ogg, fellow 1914–56, by Kenneth Knowles, 1958.*

Right: *The interior of Sir Christopher Cox's set, 1982, a vision not untypical of many dons' rooms.*

the old-style tutors in New College, E.C. Yorke, retired in 1969: he had shunned publication to devote himself to the task of teaching classical languages and literature and to the role of domestic bursar. In almost every college research and writing had by then become the favoured routes to reputation and promotion. While college-based tutorials remained the principal method of teaching, dons were encouraged to lecture regularly and were paid by their faculty for doing so.

Indeed, the faculty was becoming increasingly important in the life of the dons as the number of graduates studying for higher degrees increased. By 1979 about one-fifth of New College students were graduates; the proportion is now one-third. The role of graduate supervisor became an important part of the don's life and reflected the growing professionalism of academe. 'Getting on with the men' was giving way to the publication of books and articles. The tendency was reinforced by pressure from

the central government funding agency (HEFCE), which instituted the notorious Research Assessment Exercise. The prestige and prosperity of faculties and indeed of universities now depend on the quality and quantity of their research and publication. The tutorial system has survived but has become an endangered species.

Over the same period, the social life of colleges has changed. Few dons now live in college, and SCRs have lost most of the clubland atmosphere of the 1920s and 1930s. In New College, where there were two formal guest nights a week in 1964, there is now one a term. Financially dons have lost ground compared with such rival professions as the law, medicine and the civil service. Above all, the pressures of academic life have increased. It is hard to imagine a tutor today taking 10 or more undergraduates on a four- or five-hour walk through the Oxfordshire villages every Sunday during term, as did the Rev. K.N. Bell, history tutor in Balliol in the 1920s and 1930s.

SPORT

CHRISTOPHER TYERMAN

The Founder recognized the attraction of informal recreational games when he banned the playing of football in Hall and the lure of field sports when he prohibited keeping ferrets, dogs and birds of prey. Such was the austere academic concentration he wished to promote that he even forbade chess, a popular pastime among medieval elites, but always distracting and time consuming for the young scholar. Whether much of this had the desired effect on the younger fellows may be doubted. Certainly by the sixteenth century, the college had acquired a bowling green (in 1500) and the fellows were playing cards, historically the most consistent of all college entertainments. For much of the ensuing three centuries, once a fellow had gained his BA the college became a sort of luxurious waiting room for those interested in a college living. Formal academic work was discretionary. Inevitably, in the absence of a curriculum, fellows indulged their extracurricular fancies, depending on taste and aptitude. For many, this included games and sport – James Woodeforde's diary of his time as a fellow (1759–76) records a regular diet of bowls, billiards and cricket. Given that many fellows, like Woodeforde, did not reside in college much, even in term, no specifically collegiate sporting or gaming tradition can be claimed. The habits of fellows were those of their class: field sports, some genteel field games, such as the increasingly regulated game of cricket, and the domestic pleasures of cards, billiards and, of course, in New College, bowls.

The early nineteenth century saw the beginnings of a radical change in the nature and role of sport and games in education and academic life. Some elements remained constant – hunting, shooting, racing and the domestic pastimes of cards and billiards. Culturally, however, there was a formal retreat from the ubiquity of gambling, which affected attitudes and behaviour as regards games like cricket or activities such as card-playing, and rendered following horse racing officialdom's synonym for being a wastrel. More significantly, games were becoming codified and were taken up in the socially elite public schools as a way of imposing discipline by channelling and controlling pupils' energies. This essentially managerial process was increasingly endowed with moral value. Two generations before Thomas Hughes and Charles Kingsley and the bizarre excesses of muscular Christianity from the 1850s,

Below: The college's bowling green, converted to lawn in the eighteenth century, detail from David Loggan's view of the college, c.1670.

the games field was already being elevated into a metaphor for life, a testing ground for honesty, bravery, chivalry, competitiveness, endeavour, self-control, manners and masculinity, supposedly without taint of sexuality. Sport and games were deemed suitable preparation for social and political power, *noblesse oblige* and the habits of a gentleman. Educational reformers of the 1820s and 1830s, like Dr Arnold of Rugby, might have had no time for the cult of sport; for Arnold and his disciples 'exercise' meant prep. However, the culture of the public schools that provided the overwhelming majority of Oxford undergraduates and hence college fellows inexorably embraced games as an integral part of their training, effectively as part of the syllabus. At Winchester, New College's sole feeder school until the 1860s, organized football, fives, cricket and cross-country running were all features of school life by the 1820s. The universities did not remain immune: the Oxford and Cambridge cricket match was first played in 1827; the first Boat Race was rowed in 1829.

New College initially remained less infected by the nineteenth-century games craze than other colleges because of its restrictive statutes and small numbers of undergraduates. However, with reform, the opening of college admission to non-Wykehamists and the consequent massive increase in undergraduate numbers, the college rapidly conformed to Victorian type. Typical of the change in manners was Alfred Robinson (fellow 1864–95, bursar from 1875), a Marlburian and enthusiastic cricketer, who bought the playing field by the Cherwell from Merton and donated it anonymously to the college. Before that, college sportsmen had to trek out to Cowley Marsh. Robinson attracted undergraduates from the elite public schools, such as Eton. The sporting results, at any rate, were exceptional. By the 1880s organized games of all sorts had become not just the norm but an integral part of undergraduate life. New College rowing eights began to win the Head of the River trophy and be photographed with it in the cloisters, a conjunction of the old and new

that probably bewildered Warden Sewell even if he noticed. Between 1885 and 1906 New College was never out of the top three places in the summer Eights.

In continuation of familiar school structures, sports and games were organized on competitive collegiate bases, confecting often strident corporate loyalty. Adult sport was aped by the creation of college clubs for individual sports, notably the Boat Club, thus preserving a sort of semi-detached relationship with the college, allowing the undergraduates, as in other non-academic activities, to manage their own affairs. Even non-competitive field sports, such as beagling, began to be arranged on a collegiate basis (in this case in alliance with Magdalen). Investment in sport, such as the college barge on the Thames, boatmen, groundsmen and the like, matched the enthusiasm of the young. In the years before 1914 the range of college teams, formal and informal, was huge: cricket, rowing (eights and fours), athletics, association and rugby football, hockey, lawn tennis and even ice

hockey. In addition to competitive sport, informal teams grew up, such as the New College Nomads who played cricket against local villages. While official team games garnered most acclaim, so-called minor sports equally flourished. Nonetheless, beside all this strenuous quest of *mens sana in corpore sano*, over breakfast tables in rooms across the college racing form was still as widely and avidly studied as ever.

This too was the era of public achievement. New College Olympic medallists included George Robinson, bronze in tennis men's doubles in the first of the modern games in 1896; John Jacob Astor, later proprietor of *The Times*, gold medallist in rackets singles and silver in rackets doubles in 1908; and Patteson Nichols and Herbert Wilson, gold medallists in polo in 1908. Most notable, as well as revealing of the then social complexion of certain public sports, the New College eight who rowed Head of the River in 1911 competed in the 1912 Stockholm Olympics. They took the silver medal, on the way beating

Above: *The Head of the River crew, 1887.*

Inset: *Head of the River medal, 1911.*

Below: *J.J. Astor, gold medallist in rackets in the 1908 Olympics, third from right, photographed in the New College steeplechase, 1910.*

Norway but losing to Leander. The eight was stroked by Robert Bourne, who had also rowed in four consecutive victorious Boat Races. Even more remarkable was the coach, Robert's father Gilbert Bourne (1861–1933), at the time Linacre Professor of Zoology at Oxford and an FRS. The elder Bourne had also been at New College and had rowed for the college and, twice, for the university (1882 and 1883). He was fellow in physiology at New College 1899–1906. Aside from his research into zoological morphology, Gilbert Bourne was a soldier, pioneering designer of racing boats, author of

a definitive technical *Text Book on Oarsmanship* (1925), as well as an outstanding and dedicated rowing coach who helped the college's oarsmen for half a century.

After 1918 the democratization, nationalization, professionalism and expense of public sport combined to extinguish its Corinthian character. Yet for as long as the public schools exerted a near-monopoly on admissions, the traditional sporting ethos was unlikely to fade. Later notorious for the promotion of 'bodyline' bowling, Douglas Jardine, a Winchester and New College man (getting a fourth in history in 1923), epitomized the lingering amateur code with his signature I Zingari cap and scarf, even if his austere batsmanship and even drier captaincy spoke of a more utilitarian attitude. University remained a finishing school in which playing games was entirely normative, even if, after the Somme, it was now shorn of its sentimental and corrosive Victorian Newbolt-esque notions of character-forming virtue.

The small grammar school intake joined in. Goronwy Rees (1928–31), from a Welsh grammar school and later a fellow of All Souls, was an enthusiastic rugby and soccer player. Like a number of his contemporaries, Rees continued to give the lie to the inevitability of

the hearty–intellectual divide. In the late 1920s Richard Crossman, soon to become fellow in philosophy, played brutal games of rugby for the college. John Sparrow, future warden of All Souls, and John Maud, later a politics fellow and later still master of University College, played soccer for the college. Crossman and Sparrow were Wykehamists; Maud was an Etonian. Obviously, there remained a gulf of bafflement between the sports-obsessed athletes and the aesthetes or simply those who had loathed compulsory games at school and were delighted to be rid of them. Of course, among the fellows over the years a number were obsessed with cricket and cricketana, a familiar English middle-class intellectual vice, although by 1950, lamented one leading New College rower of the time, no fellow was interested in what happened on the river. For many years each summer a fellows' XI would take on the Choir School at cricket, to the amusement of many and subsequent incapacity of some.

Modern New College retains many of its traditional sporting attributes, even if they possess rather different cultural resonance, fitness and fun replacing ruling-class moral values. Sport is now socially normative only in the sense that it is an option of individual choice, no longer an expectation or a conformist activity to be deliberately pursued or rejected. Consequently, participation, notably in rowing, is broad across the college, taken for granted but not forced, nor regarded as a central feature of collegiate identity as it was a century ago. Whereas in some generations (such as the much maligned 1970s) sport was more the preserve of the committed and keen minority, in recent years the vigour and diversity of athletic pursuits have flourished, enhanced by new disciplines as well as new teams and crews of women. The college still maintains a boathouse and one of the most

Above: *Keble versus New College, 1920.*

Below left: *The New College team which won silver the silver medal* (below) *in the Eights, at the Stockholm Olympics, 1912.*

Right: *An overloaded New College barge, c.1911.*

Below right: *Women's VIII, 2010.*

envied central sports grounds in Oxford. New College men and women win blues and half-blues. The most outstandingly successful coach of the university crew, Dan Topolski, was at New College. Along with rowing, cricket, rugby, soccer, hockey, swimming, tennis, squash and the rest, what would once have been seen as exotic imports are now commonplace, such as yoga. Even what used to be domestic recreational pursuits have succumbed to the modern competitive league syndrome. A college competitive darts team has recently been formed, and there is even a highly committed pool team. That, at least, might have attracted nods of approving recognition if not from Edwardian Corinthians then, perhaps, from Parson Woodeforde.

THE COLLEGE AT WAR

JENNIFER THORP

One New College man, Richard Hankford, may have fought at Agincourt. It is not known how many other members of the college during its early history went off to fight in the wars in France or were influenced by the military career of former fellow Nicholas Upton, whose study of heraldry and the arts of war, *De Studio Militari*, was written in 1447 and dedicated to Humfrey, duke of Gloucester. Two hundred years later, however, the entire college was caught up (as was the whole of Oxford) in the English Civil War. Between 1642 and 1646 Charles I made Oxford his headquarters, and Warden Robert Pincke, in the absence of Vice-Chancellor Prideaux (who had fled), allowed the university's trained bands to drill in the front quadrangle of New College, much to the delight of the choristers. Anthony Wood describes how the Bell Tower and cloisters were turned into a magazine 'for arms and furniture, bullets, gunpowder, match' and the like, and the college today still owns breastplates and helmets dating from that time.

Left: *One of the remaining sets of armour ordered for the Fellows by Robert Pincke, warden 1614–47.*

Right: *The memorial to the New College fallen of the Boer War, c.1905.*

Below: *An account for repairing muskets, 1799, paid in 1802.*

During the French invasion scares between 1798 and 1803 the college ran an armoury near the chapel, employed an armourer (at nine shillings a week) to clean the arms and accoutrements and a gunsmith to repair three dozen muskets, and it paid armoury expenses to Serjeants Beckley, Whitaker and Carrick of the university volunteer corps.

The half-century after 1900 saw the involvement of New College men in the Boer War, two world wars and the Korean War, and the war memorials in the ante-chapel and cloisters, as well as documents in the archives, bear witness to those commitments. Drury's bronze memorial to the New College men who died in South Africa lists seven names: three of them died of wounds sustained in action, four of sickness caused by the climate and living conditions of the Transvaal. The British High Commissioner was Alfred, Viscount Milner, a fellow of New College since 1876, who had proved a less than sensitive negotiator with Kruger or with local officials in South Africa, but he was applauded in England for bringing the war to a conclusion and setting up long-lasting administrative and agricultural improvements in the Transvaal and Orange River Colony. He was not, however, popular with all his colleagues at New College – Warden Sewell, for instance, refused to allow the college bells to be rung after the relief of Mafeking in May 1900, ostensibly, as he insisted he remembered, because they had not been rung after the battle of Waterloo.

The First World War saw the strange phenomenon of a near-empty New College, as large numbers of its members flocked to serve in the armed forces when war broke out in September 1914. In their place came the military: a succession of battalions of the Oxfordshire & Buckinghamshire Light Infantry established their headquarters on the sports ground, with their armoury in the cricket pavilion, while from 1916 to 1919 the college

Right: *3rd Southern General Hospital, New College Gardens, 1914–15, by Walter Spradbery, 1919.*

housed nearly 200 officers, men and orderlies of the Officer Cadet battalions. From an early stage in the war the college worked closely with the base hospital in the Examination Schools, transforming the college garden into wards of four tents, each containing eight beds. Within a year the number of beds under canvas had risen to over a hundred, and there was also an area at the northeast corner of the garden for treating septicaemia cases. College properties at 6 Holywell and 8 New College Lane housed Belgian refugees throughout the war. Professor Hugh Allen organized organ recitals in the chapel, singsongs in the Hall and concerts in the Town Hall for them and for the many servicemen in Oxford at the time.

Over 800 junior members of New College enlisted in the armed forces during the first year of the war, and a number of fellows also joined up or undertook military intelligence work. Warden Spooner and tutors such as Ernest Barker, who remained at New College, kept up a correspondence with students serving in France, Italy and Greece, responding sympathetically to the young men who took copies of Virgil and Homer into the trenches or out to Gallipoli and with those who were prisoners of war. Robert Gore-Brown, in the PoW Camp at Stralsund (Dänholm), was particularly grateful for books. 'One reads such a lot – chiefly a scratch collection of stuff from Shakespeare thro' Paul Bourget to Agricultural Manuals. I should be most awfully grateful if you would send me some sound books … any good book is a godsend,' and he also passed on news of his myopic fellow student Lionel Abel Smith, who 'is now in the Grenadiers, having eventually passed the eye-test, he says, by reciting the alphabet and being stopped by a benevolent board whenever he got to the right letter'. Several New College servants and choristers enlisted in the early days of the war, some of them to join the ranks of the army while others became hospital orderlies or munitions workers.

The losses for New College were enormous, as may be seen in Eric Gill's austere memorial, placed in the ante-chapel in 1921, to the 228 New College men who

Left: *Captain Esdale, in the Front Quad, in Saucy Jane towing 'Esdale's Whale', 1918.*

Below left: *The Armistice Day cup, engraved with the names of the four New College fellows, who fell in the first world war, presented by Percy Mattheson, 1919.*

'COMING FROM A FOREIGN LAND'

On the southeast wall of the ante-chapel is a memorial to three German members of the college who had been killed in the early months of the First World War in 1914: Prince Wolrad-Friedrich zu Waldeck-Pyrmont, Freiherr Wilhelm von Sell and Erwin Beit von Speyer. On learning of their deaths, Warden Spooner had placed their names on the lists of war dead headed 'Pro Patria' that were regularly placed on the chapel door. When a visiting American broadcast this in the *Morning Post* in June 1915 it provoked a brief public storm of protest at the warden's and college's perceived lack of patriotism. Spooner's reply transcended collegiate solipsism in a courteous but defiant statement of liberal humane principle: 'The Germans had done no disgraceful act in fighting for their own country.' One had 'died in the act of carrying a wounded comrade'. He ended: 'To carry on a spirit of hate against those who passed into another world can make us neither better patriots nor better men.'

In 1929 the philosophy tutor H.W.B. Joseph initiated moves to erect a memorial. He enlisted the help of Ernest Barker, a former fellow, by then Professor of Political Science at Cambridge, who drafted the wording. The memorial, deliberately carved in the same stone as that used for the main college war memorial nearby, was in place by October 1930. It reads: 'In memory of the men of this college who coming from a foreign land entered into the inheritance of this place and returning fought and died for their country in the war 1914–1919.' It stands as testimony both to the bravery of the fallen and to the courage and values of the warden and college who saw beyond the narrow malign hysteria of nationalism to a unifying humanity. Spooner's own memorial looks on from the opposite wall. It is one of the most moving sites in all Oxford.

Christopher Tyerman and Keith Butcher

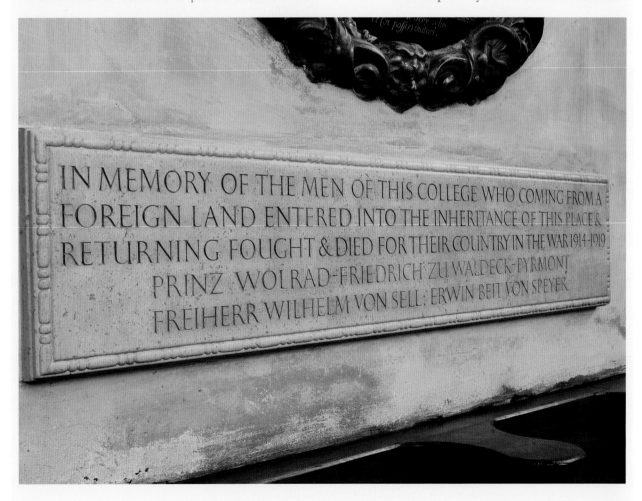

13. July.   Mr. Casson bets Sir Hugh Allen one bottle of Veuve Clicquot – that Herr Hitler will be bumped off by Dec. 26th 1934.

Above: A bet from the Senior Common Room Betting Book that Sir Hugh Allen would probably have preferred to have lost.

died fighting for the Allies between 1914 and 1919, the largest number of losses from any Oxford college. Another memorial by Gill and H.J. Laurie Gibb, erected amid some controversy in 1930, records the names of the three German students of New College who died for their own country in the 1914–18 war.

It is ironic that Hubert Worthington's new library building, created as a memorial to the fallen of the First World War, was not ready for use until 1941, by which time another world war was raging. The warden in 1939 was Herbert Fisher, and one wonders what he, as a respected commentator on the history of Europe, might have thought of the counterintelligence operation carried out after his death (in 1940), by which the corpse of a fictitious major of the Royal Marines ('the man who never was'), was dressed in Fisher's undergarments and washed ashore off Spain, with a briefcase attached to his wrist containing false documents to fool the German High Command into thinking that the Allies were about to invade Greece rather than Sicily.

The 1939–45 war made a quite different impact on life at New College to that of the First World War, not least because the German bombers threatened British civilians to a much greater extent than had been the case in 1914–18. Valuables from the chapel, including the misericords, all the medieval stained glass windows and Reynolds's west window, were removed to places of safety. Makeshift air raid shelters were created in the cellars

of the New Buildings, the passage under the Hall was turned into a first aid station, Holywell Lodge became Air Wardens Post A17, and an observation post was set up on top of the Muniment Tower. Acting-warden Alic Smith's papers reveal his own determination to take part in war work, when in 1941 he joined the Home Guard and volunteered for fire-watching rotas in Manor Road, and he also took up small arms training at which he became very proficient. Students under the age of 20 were not eligible for call-up and so continued their studies as best they could, while a succession of military and naval cadets also came into residence for short courses.

Large numbers of college members volunteered for service in the armed forces and associated war work from 1939 onwards. Stanley Casson, fellow in classical archaeology, cinema buff and veteran of the First World War, went off to work for the War Office and 'has had an adventure in Holland' as the *New College Record* coyly referred to his intelligence work. Later he was witness to the Allied campaign in Crete and in April 1944 became the first New College fellow to be killed on active service in the Second World War. Undergraduates and college servants enlisted in their hundreds, and three plaques set into the south wall of the college cloisters pay tribute to the 159 college members who died, among them one former lay clerk and seven former choristers. When news of the German surrender came on 8 May 1945 the college celebrated with a chapel service of thanksgiving, the king's health was drunk at dinner, and the bell tower was illuminated although 'lack of fuel precluded a bonfire in Garden Quad'.

The Korean War of 1953 also saw the involvement of New College men within the United Nations forces. One such was Frank Booth, who matriculated in 1942 as an RAF cadet, served with the 79th Squadron of the RAF in Korea in 1953 and went missing there during a flight on 27 January. A plaque to his memory is in the south walk of the college cloisters.

Right: *Papers relating to Alic Smith's service in the Home Guard, including his small arms target, 1941.*

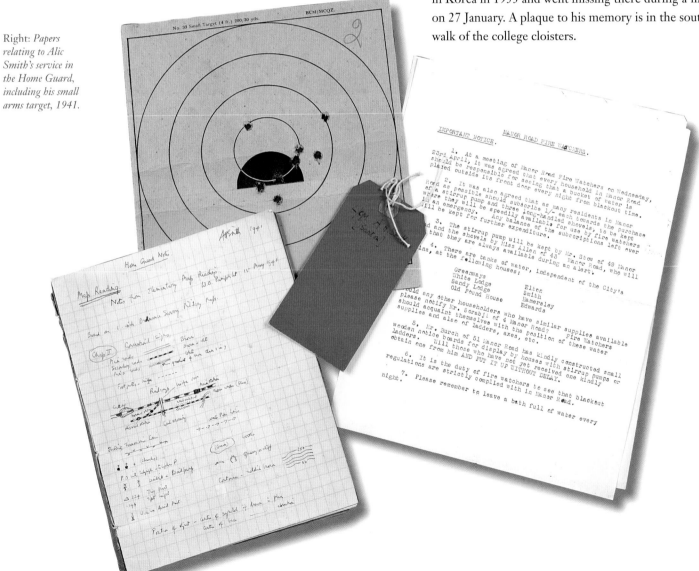

WARTIME NEW COLLEGE
Sir Roger du Boulay

When I came up to Oxford as an exhibitioner in 1940 I had the good fortune to be given rather grand rooms on the first floor of the Robinson Tower. Immediately above me lived Sir High Allen, and above him lived H.W.B. Joseph. My tutor was Sir John Myres. My 'moral tutor' was Lord David Cecil. I was to read for a war degree in Lit. Hum. (Greats), taking four papers on philosophy and ancient history. For philosophy I was assigned to the up-

and-coming A.H. Smith. Can any 18–year-old ever had a more starry welcome to higher education?

Sir Hugh Allen, who was described in the old *Dictionary of National Biography* as not just a musician but a musical statesman, had been Oxford's Professor of Music since 1918, and his main purpose in life was to inspire the young to make music. I was a hopelessly incompetent would-be pianist. The ceilings in the Robinson Tower were not soundproof, and in despair over, or pity for, my all-too audible fumblings, Sir Hugh called me up to his room night after night and did his best to instil the basics.

Below: *Sub-Warden Alic Smith with the Junior Members, 1942.*

A moral tutor made a point of seeing his charges as soon as they came up, and I quickly found myself in Lord David's rooms (then in the southeast corner of the Front Quad) facing a barrage of questions and *bon mots* and a fusillade of spent matches and half-smoked cigarettes. 'What are you here for?' he demanded.

'To work for a degree, I suppose,' I answered priggishly.

'Work!' he shouted. '*Work*? If all you want is to do work, you might just as well go to one of those dreadful places like Manchester or London! No – you're here to get educated. Go and enjoy yourself.' And he proceeded to tell me in detail how to get the best out of the university.

John Myres and Alic Smith were the major influences. Tutorials were then tutorials – one to one, lasting at least an hour and in their case often two or three. And they both had the capacity, no matter how ignorant, foolish and young their pupils, of treating them as adult, serious equals. Each week the subject for an essay was set, relevant lectures indicated and a (formidable) reading list sketched out. You began by reading your essay. Before the first sentence was complete – 'Now, that *is* interesting! Why do you say that? … How do you explain so-and-so in that case?' And often the reading got no further, and an hour or more later you would leave the essay with the tutor and it would come back next week scrawled all over with red or green ink and marked with anything from the coveted alpha to the more usual beta or dreaded gamma.

Alic Smith was then sub-warden but in effect warden, since the actual warden, H.A.L. Fisher, had died in April 1940, though Mrs Fisher was still very much there, entertaining all freshmen to tea in the Warden's Lodgings. But, busy as he was, Alic Smith never lost his absorbed interest in every single undergraduate who came to New College, and he corresponded with most of them individually, including myself, in subsequent years, to persuade them to come back and finish their education

Above: *John Myres, fellow 1910–54, by Albert Rutherston, 1946.*

Joseph, at 73 a couple of years older than Sir Hugh, was more remote. No longer senior tutor in philosophy, he was at the time writing the fifth and last of his great books, *Knowledge and the Good in Plato's 'Republic'*. But since the *Republic* was at the heart of my course, he provided in person as well as at his lectures, invaluable guidance on what to read, look for and think about.

> 24th April, 1948.
>
> Dear Sir,
>
> Now that we have burgundy to drink with our bread and cheese, perhaps it will be possible to obtain some cheese to eat with our bread and burgundy?
>
> Yours sincerely,
>
> S. Solomons.

when the war was over. That, even more than *Lazarus* or the Old Library, should be his memorial.

John Myres was the ultimate Oxford phenomenon. Originally a classical scholar, moving naturally into archaeology, his interest in the Persian Wars took him to sea in the Aegean, where he became a leading hydrologist and acquired his own ship. In 1914 he and his vessel were recruited into the Mediterranean Fleet and were used to scout ahead of the main body and locate enemy units, Turkish or German, or blockade runners. Myres was known personally to every islander in the Aegean and was in the habit of lobbing a shell into the harbour from a mile or two away to announce his imminent arrival and to let them know to have his slippers and a glass of wine ready for him. There were harsh words on the day the admiral's flagship was in harbour when his shell dropped. But the Greeks – and Myres – laughed. Myres was as fond of Aristophanes as he was of Herodotus, and to hear him you could believe he had spoken personally with Themistocles, Pericles and Alcibiades. 'You know why Themistocles turned to starboard at that exact point to win the Battle of Salamis? Because that's the way the wind and current sets at that time of day and the trireme rowers were getting tired.' His tutorials were crammed with such illuminating sidelights that it was not possible to be other than absorbed, enlightened and inspired. Uniquely, I believe, Myres added to his DSc for hydrology a DSC for gallantry. And recalled to the Admiralty after 1940, he was deservedly knighted. A lovely man and my fondest memory of the true genius of Oxford.

I have mentioned five people because Oxford, lovely as its buildings are, is its people. There are so many others who should get a look. I shall always regret not overlapping with Warden Spooner. But Lightfoot, with the lovely rooms in the Garden Quad, who was, after Lord David, my moral tutor and very conscientious at that, was another incomparable character. With him there was always a marginally risqué tinge. The Australian ex-service Rhodes Scholars got it rather crudely right after the First World War when they 'crucified' him on the lawn with croquet hoops, watered him and bellowed, 'Grow, you little bugger, grow!' But, if at all, he was only a bugger in spirit, not remotely in act. His fondness for young men had the strictest physical limits, but he plied them with excellent sherry and even better advice and reminiscence, and I cannot imagine that anyone ever misunderstood

Above left: *From the Junior Common Room Suggestions Book, 1948.*

Above: *Holywell Quad, with prefabs, c.1952.*

him. As dean, which he improbably became, he more than tempered justice with mercy.

It is hard to imagine nowadays how cold and hungry healthy young growing boys could be in the sensationally icy and austere winters of 1940 and 1941. Your scout brought you hot shaving water at 7.00 am, but you had to be quick up or you would find it frozen in the can. Your ration of coal might help in the evenings, but I remember with gratitude that the librarian (in the new library) had to keep his books warm, and there was always a snug corner there for the cognoscenti. No method has ever been invented for inducing hypothermia more quickly than sitting still for hours on end reading or writing in a New College sitting room. As for hunger, college food in those days may have been healthy, but it was not filling. Who of my generation can forget the debt he owes first to Fuller's in the Cornmarket, but more importantly to the cake factory in Summertown, where day after day the queues formed at first light and waited, studying Thucidydes or Aeschylus, for the doors to open at 7.30 am? Cakes – and peanut butter – kept many a young man just this side of starvation in the 1940s. Such were our real preoccupations while we concocted our essays on Plato and Herodotus.

NEW COLLEGE AFTER THE WAR
Sir Marcus Worsley

One thing that kept me going in those unhappy years in the army was the promise of a place at New College. My grandfather, a man of scholarly disposition, had gone to New College. My father, who was not of a scholarly disposition, also went there but, as they say, did not complete his studies. My son won an exhibition there. So, there were four generations. A.H. Smith, the admirable warden, strained every nerve to get people into New College, and its numbers doubled. I lived in a (really very comfortable) prefab in the quad adjoining the new buildings and studied history. There were outstanding lecturers, including A.J.P. Taylor and Asa Briggs. It certainly loosened my brain up and rubbed off the rust. 'He in whose heart no history is enscrolled cannot discern in life's alloy the gold' ran the tag on our Eton history notebooks. I believe that to be true. The lack of a sense of history is the cause of much folly.

When I came up to New College in the autumn of 1947 Alan Bullock was very much in evidence. I came across him in two ways. First, he was tutor in history for the most modern third of the modern history syllabus, which was almost xenophobic in its emphasis on British history. We had Harry Bell as tutor for the medieval period, David Ogg for the Tudor–Stuart period, and Bullock for the modern period. Both Bell and Bullock were Yorkshiremen. Harry Bell was once teaching Aristotle, a part of the syllabus introduced I suppose for intellectual rigour, when his attention wandered and he turned to me and said: 'I remember the time your father hit a six over the pavilion at Bradford.' (My father had then been captain of the Yorkshire cricket team.) Bullock was perhaps more obviously a Yorkshireman, with a Yorkshire accent and Yorkshire bluffness. I remember him describing how his wife took woollies home to Yorkshire to wash because the water was so soft, this being the reason why the wool trade settled in the West Riding. David Ogg was a very different figure, Scottish and dour and, I think, a little world-weary by that time, but a great scholar and writer.

Alan Bullock's teaching of modern history was the opposite of dry-as-dust. He was a radical, political man, so his teaching of, say, nineteenth-century politics was related to contemporary politics and the more enlightening for that. He was, I think, an understanding teacher with the key quality of arousing enthusiasm. He viewed with alarm the possibility of a Conservative government. 'They'll put in a hard-line Home Secretary just like a continental minister of the interior,' I remember him saying. The other way I came across Bullock was in his capacity as dean, in charge of discipline. Not that I was particularly undisciplined, but we did have to get permission to go to London for the night and say where you were staying. In retrospect, it seems odd that a 22-year-old after four years in the army was so required. I used to give an address in St John's Wood. He always made out that I was visiting a nice, cosy mistress, but sadly it was just a favourite aunt. It was not only in academic matters that Bullock was a great encourager, and after four dreary years in the army I valued that. He got me a job in the BBC European Service – he had worked in it himself – and I kept in touch with him for a bit, until time washed that away. But I owed him a lot at a critical time.

Right: *Alan Bullock, fellow 1945–52, by Tom Phillips, c.1995.*

WARDENS

WILLIAM POOLE

The original statutes of New College place at the head of the college a *custos* or warden. There have been 45 wardens of New College from the foundation to the present day. All have so far been men, although nothing would prevent a woman from becoming the next warden. Some served for a matter of months; others for decades, the two most tenacious being Robert Pincke (1617–47) in the seventeenth century and J.E. Sewell (1860–1903) in the nineteenth and early twentieth centuries. A few figures have been nominated or elected warden who did not in the event take up office and are therefore not counted among the 45. One warden, George Marshall (1649–58), who is so counted, was imposed on the college by the parliamentary commissioners after the end of the Civil War. Marshall's custodianship may be judged invalid under the statutes, and much was retrospectively blamed on his apparent mismanagement, but Marshall was in office for a full decade, and a decade of supposed depredation is just as much a part of the college's history as a decade of thrift or splendour.

The warden's rights and duties were carefully set out in Wykeham's statutes. He was elected for life by a majority of the fellows; he had to be a fellow or ex-fellow in his 30s or older, with a degree in the higher faculties of theology or law or at least an MA; and he had to take holy orders if he was not already in them. He received allowances and a salary of £40 on top of the normal emoluments granted to fellows. In addition,

he could hold as many ecclesiastical benefices as he liked, meaning that a warden could, in theory, become a wealthy figure while in post, something denied to the fellows. Strictly speaking, the warden was (and remains) outside the fellowship, with his own household and staff and restricted rights when he ventured into the fellows' territories, the college Hall and later the SCR.

Some of these restrictions are observed today in order to underline the sovereignty of Governing Body. The warden still does not preside in Hall and wears his gown in the SCR to symbolize that he is the guest of the

Below: *The Warden's Lodgings as depicted by William Nicholson, c.1910.*

Above: *The Warden's stableyard, by Hort New, 1907.*

Right: *The flagons given to the college in 1606 by William Ryves, warden 1599–1613.*

fellows when on their turf. New College has thus always in theory been a notably democratic institution. Major decisions were taken by consulting the entire fellowship, and Wykeham insisted that in matters involving external negotiations with possible legal ramifications, the warden had to obtain a majority vote, additionally subscribed to by at least 10 lawyers. On the other hand, internal college business was largely conducted by the 'Warden and Thirteen', the name for the senior figures who acted as the college executive council. This group usually, but not always, comprised two deans, four bursars, five senior fellows, the sub-warden and the warden himself. This was the *de facto* college executive from the sixteenth century and is not dissimilar to the way in which certain of the older Cambridge colleges are still run today, where a 'council' is in theory accountable to, but in practice rarely challenged by, the entire Governing Body. Indeed, in one sense New College wardens functioned more like the modern college bursar, administrating the college assets and undertaking annual reviews ('progresses') of the college estates. But the original wardens also acted somewhat in the manner of monastic abbots, examining the fellows on their moral conduct in a solemn, termly meeting of the fellowship in the ante-chapel, and hearing complaints between fellows. If discipline ever threatened to break down or if a dispute broke out among the senior fellows, the warden was to call

in the college's Visitor, the bishop of Winchester. For most of the college's history, the warden has, therefore, occupied a fascinatingly ambiguous position: the head of the college, yet socially distinct from the fellows; the leader and arbiter of the fellowship, yet bound by the advice of the Thirteen in internal, and the voice of the entire fellowship in external, matters. This spirit of a 'mixed constitution' survives today, despite the many formal changes the statutes have undergone in recent centuries.

Like Wykeham himself, Wykeham's ideal warden was more of an administrator than a scholar. The oath taken by a new warden in the presence of all the fellows was long and pernickety, almost completely barren of promises to promote intellectual inquiry. Instead, it was replete with minute and legalistic formulae of how the estates were to be administered and who to turn to in times of trouble.

In 1402 the Warden's Barn was constructed, with an adjoining paddock for grazing six horses, also provided by college for the purposes of the warden's annual progress. On the south side of the Barn still survives an otherwise puzzling outdoors staircase leading nowhere – these are steps to allow the warden to mount his horse. (Today, the Barn largely houses teaching rooms for fellows, and the paddock is now the warden's garden.) The ideal administrator-warden spent much of his time on horseback visiting the estates, accompanied by the outrider and a clerk, setting out each September on the annual tour.

Perhaps the most diligent warden in this respect was Michael Woodward (1658–75), in many ways the ideal Wykehamist warden. He had no pretensions to scholarship, but he was a keen administrator and an obsessive note-taker, and he settled an annuity on the library so that new books could be bought each year. The register for Woodward's benefaction survives and shows how the college's intellectual tastes developed throughout the seventeenth and eighteenth centuries and at least partially qualifies the common view that the eighteenth-century college was intellectually moribund. Woodward also reorganized the college's archives. His fussy little secretary hand is visible on thousands of archival items, and it is largely thanks to him that the archives were intelligible to future centuries. Woodward also kept little notebook-cum-diaries of his progresses arranged by estate, and these provide us with the most detailed accounts of the life of a diligent head-of-house on progress. He recorded the minutiae of each meeting with his tenants, but he also now and then turned to more personal reflections. On progress in Wiltshire in the 1660s, for instance, Woodward recalled, 'the morrow being Sunday Mr Budd [William Budd, BCL, fellow] did preach in the morneing upon the subject that the world should have an end, bee burnt up with fire and utterly annihiliated. But whether soe, or noe I doubted'.

Despite his diligence, Woodward has failed to gain an entry in the *Oxford Dictionary of National Biography*, and

indeed, partially because of the administrative nature of wardenship, it must be confessed that few New College wardens over the centuries have achieved great distinction over and above their office. Wykeham himself put in place the first two wardens – the first, Nicholas, being a Wykeham himself – but thereafter the fellows chose their head by election. Thomas Cranley (*c*.1337–1417), the second warden, had served as warden of Wykeham's other foundation at Winchester before moving to New College (warden 1389–96); he later rose to become the archbishop of Dublin and the chancellor of Ireland. Two generations later, Thomas Chaundler (*c*.1417–90), had likewise already served as warden of Winchester when he took up the wardenship of the parent college (1454–75). Chaundler was the first example of a warden who had a decisive effect on the intellectual culture of his college: the 'Chaundler manuscript' is a collection of literary works by Chaundler and a few others, a compendium of what has been called 'Wykehamist culture'. The manuscript contains a Latin drama, as well as poems and dialogues in praise of the cities of Bath and Wells and of the life and virtues of Wykeham himself. Chaundler was a proselyte of elegant Latin style, and as both an academic politician and an educational reformer he is the most significant of the early wardens.

The notable sixteenth-century wardens are less attractive figures, mainly because of the religious fluctuations of the age. Up to the advent of Warden

London (1485/6–1543, warden 1526–42), all the wardens had been academic theologians. John London, however, was a lawyer and a notary public. He had attended Winchester and New College, to be sure, but in the 1530s he had been one of Henry VIII's Visitors of the monasteries and as such was responsible for many dissolutions in the locales of Oxford, Reading, Warwick and elsewhere. London was on this account an odious figure to many, but he was doctrinally conservative. London persecuted heretics to the stake in Windsor, where he held a canonry, and was pilloried by John Foxe in his *Book of Martyrs*. Desecrator of monasteries and burner of evangelicals, London was for some time going to be remembered with nothing but hatred. Modern historians have attempted to be kinder, recognizing that conservative administrators such as London were in an impossible position. Fellows of New College, however, may also reflect that in 1528, when faced with the heresy of the young fellow John Quinby, London imprisoned him in the Bell Tower and, neither

Above: *John Oglander, warden 1768–94, by George Romney, 1775.*

Right: *Oxford as depicted by Jane Mary Oglander in 1786; she was tutored at John Oglander's behest by William Malchair of Oxford.*

man repenting, left him there to die. London himself was to die in incarceration 15 years later.

His successor, Henry Cole (1504/5–1579/80, warden 1542–51), was also religiously slippery, but in Elizabeth's reign he finally consolidated his conservatism into recusancy, and he too died in jail, having spent two decades in captivity. The fates of London and Cole attest to the difficulties of holding a perhaps inherently conservative office in times of state-led radicalism.

The wardens from the late sixteenth century to the Civil War were on the whole more peaceable, and the consecutive tenures of Wardens Culpepper (1573–99), Ryves (1599–1613), Lake (1613–17) and Pincke (1617–47) represent the halcyon days of the college in literary and social terms. These were the decades in which New College men wrote great quantities (if not qualities) of poetry and in which the Wykehamist identity was consolidated. The Ryves surname would long feature among New College fellows, and of George Ryves's family we may recall his younger brother Thomas, civil lawyer and naval historian, and his first cousin Bruno, singing clerk and Royalist journalist. Warden Lake worked on the King James Bible and became bishop of Bath and Wells. The fellows were so proud of Lake's elevation that they commissioned his portrait and hung it in the Founder's Library; in recent years it has adorned the Chequer. Lake was another of the intellectual wardens. He established college lectureships in Hebrew and mathematics, and he gifted a substantial quantity of books to the library, including works on Arabic. His own sermons were published in 1629 with a biography written by a fellow of the college in which it was claimed that Lake never dreamed – sleeping, he said, with an easy conscience. Pincke became the right-hand-man of Archbishop Laud and on the outbreak of the Civil War led a muster of the fellows. He was a senior figure in the university of his age, serving on multiple occasions as vice-chancellor, as well as a delegate to the Press. But he did quarrel with his fellows in the 1630s and met his end in 1647 in the Warden's Lodgings at the bottom of the stairs.

The next two centuries did not see great wardens, although we may celebrate the fine artistic taste of Warden Oglander (1768–94) and the mechanical wit of Warden Shuttleworth (1822–40), inventor of the Port Railway, based on the contrivances of Durham collieries. Perhaps we should better remember Shuttleworth as instigating

Left: *Alic Smith, warden 1944–58, by Jacob Epstein, 1950.*

the abolition of the long-misunderstood custom that New College men were exempt from university examinations. Warden Sewell (1860–1903) let his senior fellows preside over the greatest intellectual reforms the college has seen, and it is to his credit at least that this exceptionally long-serving warden did not get in the way. He was an antiquary in the vein of Woodward and took pleasure in putting the

WARDEN SMITH AND THE SQUATTERS

I think it was in the Michaelmas Term of 1948 that the New College JCR, stirred to unusual activity by high charges and disgusting food, petitioned the Governing Body for redress of their grievances. Alic Smith (warden 1944–58) came to address us. He seemed to us rather an unworldly figure, devoted to the buildings of the college but probably innocent of college politics. We were soon to learn better. He began by explaining how the college had done its utmost to accommodate the men who were coming back from war service, building a set of prefabricated hutments, as he called them, on Balliol sports ground. He described how squatters had occupied them and how he had himself gone to reason with the occupiers, accompanied by a local, communist, councillor. 'Well, you see,' most sentences began with that phrase, 'all seemed to be going well until a very large lady came up to us and demanded to know "What

about us expectant mothers?" Well you see, we had no answer to that, so the college had to build new hutments in the back quadrangle.' There was a good deal more, but he had already won the day. Here was this frail old man who had gone to grapple on our behalf with a crowd of angry squatters – and we applauded him to the echo. The story he had told was, of course, no response to our grievances, but it had served to win us over. We were the innocents. Had Epstein's superb bust of the warden then been completed and had we been able to see it, we might have learned better. What Epstein perceptively saw was a man of toughened steel and abundant guile: Machiavelli could, as P.G. Wodehouse might have written, have taken his correspondence course. But Warden Smith was an original, and we loved him for it.

Penry Williams

Above: *The installation of Curtis Price as warden, 2009.*

college archives in order once again and compiling a huge manuscript register of every member of New College up to his own day. His famous successor Warden Spooner (1903–25) was again a man who did not originate, but who equally did not obstruct, the great changes being introduced around him. Whether Spooner actually said things like 'Who has not nourished in his bosom a half-warmed fish?', he nevertheless has the unique distinction in the history of the college of having a type of verbal joke named after him. But Spooner's significance rests upon his ecumenism: he was the first non-Wykehamist scholar of the college, and he later insisted upon memorializing in the ante-chapel the college war dead who had fought against the Allies. Accused of unpatriotic behaviour, the mild Spooner magnificently held his ground (*see p.117*).

Spooner's successor, H.A.L. Fisher (warden 1925–40), was an intellectual giant in comparison to all of his predecessors, bar perhaps the remote Chaundler and Lake, and his *History of Europe* (1935) was the most

distinguished book by a head of house ever to emanate from New College. Alic Smith, his successor (1944–58), wrote the standard book on New College architecture but was regarded by the likes of Hugh Trevor-Roper as a bit of a bore with an unhealthy obsession with Gothic architecture. There is a hilarious letter from Trevor-Roper to Bernard Berenson, recently published, about that one Gothic window in the northeast corner of the Old Quad, which Smith managed to wrestle out of an unwilling Governing Body (*see p.19*). Smith's successor, Sir William Hayter (1958–76), was a distinguished diplomat, returning the college to the oldest tradition of statesmen heads-of-house.

Of the years of Wardens Cooke, McGregor and Ryan, however, perhaps too many of us are still living who knew or know these men, and so we leave them respectfully to posterity. But Warden Price (from 2009) is an entirely new departure. He is a musician, an American and has had no previous formal membership of the college or even the university. Three firsts in college history.

WARDEN HAYTER AND CHANGING TIMES

Warden Hayter looked and sounded exactly what he was: a pluperfect Wykehamist mandarin. Yet, like many of his generation, his conventional exterior was not matched by any inherent or insistent conservatism. By accident or design he proved surprisingly suitable for the times in which he occupied the Lodgings. Not merely presiding over change, in many respects he embraced it, notably the admission of women, a cause pioneered in the 1960s. Although initially unsuccessful, the first woman fellow was elected in his final years; the path to full co-education being firmly set before his retirement. In his time, the expansion of numbers of graduate students was matched by provision for them, notably the development of the Sacher Building. The Hayters, with their extensive international diplomatic experience, seemed especially comfortable with entertaining graduates from around the globe, many of whom became firm friends. Relations with undergraduates tended to be more distant and formal, yet the Hayters were irrepressibly hospitable. Iris Hayter's inimitable style as a hostess, while superficially redolent of a past age of embassies, grandees and high society, in fact betokened a genuine interest in people, an open social warmth and energy that frequently seemed to the young to be at odds with William's apparent sub-fusc reserve and diffidence. Insensitive and unobservant guests may have failed to detect the sharp, shrewd, and humane appraisal behind Iris's characteristic, at times seemingly self-parodic outbursts of effusive conversational apostrophe. Unlike the warden, she realised that social encounters abhor silence.

Quietly, however, Warden Hayter, despite or perhaps because of his non-academic career, perpetuated the tradition familiar from his own time as a New College undergraduate in the 1920s of a head of house closely committed to the college. Unlike his predecessor, Warden Smith, he played little part in university politics. Unlike Warden Fisher, he did not harp on about his earlier life in public affairs. Instead, he acted as the college's Tutor for Admissions, a traditional but increasingly onerous warden's role. More than one applicant never realised that disguised behind the illegible signature of the Tutor for Admissions on the letter offering a place was the warden himself. While lacking the studied charisma of more gaudy Heads of House, such as Maurice Bowra of Wadham (who had been an undergraduate at New College 1919–23), Hayter was liked by the junior members, even if, as with many in such positions, he occasionally attracted the frustration, irritation and condescension of the fellows, whose number and diversity of subject greatly increased under him. There clung to Hayter some hint of palmier days. His advice to freshmen was as much aesthetic as academic, including an exhortation to 'look up' at their surroundings and to visit all Oxford's halls and chapels, a witness to his sincere enthusiasm for architecture. While few penetrated what has been described as his 'canopy of charm', he allowed the college to develop with its own momentum.

The college of the 60s and 70s, as probably in most other periods, combined the extremes, compromises and contradictions of old and new as **Richard Compton Miller** (1963–6) recalls:

Dean Thomas (Merlin Thomas, fellow in French) was shocked or, in his words, 'completely dumbfounded'. For there displayed on the Front Quad lawn were dozens of garishly-decorated garden gnomes, toadstools, Little Red Riding Hoods, elves with fishing-rods, Snow Whites, Father Christmases and reindeer. It was early one morning and one of the college scouts had woken the dean to warn him about 'an unusual break-in' that had occurred overnight. If this prank was a surprise, even to blasé undergraduates occasionally used to seeing frilly knickers temporarily flying from college flagpoles, it was a mini-scoop for the university newspaper *Cherwell*, of which I was then editor. The gnome-robbers were never caught, although the fellows had their suspicions. Instead

they spent many weeks trying to reunite these kidnapped concrete and plastic gargoyles with their owners. They even advertised in the *Oxford Mail* and circulated 'Not Wanted' notices around local council estates. How their owners were able to prove good title remains a mystery. The college was just keen to rid themselves of this metaphorical dog turd on its greensward.

New College in the mid-sixties under Warden Hayter was a quirky place. Laid-back, liberal and convivial, most of us felt gloriously liberated, particularly if we had suffered the restrictions and uniformity of life at boarding school. As long as you avoided hurting anybody, playing your Rolling Stones 45s too loud or damaging college property (perhaps after too many shandies in the Buttery?) you could do pretty well what you wanted. In between history tutorials with Harry Bell,

Garry Bennett and Penry Williams I managed to create for myself an agreeably schizophrenic existence. During Trinity term I would spend at least two nights a week in London partying at deb cocktail parties and balls. For a broke undergraduate like me this was a glorious form of free entertainment, with an endless supply of glamorous girls, vintage champagne and smart venues where you could dance until dawn. All you needed to join this Brideshead Revisited-lite were a dinner jacket, a plausible manner and some key Society sponsors. John Buxton, my moral tutor (surely an anachronistic title in the so-called Swinging Sixties?) readily granted me the necessary leave of absence. Indeed he never seemed to worry about my louche, sometimes controversial, behaviour both as a socialite and journalist. He and his wife would occasionally invite me for tea on the lawn at

Above: *The Front Quad as depicted by Edward Ardizzone, c.1960.*

their rather grand house outside Oxford. I think John realized that my wayward lifestyle was actually rather more innocent than some of my boozy contemporaries, particularly as I rarely missed a tutorial or lecture. One of the most brilliant undergraduates of my generation, an Old Etonian scholar now sadly dead, devoted most of term-time to losing the family fortune. After tutorials he would set off for the gaming tables of Mayfair, playing blackjack, backgammon and chemmy. 'Up another grand last night', he would boast as he lowered himself sleepily into the college eight the next morning. He never mentioned his losses. Funny that.

One college rule that was rarely enforced was that all female guests must leave by midnight when the gates were officially closed. To disobey meant being 'gated' for several weeks. I remember the night porter at Holywell Lodge shaking his head just before this curfew once. 'I've seen more than a dozen young ladies enter the college in the last few hours, but only two leave', he muttered. The fellows were too cool to order a *cherchez les femmes* raid on the most likely offenders. You just had to be careful to remove any evidence of a female presence when your scout knocked on the door and drew the curtains at 8am. But most scouts, particularly after a generous tip at the end of term, turned a blind eye. 'You'll be wanting two cups of tea this morning, Sir ', was the usual response. One rather dashing undergraduate whom we rarely saw in college was a young maharajah. Rumour had it that he was allowed to have a double bed and a garage for his E-type Jaguar. This bending of the rules, with the connivance of the warden, made all of us who had to sleep in single beds and ride bicycles very jealous.

When it came to the Commem Ball a remarkable collusion occurred between the fellows and JCR, a bit like the Brits and Germans playing football in no-man's land at Christmas during World War One. All known 'secret' entrances to New College were blocked up so that no-one could gatecrash the festivities. One of the metal bars on the window of my Front Quad rooms had been replaced with a wooden one, which enabled me to squeeze through if the gates were closed. I was put on scouts' honour not to reveal this Colditz-style escape route. But the commonest point of entry was the old bone-shaker permanently placed by the Sacher Building to enable you to climb over the gates without disembowelling yourself.

In my third year I was nearly sent down when the Proctors accused me of 'bringing the university into disrepute'. It happened after Joshua Macmillan, grandson of former Prime Minister Harold Macmillan, was found dead in his room at Balliol following an overdose. A 'mole' told me about this tragedy shortly after his body was discovered and I was able to splash this extraordinary scoop over our front page. A deluge of 'Drugs Tragedy at Oxford' headlines followed next day, with Fleet Street's finest descending on the university looking for evidence that Britain's Bright Young Things had turned into heroin and coke addicts. As *Cherwell* editor I was their first port of call, along with the President of the Union. I gave interviews expressing my surprise that drugs existed in the university. Indeed such was my ignorance that I memorably mispronounced cocaine (rhyming it with the Cockaigne Overture) on the BBC's Nine O'Clock News. Unfortunately the authorities took a dim view of me pontificating about university business. The Senior Proctor summoned me to appear before a disciplinary hearing. As I nervously walked to the Clarendon Building dressed in subfusc I feared that my whole academic career was dissolving in front of me. If I was sent down from Oxford without taking a degree my chances of reading for the Bar afterwards were nil. Fortunately the Proctors realized that the circumstances were unusual – PM's grandsons don't normally die from drug overdoses and attract huge media interest. There was no point in making me a martyr and so they gave me a ticking off and gated me for three weeks. It was a timely reminder that the purpose for me being at university was to study. And so headline-chasing and debutante excesses were reluctantly replaced with swotting for my history Finals.

COLLEGE SERVANTS

MICHAEL BURDEN

Of course, all members of the institution, from the warden to the bottle-washer, are servants of the college. The division however is best understood by thinking of it as one between the learned (or those attempting to be learned) and those who care for them, and without whom the former would frequently be lost. No Oxford college is complete without its support staff; they are an ever-present contingent, counselling, moving, building, tidying, gardening, ensuring the smooth running of the Foundation at every level. Historically, they had greater status and authority than their counterparts in private service, which added to the already complicated and ever-changing inter-relationships between the college and its servants. This is exemplified by the position of the trebles of the choir, who were in effect servitors, the Oxford title for poor scholars who earned their fees in service. The New College statutes declared that:

> there shall be sixteen poor and needy boys less than twelve years of age, of good standing and honest conversation, who are sufficiently competent in reading and singing to assist with serving, reading and singing in the said Chapel, to assist the Priests and Fellows in Holy Orders who celebrate in the Chapel, to serve at the other Divine Offices there, to prepare and arrange the readings for the Scholars and Fellows of the College, and also assist the College servants in Hall by attending the Fellows at table in a humble and honest manner as

Below: Medieval carvings of the trebles with bread and black jacks of beer.

Right: *The donations box for the Junior Common Room servants.*

Below: *The recipe for Ralph Ayres's pancakes, from his cookery book started in 1719.*

befits those who have been received and admitted to our College out of charity. We also ordain that these poor boys be fed from the leftovers of the food they have served to the scholars and fellows, if that be enough; otherwise, if there is not enough, we ordain that they be provided with sufficient food for their needs, paid for out of our College Chest.

Today's trebles are in clover, indeed. But it is also the case that until about 15 years ago, the chapel congregation did not stand on the entry of the choir at Sunday evensong on the grounds that the members were 'servants of the college' and the congregation consisted of college members. The trebles can be seen in the medieval carvings over the Hall's buttery door, each carrying blackjacks of beer and baskets of bread; they were required to wait on the scholars of the college. The carvings themselves are miniature miracles; the choristers' heads until recently were covered in brown varnish, but during the recent

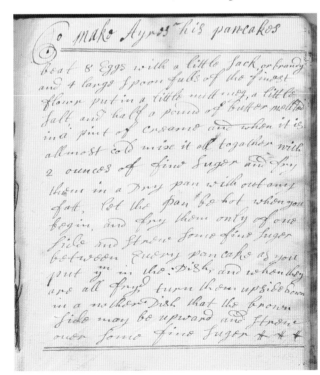

Hall restoration, were revealed to be made from carved bone. The college's employees have included some of the great characters in the college's history: Ralph Ayres, the seventeenth and eighteenth century cook, a copy of whose cookbook is still held by the college; John Louch, the butler of New College for 45 years, from about 1785, who seems to have been suspiciously wealthy, and who in 1789, had to be ordered not to lend college silver to fellows for dinners in their rooms; the redoubtable Rose, who worked in the Lodgings and waited on Warden Smith; and the gardener, Ervine Schoen, who seemed to have been part of the garden itself, and was known to the undergraduates by many affectionate nicknames.

The college kept its servants disciplined through various systems of fines and deprivations. The head butler Field seems to have been particularly problematic. He and the second butler, thought to be Vickers, were fined on account of 'great Deficiency in ye Beer and negligence in the Buttery' on 20 December 1729; he was later given until Lady Day to provide proper security of the plate and to undertake his duties with more care; and there was yet more consternation when an audit of the silver in 1730 showed that Godfrey's Pot and St Loe's pot were missing from the vault since 1727. The college's concern is understandable; the silver represented cash in form of bullion, and such losses could represent sizeable sums of sums of money. Not surprisingly, the college records detail mostly disciplinary offences such as these; for the most part, the institution has been, and continues to be, served loyally and diligently by its servants.

THE PORTERS

A visitor to the college first encounters the porters in the Lodge, known to generations of senior and junior members alike as the repository of knowledge, assistance, and generosity. The Founder was well aware of the role of porters as gatekeepers to the college; an illustrated copy of the college's statutes from the Founder's own day shows a porter expelling an unwanted visitor from the precincts. The New College Lodge finally moved in the 1980s from New College Lane to Holywell Street, a move still regretted by some, but borne of necessity. Using the small glazed box, the porters keep an eye on cyclists, the arrival and departure of college guests, and on the tourists, required to use the New College Lane gate, but who frequently 'chance it' through the back door. The affection in which the porters have always been held is reflected in the cartoon by Giles Pilbrow, drawn while he was a Junior Member.

Above: *An unwanted visitor being ejected from the College, c.1390.*

Left: *The New College porters as seen by Giles Pilbrow, c.1988.*

NEW COLLEGE GARDENS

The gardens have always been one of the college's great glories, and in general, have followed the broad trends in garden design from formality to informality, and (partly) back again. The staff required to maintain the formal Baroque garden seen in Loggan's famous late seventeenth-century print of the college was more extensive than that required to look after the broad lawns which replaced it. Supervising the gardens' staff was a mixture of stick and carrot; on 2 December 1730, it was agreed to withdraw the gardener's extra allowance on the grounds that he neglected the garden '& did not deserve such encouragement another year'. Many of the tasks undertaken have been made simpler by mechanization; the lawns are, for example, no longer constantly scythed and rolled, and the time-consuming business of raking leaves is a thing of the past; the college does not now maintain a permanent staff in the gardens. But as always, they remain on the tourist trail, and the college still fights a running battle with visitors, most of whom were (and are) well behaved, but all of whom are in need of supervision: on 23 March 1836, the college resolved to 'employ a person to let respectable people into the Garden', when the garden gate was shut on Sundays.

COLLEGE SCOUTS

The bond between members of college and their scouts is at once obvious and mysterious. For most of the history of the college, the scout's main tasks were to deal with the fires and grates, the delivery of hot water, and

Right: *Rolling the grass, by William Delamotte, 1821.*

Far right: *William Hodges serving the chaplains' rooms, by L.L., 1768.*

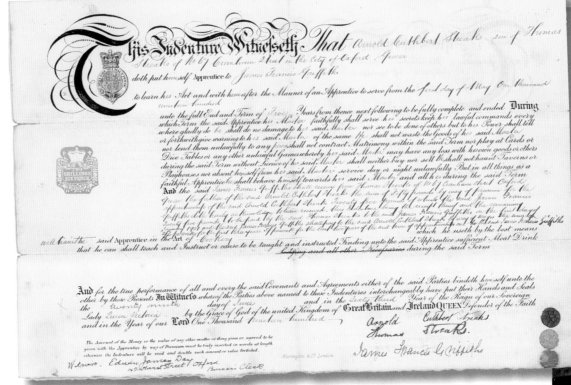

emptying chamber pots. Central heating and running water have put paid to such thankless tasks, but at the same time, it has created a considerable distance between college member and scout; after all, no relationship is closer than the one between the student and the person who wakes you in the morning. Few images survive anywhere of scouts at work – most pictures tend to be of upper servants, such as the butler – but during the eighteenth century, the college was served by the Hodges family dynasty. Hodges' father (or possibly grandfather) worked as a college porter, but his son William worked as servant to the chaplains' rooms. The 1768 painting by the mysterious 'L.L.' of William shows him wearing a coat that appears to be a cast off from his grander employers. The painting adds 'a new twist to the tradition of the emblematic servant'; it shows him carrying a flat-topped tankard – in a late seventeenth-century style – and a bundle of clay pipes under his arm. The picture is significant in itself, for William was born crippled on the left hand side, and the artist has carefully captured this fact. The picture may be part parody, for its form is a nod to the famous portrait of the Eton butler depicted with the symbols of strangers' hospitality; the tankard and pipe are indications of a much more domestic kind of hospitality, and is possibly a reference to the rather lax attitude of the college's eighteenth-century chaplains.

THE KITCHENS

The kitchens are one of the most sensitive areas of support for college members. The buildings, as known from the outside by generations of undergraduates, consist of one main, lofty, cooking space, with a warren of dependencies; vulnerable to fire, they were constructed separately from the Hall they were designed to serve. The medieval roof by Hugh Herland survives, and the room is still in use today, albeit with modern equipment, even if a splendid showing of copper pots remains in situ. The (all male) staff lined up in the nineteenth-century photograph may well have followed the career trajectory of one Cuthbert Streaks which is as touching as it is instructive. He was apprenticed to the chef, James Griffiths, for five years from 1 May 1900 to 'learn the art of cookery', the college recording the receipt from 'Mrs Streaks' of a premium of £50. Whether by custom or by position due to his own diligence, he was invited to the Staff Christmas party in December 1904 in anticipation of his imminent departure, and by 1905, we read: 'His indenture has been completed to my entire satisfaction, the apprentice mentioned has had a thorough training in all departments of this kitchen and I consider him well versed, also painstaking in his profession, hoping at some future date he will rise to a high position, he is most obliging, willing and punctual.'

COLLEGE LEADERS

ALAN RYAN

New College's Founder was a leader of men. Although the college has subsequently produced its fair share of such men, it has more often been a refuge from the world where leaders of men are held in high regard. In the early nineteenth century this process had gone too far. In H.A.L. Fisher's words, the college had become a society 'at once contracted, indolent, orthodox and obscure'. The astonishing transformation that took place after the college's acceptance of the commissioners' statutes in 1857 required real leadership within the college. This was provided above all by three men: Edward Wickham, Hereford George and Alfred Robinson, whose work was later sustained by William Spooner and Hastings Rashdall.

History is chronically unkind to near-misses, and this glimpse of the college's leading figures from 1858 to 1945, the years when the modern college was created, should begin with Augustus Hare. Hare was born in 1792 and died in Rome in 1834. He became an undergraduate fellow in 1810 and made himself unpopular by attempting to extinguish the privileges of Founder's Kin – who, in spite of repeated attempts to restrict their numbers, made up almost half the 70 fellows – and publishing an open letter denouncing the privilege that allowed the college to present its members for degrees without examination. The privilege was given up in 1834, and years passed before a New College man secured a first class in finals. Sweet-natured and not combative, Hare was a well-liked tutor between 1818 and 1829, when he refused the gift of a rich

living, married and settled in Alton Barnes to serve his remote rural parish until ill-health drove him to Italy.

Before the royal commission made its own recommendations, the college had tried half-heartedly to change its statutes for itself. Once change was inescapable it was welcomed, and E.C. Wickham led the charge. Wickham was born in 1834, became an undergraduate

Left: *E.C. Wickham, fellow 1852–74, by William Richmond, c.1905.*

Right: *Bursar Alfred Robinson, fellow 1865–95, by Hubert Von Herkomer, 1895.*

fellow in 1852, took holy orders, and after two years teaching at Winchester became a tutor in 1860. He arranged with his friend Edwin Palmer of Balliol the system of intercollegiate lectures that became the pattern for the contemporary system of university-wide lectures, and with Alfred Robinson persuaded the college to remove the prohibition on fellows marrying, foreseeing that a career in teaching and research could be as attractive as the traditional careers of law and the Church, but only if it demanded no sacrifice of family life. He himself married Gladstone's daughter when he left the college to become headmaster of Wellington in 1874.

Far left: *Hereford George, fellow 1858–1910, photographed by Stillyard & Co., Oxford.*

Left: *'The Rasher Bill'; Hastings Rashdall, fellow, in caricature by G.E.D., c.1910.*

THE RASHER-BILL ('DIVERS OXONIENSIS').

If the baton was not exactly seized by Alfred Robinson, he was unequivocally the leading figure in the college between his arrival in 1864 and his death at the early age of 54 in 1895. He was not a Wykehamist, but studied at Marlborough and University College; he was formidably intelligent, with a double first in mathematics and Greats, and the public presence that made him twice President of the Union and a longstanding senior treasurer. As bursar from 1875, he husbanded the resources that allowed the college to expand its number from fewer than 20 undergraduates in residence in the 1850s to almost 300 three decades later. He was also personally generous. The new statutes that allowed the college to elect non-Wykehamists removed the means tests on holding fellowships. Robinson bought the riverside sports ground from Merton and gave it anonymously to the college. He was an enthusiastic cricketer; he was also an excellent lecturer on Aristotle's Ethics and Politics, a supporter of university expansion for working-class students, a devoted Liberal, a passionate supporter of Gladstone and a man of immense clarity of vision. As Gladstone became more radical in his later years, Robinson followed him, to the dismay of more conservative colleagues, such as Spooner.

He had the enthusiastic, if slightly intimidated, support of his colleagues. The most prominent of these after Wickham's departure was Hereford George, whose indispensable history of the college from 1856 to 1906 frustratingly omits all mention of his own role in the changes he recounts. But all accounts of George emphasize not only his extracurricular activities in the Alps, where he was a founder-member of the Alpine Society, but his work both inside and outside the college to make the newly created school of modern history something more than the study of medieval charters. He was also the first Oxford fellow to marry and keep his fellowship. Spooner, too, played a leading role before he became warden in 1903, though his gentler approach was inevitably overshadowed by Robinson's.

By the end of the nineteenth century something very like the modern college was in existence. With the election of fellows of the quality of H.A.L. Fisher and Gilbert Murray, the college no longer needed anyone to pull it out of the academic doldrums. Perhaps the most important figure for undergraduates in the transitional period before the horrors of 1914 was Hastings Rashdall, whose tutorials were as often given on long walks or impromptu in the Cornmarket as in his rooms, though neighbouring students sometimes discovered that he had borrowed most of their furniture for a

seminar. In addition to writing *The Theory of Good and Evil*, he served for many years as a canon of Hereford Cathedral and was a powerful influence on the liberal side of the Church of England.

The interwar years were a golden age. Figures who made an impact on the outside world include Frank Pakenham, Hugh Gaitskell, Douglas Jay, Richard Crossman and Evan Durbin, as well as Rhodes Scholars such as Robert Penn Warren in one way and Bram Fischer in quite another. Among the fellowship, the college nurtured numerous distinguished thinkers whom it did not retain, including Lionel Robbins, perhaps the most distinguished economist ever to grace the college.

If it no longer needed leadership in the sense in which it had in 1858, some extremely distinguished fellows set an intellectual tone and standard. Comparisons are invidious, but G.H. Hardy always said that his years at New College (1919–31) were the happiest of his life, even if one thinks of him as quintessentially a product of Trinity College, Cambridge, where he eventually returned. Lionel Robbins recalled him as a man who called out all one's powers, but he could be unnerving. He once asked a new tutor in chemistry to name a cricket team made up of first class cricketers all of whom had committed suicide. The Haldanes, father and son, though hardly visible to the undergraduates, were only two more of the distinguished scientists whom the college sheltered. J.S. Haldane (1860–1936, fellow 1901–36) began with the traditional Scots prejudice against the collegiate system and ended by valuing New College as a refuge from the colleagues in the university with whom he had fallen out. J.B.S. (1892–1964) was a fellow from 1919 to 1923. Among others, Julian Huxley replaced his former tutor Geoffrey Smith as a biology fellow from 1922 to 1925

Below: J.B.S. Haldane, centre of back row, fellow 1919–22, c.1913.

opened his family homes in Oxford and Somerset to 30 generations of his pupils and whose private self emerged in the poetry he wrote to his wife. Until he left under a cloud for the more congenial world of politics, his younger colleague Richard Crossman (1907–74, fellow 1930–37) was a renowned lecturer and an inspiring tutor, if less meticulous and less demanding than Joseph. The Plato described by Crossman was very like the proto-Fascist described a decade later by Karl Popper, but *Plato Today* was very much meant for the 'today' of 1937.

Christopher Cox was for a decade their opposite number as ancient history tutor. Born in 1899, he came to

before leaving for London and a career that included the founding directorship of UNESCO.

The leading figure within the college, though remembered by many students with something close to terror, was H.W.B. Joseph, born in 1867, a Wykehamist, who was elected as a fellow and tutor in philosophy in 1895 on Alfred Robinson's death. He gave up his tutorship 37 years later but continued to teach almost until his death in 1943. His tutorial style took no prisoners – absolute clarity was the goal, and he was unwilling to stop his questioning until his student had removed at least some of the fog from his mind. He was in all senses a good student of Plato. Maurice Bowra maintained that the shellfire of World War One was less terrifying than Joseph's tutorials. Outside the tutorial setting, Joseph was a warm and friendly man, who

Left: Christopher Cox, fellow 1926–82, by Michael Noakes, 1972.

Below left: H.A.L. Fisher, warden 1925–40, in caricature by Powys Evans, 1926.

Above: *Bursar
George Radcliffe,
fellow 1920–59, by
C.C. Ironside, 1959.*

employed as a lecturer from 1932 and fellow and tutor
from 1938; another was Lord David Cecil, who arrived
as English tutor in 1938 and stayed until retirement from
the Goldsmiths' Professorship in 1969. In the nature of
things, young tutors do less to 'keep the show on the road'
than do bursars. From 1924 to 1956 that meant Bursar
Radcliffe (G.Y.R. Radcliffe, 1886–1959), unusual in New
College history in having solidly Conservative leanings
and an unfulfilled desire to be a Conservative MP. He
was a stalwart of the Landed Charities Association, which
was wholly appropriate at a time when the college was
still a substantial landowner. Keynes thought he was the
only competent bursar in Oxford. He was also a generous
benefactor, who gave the college the two paintings by
Bartolomeo Montagna of Vicenza that now hang in Hall.

Radcliffe's domestic bursar from 1946 to 1958 was
Eric Yorke (1901–77), remembered quite unfairly as a
man who kept the college on the shortest of short rations
in those austere years. Saying 'no' when he wished he
could say 'yes' did not come easily. He was a Mods tutor
of infinite kindness and possessed of a streak of mischief
that was not perhaps the going style of the college when
he joined it in 1927. A sign of his real virtues was the
great affection with which not only his pupils but also the
domestic and maintenance staff remembered him.

Since the 1960s with growing numbers of fellows,
increased managerialism and intrusion from university
governance, college leadership has become more diffuse,
a matter of shifting coalitions rather than dominant
individuals. As fellows did more research and spent more
time with their families, so their energy to devote to
the intricacies, minutiae and expanding technicalities of
college administration diminished, much of the work of
running the college devolving on to full-time bursars,
accountants and clerical staff. Consequently, although,
as throughout the college's history, there has been no
shortage of powerful personalities, none have stamped
their own mark on the place in quite the same way as those
who went before.

New College in 1926 via Clifton, Balliol and Magdalen.
He went off in 1937 to an extraordinarily productive
career in the education branch of the Colonial Office,
in which new universities seemed to spring up wherever
his feet had trodden, but New College was his home
until his death in 1982. He had done distinguished
archaeological work in Asia Minor as a young scholar, but
the monograph was not his forte – rather, the monologue
and wonderful rambling letters that ended with the Duke
of Wellington's apology 'too busy to be brief'. He was
subject to periods of depression that he christened 'the
fumes', but his effect on everyone he met, in and out of
the college, was like champagne.

When H.A.L. Fisher became warden he complained
that the college felt like 'a vast maus-o-leum'. One
rejuvenating influence he imported was Isaiah Berlin,

ROGUES AND ECCENTRICS

WILLIAM POOLE

Early accounts of eccentric or unruly behaviour in the college are few, because the kinds of material that survive from the first centuries of the college tend not to record such aberrations. But it was not all work, of course. There is a fourteenth-century image of New College fellows tilting on horseback, for instance, and the statutes are strict about not playing football in Hall, as well as banning the ownership of birds of prey, dogs and ferrets. Chess was also forbidden. Yet one practice that now strikes us as extremely eccentric was not only encouraged but stipulated: the ritual of the 'boy bishop', something we also find at Magdalen College and at King's College, Cambridge. Each year, on the Feast of the Holy Innocents, a young boy, usually a choirboy, was dressed in full episcopal regalia and officiated in chapel. This annual inversion of authority lasted probably until the Reformation.

The most celebrated rogue of the sixteenth century is probably Warden London, perpetrator of the imprisonment and subsequent death of a young fellow with questionable views on transubstantiation. London was, however, acting out of disciplinary and religious dogmatism and would not have appreciated or perhaps even recognized his later reputation. After the Reformation the 1566 visitation was the next point at which vice and odd behaviour was detected and recorded. During this visitation by the bishop of Winchester, for instance, Thomas Hopkins, a junior member of the college, admitted to possessing 'a book of conjurations' that had been given to him by John Fisher, another New

College member. (Fisher, in turn, had been given the book by an MA of Christ Church.) The Visitor warned Hopkins to desist from the art of magic. Warden White himself was heavily attacked in the visitation, variously being accused of keeping 'Rybaldes and Roysters' and even a woman among his personal staff and of seducing and

Left: *Entering the college in an unorthodox manner, under the eyes of the police and Warden Spooner, an incident of February 1906.*

Opposite: *The fraudster Richard Haydocke's presentation to the college; John Percival's 1630 allegory of the Guy Fawkes plot, with the eye of Fawkes (left) keeping watch on the gunpowder under Parliament.*

killing a maidservant in one rectory and keeping a mistress at another. (The warden thereupon counter-accused various senior fellows of the like offences.) A common vice in the period was venturing out of college after nightfall. These *obambulatores*, as the visitation heard, regained entry to college by opening the lock of the door to Hall by the kitchen with a knife. Other crimes detected included wearing a yellow doublet, keeping birds and seeking out opportunities to go dancing. A decade later the next visitation revealed that such vices were still standard in the college – playing cards, keeping dogs, night-walking, tavern-frequenting and brawling top the lists – but the sentences imposed on the night-walkers seem rather toothless: 15 days confined to working in the library at a set time but only for an hour-long stretch.

Equally entertaining were the naughty literati of the 1580s and 1590s, Thomas Bastard and John Hoskins. The unforgettably surnamed Bastard was a promising young *artista*, 'the most ingenious and facetious person of his time', but it all went wrong in 1591, when Bastard, 'being much guilty of the vices belonging to poets, and given to libelling', was forced out of his fellowship for

some cruel epigrams. Anthony Wood later owned a collection of Bastard's manuscript poems, 'wherein he reflects upon all persons of note in Oxon that were guilty of amorous exploits, or that mixed themselves with other men's wives, or with wanton huswives'. There is a splendid manuscript poem in the Bodleian by Bastard opening 'Jenken, why man? why Jenkin? fye for shame', and a little reading serves to show that it is a witty attack on the then warden, Warden Culpepper. Bastard reformed later in life, published various sermons, but died impoverished and 'crazed'. His great publication remains the *Chrestoleros* of 1598, a collection of epigrams on various topics. As he says, 'I speake of hidden and of open things.'

Unlike Bastard, John Hoskins would proceed to a prominent legal career, but as a young fellow he fared similarly. All was well for him, too, until the graduation ceremony of 1592. As was then the custom, a notably witty student was appointed *terræ filius* (son of the earth), whose role was to provide a comic speech to offset the serious disputations on the merit of which degrees were awarded. The *terræ filius* was by tradition allowed to sail rather close to the wind in his oration, and Hoskins gloriously capsized. He had been known since his schoolboy days as a very sharp poet, but here he apparently overdid it, being 'so bitterly satirical that he was expelled and put to his shifts', as John

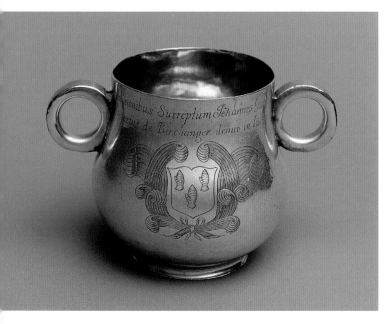

Above: *The Trapier Cup, hallmarked in 1741, but embellished and given to the college by Charlestonian William Trapier in 1845 for the purpose of drinking mint julep.*

Left: *The tun of 1675, the only piece of silver returned to the college after the 1679 raid on the buttery.*

Aubrey later recorded. Bastard and Hoskins share the twin glory, then, of having been thrown out of the college for being too funny. Alas, most of the surviving Bastard is tame by comparison to what once must have circulated, and Hoskins' suicidal speech seems to have been entirely lost.

The next notable eccentric was alas a fraudulent one, but the fraud was exposed by a king. Richard Haydocke, whose 'eccentricity' dates from just after he left the college to become a physician in Salisbury, apparently preached in his sleep. News spread of his ability, and he was summoned to court to exhibit his powers before James I, who visited Haydocke in his sleep. Eventually Haydocke had to admit that he was not, in fact, asleep. His recantation survives in the State Papers, and it is an excruciating read. Haydocke, it appears, had rehearsed sermons in bed in order to overcome a speech impediment. Overheard by the locals, Haydocke failed to explain himself in time, and let the rumour run away with itself. He remained on good terms with his college, however. The striking allegory of the Gunpowder Plot now hanging in the Chequer was not, as was once thought, painted but donated by Haydocke; it was in fact the work of John Percival.

Interregnum Oxford saw New College in some disarray. But despite the apparent suppression of music in the chapel, it appears that the choirboys persisted in some capacity, for one died while trying to climb a tree in the gardens in 1655. We know this because a young fellow of the Queen's College wrote a little poem 'On the Death of Cornish Coyrister of New. Coll: who fell in the Morning from a Mulberry Tree and broke his neck against a Stone underneath on Monday Aug 25. ([16]55)'. It is a quirky poem, in which the poet addresses first the unfortunate choirboy, then the tree and finally the stone: 'Evaporate thy selfe! In Attoms creep!' Music and misadventure were tragically combined a little later in the century, for in 1694 the college organist committed suicide in mysterious circumstances.

Restoration New College was not known for its sobriety. In Wood's famous phrase, the fellows were 'much

given to drinking and gaming, and vaine brutish pleasure. They degenerat in learning'. The lawn just to the right of the current Mound was a bowling green, and many unwritten classics were unwritten on it. The Visitor had attempted to tighten things up just after the Restoration, where among other things the vice of long hair was, as ever, condemned – it seems that the porter, though remiss in his duties, also doubled as the college barber. But the fellows were used to good living. In 1661, for instance, a young ordinand of the college, Savile Bradley, was presented at Christ Church Cathedral, but, 'having been used to eat breakfasts, and drink morning draughts, being not able to hold out with fasting, was troubled so much with wind in his stomach, that he fell into a sowne [swoon], and disturbed for a time the ceremony'. Bradley, it seems, was not used to foregoing his hearty New College breakfast. Roguery came from outside the college too: in 1675 thieves broke into the buttery and stole almost £200 worth of plate.

The seventeenth- and eighteenth-century fellows lived in relative ease, and torpor rather than roguery or vice set in. In the early eighteenth century the story was told of the notorious academician and fixer Arthur Charlett, master of University College, dining at New College. Such was the cheer that Charlett had to be

Above: *A group at a Chalet reading party, photographed by Christopher Cox, 1933.*

escorted back to his own college by a servant, tipsy Charlett bearing before him not a torch but a silver tankard. (Similar tales have been told in recent decades of another notorious head of house riding back to his own college from New College high table on one of the yardmen's carts.) The eighteenth century, however, did have its flashpoints of principle. Jacobite activity caused some unrest, and in May 1715, for instance, a group of New College Whigs clashed with a group of Tories, who had surrounded the tavern where the Whigs were celebrating the (Hanoverian) king's birthday. Later, drinking continued. Just before the college's 'Age of Reform', there were attempts to clamp down, and in 1788 the 'Warden and Thirteen' ordered that the 'beer butler' stock no more strong beer. ('But we fancy we have seen a "treble X" in New College Hall,' the college historians of 1901 mischievously commented on this ruling.) This was the period of the 'dull days', as the first full college history termed it, although at least the college generated its one famous wit at the time, Sydney Smith. Smith alas became famous for his *bon mots* long after he had left the college.

The muscular reformations of education in New College did not encourage errant behaviour, but some (slight) misrule was tolerated. In 1845 William Trapier of South Carolina visited the college and was shocked not to be able to obtain a mint julep in the SCR. He presented the college with the recipe, a tankard and (not) enough money for the college to drink that cocktail every 1 June, the anniversary of his visit. The custom continued into the 1990s, before it sank once again into another more honoured in the breach. It certainly did not obstruct misrule.

A genuine eccentric of the period of reform is often said to be Warden Spooner, on account of his peculiarities of speech and conduct. Did Spooner suffer from what is now called dysgraphia? Although 'Spoonerism' has now become a recognized class of verbal joke, many of the examples attributed to Spooner himself sound like clever student parodies of sermon-piety gone wrong ('the Lord is a shoving leopard' etc.). As Warden Ryan wrote on his predecessor: 'There is better evidence for the perpetration of physical Spoonerisms: on one occasion he spilt salt on the table-cloth and poured claret on top of it, and on another he remarked on the darkness of a staircase before turning off all the lights and attempting to lead a party down the stairs in the dark.'

In more recent times, separating eccentricity or even roguery from what passes for normal academic and collegiate (mis)behaviour requires an Olympian perspective distorted by lack of distance. The enclosed, uncompetitive environment that had for long nurtured gentle excesses of manners and living slipped into memory as the college became more open after 1918 and especially after 1945. The social boredom, claustrophobic frustration, undiagnosed psychosis or prolonged infantilism that lay behind much collegiate eccentricity wilted under the bracing heat of wider access, larger numbers of senior and junior members, co-education, professionalized scholarship and the demands of families. With the coming of a drabber, if possibly more adult utilitarianism, the scope for the quiet maturation of aberrant or abhorrent behaviour decreased, although never entirely disappeared. Some, at least in their mind's eye, regret this.

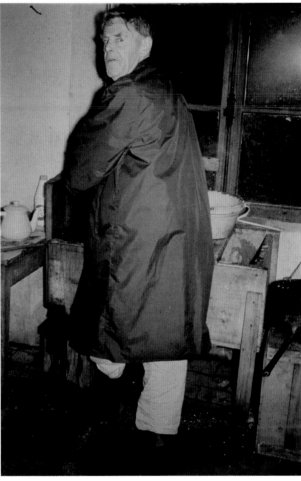

Right: *Christopher Cox, in characteristic attire at the Chalet, photographed c.1966.*

One of the last representatives of a more confident yet cloistered past was, oddly, one of the most cosmopolitan of New College figures in the mid-twentieth century, Christopher Cox, ancient history tutor, architect of university systems across the Empire and Commonwealth and life resident in OB 3. Accurately described as possessed of 'madness and magnetism', brilliant, brittle, child-like, occasionally childish, his pathological untidiness, surreal hilarity, Brobdingnagian travel arrangements, illegible handwriting (a match for Mrs Fisher's), elaborately discreet indiscretions, exhaustingly torrential conversation, taste for exotic coloured shirts (but not in college) and genuine interest in young people left indelible impressions in his wake on all who encountered him.

Cox's special field of operations lay in the on-going collective oddity that is the New College Chalet with its aficionados, the 'chaletites'. There, well into the 1970s, he presided over generations of undergraduate reading parties redolent of the 1920s, complete with bizarre traditions, like the porridge he daily brewed wearing his signature plastic mac, his style reflecting the whimsical, apparently chaotic but bulging mind of a genuine eccentric. The *Chalet des Anglais* is marked on the official French map,

opposite the Mont Blanc massif in the French Alps. It was built by an eccentric diplomat in the 1860s, passed on to his eccentric son, the socializing Balliol don F.F. 'Sligger' Urquhart, burned down by Oxford students in 1906 and reopened in 1909, and is now shared, in its all-wood, no-electricity glory, by the three colleges of Balliol, University and New College. (The Maquis took it over in the war.) It is now open to any college member who wishes to attend. Every summer two reading parties of a dozen or so students ascend the Alps to experience, as Urquhart put it, *la grande paix de la montaigne*. It is not all peace. The current writer arrived at the top of the mountain a few years ago to find a group of students at the summit of the hill wearing war-paint and each other's clothes, presided over by a vicar, enjoying champagne and canapés, and the bewildered attention of the locals, who have now spent over a century getting used to the Frankly Odd of New College, on the top of an Alp. The Progressive Dinner, for that is what I had stumbled into, eventually made its way down the mountain and back to the chalet, where a variety show followed a just dessert.

PUBLIC FIGURES – CHURCH

DAVID PARROTT

New College's statutes bear witness to the Founder's primary intention of preparing scholars for the ministry of the Church. In the aftermath of the Black Death and the population decline of the fourteenth century, Wykeham was concerned by the falling numbers of clerical vocations, and while the statutes also stressed the utility of learned men to the king and the government of the country, the main purpose of the foundation was to meet these spiritual needs. Despite the vicissitudes of the college's history down to 1850, it would be fair to conclude that the Founder's primary purpose was maintained. By the early seventeenth century the college held rights of appointment to 26 livings across the country, and throughout the sixteenth, seventeenth and eighteenth centuries these were the career destination for a large proportion of fellows. In addition, many scholars combined the holding of a New College fellowship with curacies or schoolmasterships before moving on to assume college or other benefices. For many of the fellows, membership of the college brought them into contact with patronage networks that could facilitate both initial ecclesiastical appointments and promotion.

While large numbers of fellows over the centuries followed the path of James Woodforde, who was presented to the New College living of Weston Longeville in 1774 and remained rector there until his death, others climbed further within the Church hierarchy. This brief overview begins with a number of fellows whose careers flourished during what in retrospect can be seen as a pre-Reformation Indian summer for churchmen who achieved high office in both Church and state. The combination of secular and spiritual office became rare after the sixteenth-century Reformations, and distinguished New College churchmen were thereafter more likely to combine authority in the Church with scholarly or literary achievements.

John Russell, who was probably born in Winchester around 1430, progressed from scholar at Winchester to New College in 1447. Russell took successive legal qualifications at New College up to a doctorate in canon law and was ordained only in 1460, after which

Below: The celadon bowl given to the college by William Warham, Archbishop of Canterbury. Silver-gilt mounted in the early sixteenth century, it vies for the distinction of being the first piece of Chinese celadon in the west.

Right: *William Warham, Archbishop of Canterbury, 1503–32.*

he received a canonry at Salisbury. He was promoted to bishop of Rochester in 1476 and then translated to the grander diocese of Lincoln in 1480. As counterpoint to this ecclesiastical preferment, Russell's career took off as a diplomat, when he was part of the delegation that negotiated the marriage of Margaret of York to Charles, Duke of Burgundy, and in central government, when he was named keeper of the Privy Seal in 1474. The peak of his career was reached in 1483 when Richard III appointed him Lord Chancellor to replace the archbishop of York, Thomas Rotherham. He lost the chancellorship after Henry VII came to the throne, but he continued to enjoy the respect and confidence of the new king, who made use of his diplomatic skills in Scotland and Brittany. The decline in his role in central government was compensated by administration of the diocese of Lincoln and considerably more time spent with the affairs of Oxford University, where he had been appointed chancellor in 1483. Though a lawyer by training, Russell had the reputation of being a wide-ranging scholar, with a humanist's interest in classical texts, many of which he bequeathed to New College on his death in 1494.

Russell's near-contemporary Richard Mayhew combined many similar traits of an ecclesiastical, diplomatic and university career. At New College from 1457, he took his degrees in theology rather than law, gaining his doctorate in 1478. Holding a series of prebends, he was also appointed a royal chaplain under Richard III and Henry VII. In 1490 he was sent as an envoy to Spain and was subsequently appointed to the king's council. In 1504 his career in the Church culminated in his appointment as bishop of Hereford. Mayhew's particular significance for New College lies in the decision of William Waynflete, bishop of Winchester and Lord Chancellor, to appoint him in 1480 as the first president of Waynflete's new Oxford foundation of Magdalen College. Having used the statutes of New College as his model for Magdalen, Waynflete's appointment of a New College fellow as its first head

reinforced the close links between the foundations, their organization and character. Mayhew also became chancellor of the university in 1503, but the burden of his university and ecclesiastical duties seems to have led to neglect of the situation in Magdalen, where disciplinary problems festered, and he was ultimately forced to resign in 1507. On his death in 1516 he divided his books between bequests to Magdalen and New College.

The third of these New College alumni who brought together great offices of Church and state was William Warham, born to a modest family in Hampshire, who held a scholarship at Winchester and was made a fellow of New College in 1475. Like Russell, he specialized in canon law, taking his doctorate in 1488 when he left the college to begin a legal career in London. He, too, was called on to undertake a variety of diplomatic missions for Henry VII in the 1490s and acquired a series of Church livings before being preferred to the bishopric of London in 1501. In the same year Henry made him keeper of the great seal and in 1504 was to promote him to Lord Chancellor. Parallel with this meteoric career in government, in late 1503 he was translated from London to the archbishopric of Canterbury, where he remained until his death in 1532.

Though an able administrator and a generous patron of humanist scholars, Warham's lengthy tenure as archbishop was coloured by a complex and ambiguous relationship with Thomas Wolsey and then overshadowed by Henry VIII's 'Great Matter', the divorce and the repudiation of papal authority over the English Church. As early as 1515 Warham resigned the chancellorship, immediately assumed by Wolsey. Warham may well have wished to relieve himself of an over-heavy burden of spiritual and secular office, and shedding the chancellorship after a decade in his possession allowed him to devote his attention to the Church and its needs. But the transfer was the beginning of a process by which Wolsey, progressively archbishop of York, cardinal and legate *a latere*, encroached steadily on Warham's authority and undermined his relationship with the king and much of the court. By the time of Wolsey's disgrace and death in 1529 Warham had not only seen his own authority in the Church weakened but had been heavily implicated in Wolsey's unsuccessful schemes to get the king's divorce tried in England rather than Rome. When Henry, with the help of his new servant Thomas Cromwell, adopted increasingly aggressive tactics against the Church and papal authority as a means to intimidate the pope into granting the divorce, Warham was ill placed to lead the Church in active resistance to the king's claims. He himself seems to have suffered from a personal conflict between his duty of obedience to the crown and his allegiance to the universal Church. Bolstered by the firm stance of John Fisher, bishop of Rochester, Warham rejected Henry's claim to be recognized outright as head of the English Church in 1531, yet in May 1532 he led

Left: *Thomas Bilson, successively bishop of Worcester and Winchester, who, with Miles Smith, oversaw the printing of the King James bible, painted 1611.*

Convocation in conceding the submission of the clergy to Henry's authority. Warham died in August 1532, and we can only speculate about how he would have responded to the king's subsequent demands, but the submission had critically weakened the ability of Convocation to resist Henry's formal break from Rome and his establishment as Supreme Head of the Church.

Warham was personally austere, though he had a strong sense of the dignity of his office and spent vast sums on his palace at Otford and on repairs and work on Canterbury Cathedral. He was an exceptionally generous patron of New College students: no fewer than 18 of the 53 officials in his archiepiscopal administration were from New College. His substantial collection of books on civil and canon law were left to New College on his death, a legacy of a man who enjoyed the benefits of the highest offices, but by repute died with almost no personal fortune.

New College's most notable theologians and churchmen in the mid-sixteenth century were conservative

supporters of the Marian reaction, figures typified by
John White, created bishop of Lincoln in 1554 and who
then succeeded Gardiner as bishop of Winchester in
1556. The expulsion of conservative fellows during the
first two decades of Elizabeth's reign eliminated a pool of
potential senior churchmen, and only gradually were they
replaced with men who played a role in the Elizabethan
and early Stuart Church. Of this group Thomas Bilson
was probably the most significant Church careerist. Bilson
held a scholarship at Winchester, then proceeded to New
College, where he was sustained by a trust established

*Below: Thomas Ken,
bishop of Bath and
Wells, deprived 1691.*

by Robert Nowell for the support of poor scholars.
He became a fellow in 1563, then returned to teach at
Winchester College, where he was appointed headmaster
in 1572. Bilson was to progress from the headmastership,
via a cathedral prebend, to the wardenship of the school.
His polemical writings in support of the Anglican
settlement and Protestant rights to resistance (on the
Continent) won him political support, and he accepted the
bishopric of Worcester in 1596 only to be translated to the
bishopric of Winchester one year later, which he held until
his death in 1616. Too much a controversialist, he was
passed over twice, in 1604 and 1611, for the archbishopric
of Canterbury.

With the Restoration and after, a more notable
series of New College churchmen can be identified.
Thomas Manningham, a fellow from 1671 to 1681,
seems initially to have sought comfortable obscurity
as holder of the living of East Tisted in Hampshire.
However, Manningham was not merely a serious scholar
but an impressive preacher, whose talents came to the
attention of Charles II and his court in the early 1680s.
A series of preacherships, prestigious chaplaincies and
the rectorship of St Andrew's, Holborn, fell to him, and
after acting as a chaplain to both William and Mary, then
Queen Anne, was appointed dean of Windsor in 1709,
shortly followed by the bishopric of Chichester, which
he held until his death in 1722. Though a creature of
courtly favour, Manningham was no sycophant. When,
during one of Queen Anne's illnesses, it was suggested
that Manningham, as her chaplain, should perform
his offices in an adjoining room, he refused, allegedly
saying that 'he did not chuse to whistle the prayers of the
church through a key hole'.

Near contemporary with Manningham was
Thomas Ken, who entered New College in 1657. In
1663 he was made rector of Little Easton in Essex but
returned to Winchester in 1665 where he was elected
fellow of Winchester College in 1666 and resigned his
New College fellowship, though making a donation of

over £100 to the new building works being undertaken by the college. Like Manningham he was an impressive preacher and followed a similar path, being appointed in 1679 as chaplain to Charles II's niece, the future Queen Mary. Prepared to stand up both to William of Orange in defence of Mary and to Charles II, whose request that Ken should accommodate Nell Gwynn in his Winchester house on a royal visit to the city was stubbornly refused, Ken's reputation as a man of principle became widely appreciated. In 1684 Charles II insisted that he be appointed to the vacant see of Bath and Wells.

Ken initially enjoyed the confidence and respect of James II, but he grew increasingly uneasy and hostile in response to James's initiatives towards toleration and Catholic ascendancy, preaching extensively against Catholicism and the king's policies. In 1688 Ken was one of the seven bishops who petitioned James, refusing to accept the king's dispensing authority explicit in the second Declaration of Indulgence. Sent to the Tower, they were tried before the King's Bench and acquitted. It might be assumed that Ken would be an obvious supporter of the Williamite revolution, but as an Anglican Tory he balked at the deposition of James II and argued for a regency rather than the declaration that William and Mary were king and queen, and he refused the subsequent oath of allegiance. In April 1691 he was deprived of Bath and Wells, and having set aside little money during his episcopate, was reduced to modest and dependent circumstances for the rest of his life. Though he shunned the uncompromising and hardline non-jurors and tried to work for a peaceful settlement between the factions within the church, he was nonetheless unable to bend his own conscience in a way that would allow him to resume his episcopal functions. In the short time he had been bishop of Bath and Wells he had proved an exceptionally devoted, conscientious and generous incumbent. His best writings offered sincere and straightforward doctrinal guidance for the laity, whether in the form of expositions of the catechism or his still well-known Anglican hymns.

Ambitious New College fellows continued through the eighteenth century to combine academic and administrative skills with a shrewd grasp of patronage opportunities. Robert Lowth, a distinguished scholar of Hebrew and elected Professor of Poetry at Oxford in 1741, had been a fellow of New College from 1730 to 1744. After extensive manoeuvrings around patronage

Below: *Parson James Woodforde, fellow 1759–76, by Samuel Woodforde, 1780s.*

Right: *Sydney Smith, the 'Smith of Smiths', and probably the model for Henry Tilney in Jane Austen's* Northanger Abbey, *in caricature by Edwin Landseer, c.1821.*

Woodforde, typical of New College fellows of the period, accepted the curacy of Thurloxton near Taunton, followed by further curacies at Babcary and Castle Cary. For the next decade he lived mainly as a Somerset cleric, visiting Oxford about once a year to vote in elections or to go through the formal exercises required for his MA, which he took in 1767. Woodforde was resident in New College for only five of the 15 years that he was a full fellow. His career was probably typical of many unambitious, worldly fellows, exceptional only in the detailed diary that he kept from his 18th year through to his death on New Year's Day 1803. The diary, though frequently laconic, almost completely lacking in introspection and betraying no indication of spirituality beyond the occasional perfunctory scriptural invocation, nonetheless provides an extraordinary, detailed account initially of a fellow of New College, then of day-to-day life in a rural parish at the end of the eighteenth century.

One area where Woodforde's diary never stints on detail are his accounts of eating and drinking. Christmas dinner for the senior fellows at New College in 1773 was lovingly described as 'two fine cods boiled with fried soles round them and oyster sauce, a fine sirloin of beef roasted, some pea soup and an orange pudding for the first course, for the second, we had wild ducks roasted, a fore quarter of lamb and salad and mince pies'. A decade later Woodforde is describing the food at a dinner served by the bishop of Norwich, including 'two dishes of prodigious fine stewed carp and tench, and a fine haunch of venison. Among the second course a fine turkey, poult, partridges, pigeons and sweetmeats'. Although 'the bishop behaved with great affability towards me as I remembered him at Christ Church in Oxford', a month later this affability resulted in a 'disagreeable letter', requesting Woodforde to preach at the cathedral the following February. Woodforde's response to this unwanted imposition was to travel to Norwich in order to see the bishop and to ask him to withdraw the request, which the latter refused, reminding Woodforde that it was a compliment to be

and possible preferments, Louth was successively appointed to the see of St David's in 1766, translated to Oxford and was finally nominated bishop of London in 1777. He declined the offer of the archbishopric of Canterbury in 1783, thereby depriving New College of a fourth holder of the primacy after Henry Chichele (1414–43), William Warham (1503–32) and William Howley (1828–48).

In contrast with Lowth was that best-known representative of a very different clerical tradition, Parson James Woodforde, whose career was in some respects more in keeping with the Founder's original intentions to fill benefices for the cure of souls. Woodforde entered New College in 1759 and remained a fellow until 1776, when he secured the coveted college living of Weston Longeville in Norfolk. Having taken his BA in 1763, asked and that the cathedral pulpit should be 'filled properly with able and beneficed clergy'.

In one of his few active years as college fellow he served as pro-proctor and seems to have enjoyed some of the challenges of exercising authority: 'While I was at Supper I was sent for to quell a riot in Holliwell.' Though a senior fellow, and in 1773 sub-warden, Woodforde had no responsibilities for teaching New College probationary fellows or those in pursuit of higher degrees. Indeed, his main responsibility as sub-warden, he reminds us in his diary, was to order dinner every day for the senior fellows.

Comparable to Woodforde in his liking for the conviviality of food, wine and company was Sydney Smith. Smith entered New College in 1789 and gained his full fellowship after two years. Indicative of the declining financial status of college fellowships, Smith then received an annual stipend of £100, at which point his father removed any additional financial support. His hundred pounds fell far short of an income sufficient to entertain or live with any comfort, and he passed a solitary and lonely few years in college, unprepared to accept hospitality that he would be unable to reciprocate.

Smith followed the familiar path of holding his fellowship conjointly with a curacy at Nethervon on Salisbury Plain. Acting as reluctant private tutor for the son of the local gentry family, he found himself in Edinburgh, where he formed a close circle of intellectual friends who collectively went on to found the *Edinburgh Review* in 1802. Returning to London, Smith became part of the social and political life around Holland House and attracted the patronage of Henry, 3rd Baron Holland, who used his influence to get Smith appointed to the living of Foston-le-Clay, near York. Appointed to a prebend in Bristol Cathedral in 1828, Smith managed to exchange Foston for the Somerset rectory of Combe Florey a year later. He was ambitious for further promotion in the Church, deploying both his eloquence and his numerous, well-disposed patrons to try unsuccessfully to obtain a bishopric. However, his now well-known reputation as

a wit and raconteur and his apparent lack of theological seriousness, stood against him. Lord Grey, a strong supporter of Smith and prime minister from 1830, finally obtained a canonry at St Paul's for him in 1831, which

Below: *Hastings Rashdall, by Oswald Birley, 1923.*

brought his overall income up to the remarkable sum of £2,900 a year.

Despite his social success and his sometimes impatient and irascible ambition, Sydney Smith had been a good rector at Foston, concerned with the welfare and the education of his parishioners. His social conscience emerged strongly through his writings, and he frequently deployed satire or mild ridicule to make his case. In defending the principle of women's education against assumptions of male superiority, he disingenuously suggested that: 'A century ago, who would have believed that country gentlemen could be brought to read and spell with the ease and accuracy which we now so frequently remark?' The canonry of St Paul's seems not to have interfered with a life that was largely devoted to the sponsorship of political and social causes and to a warm and extensive sociability with a rich variety of friends and acquaintances, elegantly refuting his own mischievous suggestion that 'it is a pity that we have no amusements in England but vice and religion'.

Sydney Smith's clerical style could not be more different from the seriousness and high moral purpose that becomes characteristic of New College churchmen from the later nineteenth century. Few better exemplify this trend than Hastings Rashdall, who went from Harrow to a scholarship at New College in 1877. He was appointed lecturer in Lampeter and then at Durham University and was finally ordained priest in 1886. Two years later he was elected to a fellowship at Hertford College and appointed chaplain of Balliol. In 1895 he returned to New College as fellow and tutor in philosophy, where he remained until 1917, when he was appointed dean of Carlisle Cathedral. Rashdall combined the qualities of an engaged and loquacious, if extremely absent-minded, tutor with extensive writing on the relationship between theology and philosophy. His serious scholarship in both disciplines was underpinned by an intense belief that theology should have relevance to immediate, contemporary issues, and he was directly involved in the founding of the Christian

Social Union in 1890. He accepted the deanery of Carlisle as a means to advance his practical vision of an engaged and inclusive Christianity and worked closely there to integrate Anglicans and Nonconformists within his ideal of liberal churchmanship.

Although his sense of duty led him to accept Carlisle, his attachment to New College was profound. His lengthy period as a college tutor was remembered with affection by many of his students and in a memorial placed in the cloisters by the warden and fellows. His substantial contribution to what emerged as the history of New College co-authored with R. Rait in 1901 reveals clearly Rashdall's enthusiasm for the early history of the college and is enlivened throughout both by his strong identification with numerous eccentric and heroic figures from the college's history, no less than an obvious distaste for those periods in which the institution seems to have achieved – to cite Rashdall's page headers – little more than 'disorders, drunkenness, decline in literary output, growth of idleness …'.

After the First World War, with the decline to near extinction of the ordained don as opposed to the professional chaplain, New College's tone tended towards the more resolutely secular. Support for the chapel and the continuance and flourishing of the choral tradition sat apart from engagement with the Church as a vocation or career. The college went on producing clergymen but in smaller numbers than in the late nineteenth century. Theology became a rare bird. There were redoubtable chaplains; some rose in the ecclesiastical hierarchy; many carved their own niches in college folklore and memory. Old members still became bishops, such as Cuthbert Bardsley (1907–91), the charismatic bishop of Coventry who presided over the opening of the modernist new cathedral there in 1962 in a blaze of publicity. Increasingly new forms of proselytizing now compete with the old religious ones. For example, the campaigner for atheism and Darwinianism, Richard Dawkins, has been a fellow of New College since 1970.

PUBLIC FIGURES – STATE

CHRISTOPHER TYERMAN

Warden Hayter once wrote that New College 'produced no distinguished men between the Middle Ages and the nineteenth century'. That is a bit hard on the likes of the non-juror Bishop Thomas Ken (1637–1711), whose hymns 'Awake my soul and with the sun' and 'Glory to thee, my God, this night' are still sung, or James Brydges, 1st duke of Chandos (1674–1744), patron of Handel, paymaster of Marlborough's armies (a task that netted him a personal fortune of £600,000) and benefactor – to the tune of £100 – of the Garden Quad and screen. It also ignores the fact that while the college's famed early-modern torpor may have been exaggerated, few New College men in any age after the Reformation scaled the topmost heights of public life. There have been no New College Prime Ministers. The careers of those educated at New College present a long, not ignoble but scarcely glamorous procession of clergymen, prelates, academics, writers, lawyers, businessmen, civil servants and administrators, accompanied by the usual crowd of the propertied, the obscure, the improvident, the extravagant, the ordinary, the eccentric and the dull. The restrictive entry criteria, essentially unchanged until the 1850s, rendered future distinction a pure chance, the college's contribution to it, if any, probably tenuous. Chandos spent only a couple of years at New College, possibly refining his ingratiating social skill. While he reportedly acquired his taste for books and music at Oxford, there may have been little distinctive about his college experience that he could not have

obtained at a similarly comfortable establishment. Indeed, any account of the achievements of alumni in any period must carry a general warning. Educational institutions may be significant to their members more for the period of life spent in them rather than for any intrinsic or especial corporate merit.

This may have been less the case with the succession of medieval mandarins produced by the college. The security of progression that Wykeham's statutes instituted from school to university and, once there, to a solid grounding in the liberal arts and then theology or law, civil or canon, may have bred a worldly confidence in the ambitious and able few. The model of the Founder, whose cult so pervaded his colleges, may also have served to inspire men from similarly ungrand backgrounds. If distinction is measured by office then New College produced a significant number of distinguished public servants of the state before the Reformation, most of whom, as a direct corollary or reward, advanced to the pinnacles of Church preferment as well. Aiding promotion were the early established networks of mutual Wykehamist patronage, probably originally created by the Founder himself. Henry Chichele DCL (*c*.1362–1443) became a career ecclesiastical advocate and diplomat on leaving New College in the 1390s, rising to be archbishop of Canterbury (1414–43). One of his protégés was another former fellow, Thomas Beckington DCL (*c*.1390–1465), who rose to become secretary to Henry VI and keeper of the Privy Seal. He, in turn, employed and supported a number of fellow Wykehamists, including the future Warden Thomas Chaundler and the early English humanist Andrew Holes. The expertise gained from university legal training clearly made the college's graduates attractive to government. John Russell (1430–94) and William Warham (*c*.1450–1532) were both keepers of the Privy Seal, both rising to become Lord Chancellor, to Richard III and Henrys VII and VIII, respectively.

Increasingly, New College men followed secular paths of public life or service, refusing or abandoning holy orders. One outlet were the Inns of Court, although few reached the heights of John Kingsmill (*c*.1460–1509), who capped a successful career as a smart London barrister, Wiltshire MP and Hampshire JP with elevation to the bench as a Justice of Common Pleas (1504–9). His aspirational trajectory was entirely secular, far from the Founder's intentions. The common law was to claim many subsequent alumni. The college tradition of lay civil servants was also pioneered in the fifteenth century. Ralph Greenhurst DCL, at New College 1389–1401, abandoned his clerical status and the university by entering royal service as a diplomat and getting married. By 1411 he was working in Chancery, breaking that office's rule against employing married men. A younger contemporary, Richard Sturgeon, who had left in 1405, also married and worked for more than 30 years as a clerk of the crown in Chancery.

The post-medieval dearth of distinguished New College men between the sixteenth and nineteenth centuries can, in part, be laid at the door of the unchanging social complexion of the college set against the changing nature and structure of the university. Although most New College men still came from modest backgrounds, a public school and university education increasingly became marks of gentility, not scholarship or piety. Physically, this is represented in the extension of social and domestic facilities in the college, notably the construction of the Garden Quad ranges. High minds and simple habits faded. The college was comfortably wealthy. The summit of most ambitions was to maintain social standing through a college living. In stark contrast to every other Oxford college except All Souls, New College, corseted in the Founder's statutes, did not expand or change its ways. Unlike other colleges, except for a few gentleman commoners who, from the 1670s, were allowed to reside in the college, it did not admit commoners and so avoided the need to provide additional teaching or accommodation. The tie with Winchester prevented competition, diversity or even much active control over membership. Because of long waiting lists, some fellows in the seventeenth and eighteenth centuries sold their fellowships. Significantly, in contrast with the medieval college, numbers of Founder's Kin rose in the following centuries: in 1651 the quota was put at 20; two hundred years later the number was 21 plus the warden.

After the Reformation other colleges supplanted New College as centres of learning, religious commitment or scientific debate, even though the first Bodley's librarian (1599), Thomas James, was a fellow. While far from wholly intellectually inert, the fellowship's main interests appeared social, parochial, antiquarian, perhaps increasingly so as the eighteenth century progressed. Public preferment revolved almost exclusively around the Church and the university.

With Reform in the 1850s and 1870s New College was transformed in size, structure and membership. The reduction in corporate distinctiveness was matched by an access of talent, not least among the fellowship, now in part opened to free competition. Initially, public careers hardly diverged from the traditional spheres of ecclesiastical and academic life. The law continued to be a field of achievement for alumni. However, the two twentieth-century New College Lord Chancellors, who occupied the Woolsack in succession between 1945 and 1954, could hardly have displayed more contrasting careers. William Jowitt (1885–1957) stood in the long line of political lawyers. A Liberal then Labour MP, he served as Attorney General (1929–31) and Solicitor General (1940–42) before occupying various non-legal ministerial posts chiefly concerned with postwar reconstruction In 1945 Clement Attlee, who had been at prep school with Jowitt, made him Lord Chancellor, an arduous political role in a House of Lords that was overwhelmingly hostile to the Labour government and its legislation. One lasting achievement was the piloting of the introduction of legal aid for poor litigants. Out of office, for some years he acted as Labour leader in the Lords. By extreme contrast, Gavin Simonds (1881–1971) was primarily a lawyer, a

Above: *William Jowitt, by H.R. Freeth, 1957.*

Left: *Gavin Simonds, photographed in 1902.*

Chancery KC and, from 1937, a judge and a Law Lord from 1944. His appointment to the Woolsack in 1951 came as a complete surprise – he had never even met Churchill, who had quite possibly never heard of him. Simonds proved one of the most able lawyers and least adept politicians to sit on the Woolsack. His reputation rests on his judicial standing, described as 'one of the greatest judges of the modern age', the most prominent exponent of 'judicial conservatism' or 'legal formalism' that insists that the judiciary's role is merely to expound literally existing law, in statute or precedent, and not to challenge, over-interpret, change or initiate.

Such contrasting legal experiences hardly broke with tradition. However, the late nineteenth century

Right: *Alfred Milner, 'awaiting his worst fears about the South African constitution', in a caricature by Max Beerbohm, 1913.*

and beyond offered genuinely fresh opportunities for respectable public service with the expansion of the British Empire, the elevation in status of government service in the wake of competitive reforms, the decline in aristocratic dominance of political life and the rise of middle-class politics and politicians. One example of the different post-reform world is found in Alfred Milner (1854–1925). A brilliant Balliol classicist and former President of the Union, Milner was elected to an open fellowship at New College in 1876, retaining a link with, and affection for, the college for the rest of his life, a useful source of patronage both for the college and its members. The archetype of the dictatorial colonial pro-consul, helping first to run Egypt after 1889 and then, controversially, South Africa as High Commissioner (1897–1905), Milner was an outstanding administrator, deploying his skills most effectively as a member of Lloyd George's coalition from 1916 to 1921, as minister without portfolio, Secretary of State for War and finally Secretary of State for the Colonies (1918–21). (Alongside him in government was H.A.L. Fisher, President of the Board of Education and later warden, a rare coincidence of New College fellows. Fisher always boasted that he had taught all the New College members of Milner's circle of young advisers.)

Between periods of public service, Milner was an accomplished businessman. As a founding trustee of the Rhodes Trust, he was instrumental in establishing the arrangements for Rhodes Scholars to come to Oxford. Preferring to work behind the scenes with small groups of like-minded acolytes, in South Africa Milner surrounded himself with a group of young, enthusiastic imperialists, known, initially as a slur on Milner's early education in Germany, as his 'kindergarten'. In a show of parochial patronage or favouritism redolent of an earlier age, among its earliest recruits were a close-knit group from New College, John Dove, Richard Feetham, Lionel Hitchens and, most prominent, Lionel Curtis (1872–1955). Curtis played a pivotal role in drafting South Africa's constitution (1910). He remained an indefatigable promoter of the

ideal of a united federal British Empire, a cause he
pursued through organizations such as the Round Table,
set up with Milner in 1909, and the Royal Institute for
International Affairs, known as Chatham House, founded
by Curtis and others in 1919, as well as, after 1921, from a
fellowship at All Souls.

The administration of the state interests, whether
imperial, colonial, international or domestic, became the
preserve of the products of reformed Oxbridge from the
last quarter of the nineteenth century, a near-monopoly
of possibly increasing controversy and one in striking
contrast to the backgrounds of these public servants'
political masters. In the twentieth century of the 20 Prime
Ministers between and including those Oxford men Lord
Salisbury and Mr Blair, eight were not Oxbridge graduates
and six had not been to university at all. The same
eclecticism could not be found in their contemporaries
as heads of the home or foreign civil service. Given New
College's post-reform academic status, wealth, social
connections and public prestige, it is unsurprising that
it produced perhaps more than its share of effective,
powerful and distinguished civil servants and diplomats.

On the home front few mandarins have been so
disliked yet so effective as Robert Morant (1863–1920),
who left New College having redeemed a third in Mods
with a first in theology, not the usual public servant
pedigree. After using a private position at the court of
Siam to reconstruct the local educational system when
he was in his 20s, Morant infiltrated himself into the
heart of British educational policy-making during the
1890s. A key influence on Balfour's 1902 Education
Act that set up local education authorities and widened
access to state secondary education, Morant leapfrogged
more established – and Establishment – figures to
become permanent secretary at the Board of Education
(1902–11), attracting accusations of being a grasping
and unscrupulous *arriviste*. Among his achievements
was the creation in 1911 of the forerunner of the
University Grants Committee (established by H.A.L.

Fisher in 1920). Switching to the chairmanship of the
new National Insurance Commission, he implemented
employment and health insurance and established what
later became the Medical Research Council. His final
post was as the first permanent secretary of the new
Ministry of Health (1919–20).

Morant's career possessed an unusual trajectory,
partly because his aggressively self-confident ambition
was in no way matched by the silken charm and social
skills of many successful mandarins, and partly because he
coincided with a period of sustained state-led social and
educational reform that demanded and attracted a fluid

response to bureaucratic hierarchy. In this, and in little else, Morant bears comparison with another New College example of the classic type of public servant, John Maud (later Lord Redcliffe-Maud, 1906–82), whose rise to a position of public eminence relied, as it did for so many of his generation, on the peculiar circumstances of the Second World War. The national emergency produced state control and planning on an unprecedented scale that, through a delicate combination of conscription, opportunism and merit, recruited talent from far beyond the existing civil service. After converting the standard Mods and Greats training at New College, via economics at Harvard, into an innovative academic career as one of the first full-time politics dons in Oxford (at University College), specializing in local government, Maud was plucked from the mastership of Birkbeck (1939–43) into wartime administration. So adept and successful was he that in 1945 he became peacetime permanent secretary at the Ministry of Education (1945–52), where he was one of the founding spirits behind UNESCO, and Fuel and Power (1952–9). Regarded as a safe pair of hands, Maud was then despatched to South Africa, as High Commissioner then ambassador to South Africa (1959–

Opposite: *Satirical verse on the 'Song of Songs', by Rudyard Kipling to Milner, 1907.*

Right: *H.A.L. Fisher, warden 1925–40, by William Nicholson, c.1932.*

63), before returning to University College as Master (1963–76). Here he remained available for public service, most notably chairing the royal commission on local government (1966–9) whose radical recommendations, as is usually the case with such commissions and their initiatives, fell foul of the government, in this case Conservative (1970–74), that produced its own scheme, implemented in 1974, which Maud regarded as ugly.

The management of the vestiges of empire and the challenges left behind in the wake of its collapse similarly attracted New College men. The influence of Milner was evident in the career of Edward Grigg, 1st Baron Altrincham (1879–1955). After involvement in both the Round Table and the Rhodes Trust and sporadically an MP, Grigg was governor of Kenya (1925–30). A generation later Evelyn Baring, later Lord Howick of Glendale (1903–73), could be described by his biographer without irony as 'the last proconsul'. Born into the imperialist purple, the third son of Lord Cromer who had entrenched British power in Egypt so effectively between 1883 and 1906, Baring spent much of his career upholding British interests in Africa as governor of Southern Rhodesia (1942), High Commissioner to South Africa (1944–51), when the Malan's Nationalists won power, and governor of Kenya (1952–9) during the Mau Mau crisis. As a sign of the times he subsequently chaired the Commonwealth Development Corporation.

In a different register, Christopher Cox (1899–1982), a fellow in ancient history from 1926, spent over 30 years before his retirement in 1970 shaping higher education across the empire and its successor states. The diplomacy of Europe and the Cold War provided no less scope for New College diplomats. William Hayter (1906–95) was ambassador to Moscow (1953–7) at the time of Suez and the Russian invasion of Hungary. His immediate successor in Moscow (1957–60), Patrick Reilly (1909–99), had to cope with the volatile Mr Khrushchev and, later, as ambassador to Paris (1965–8), the hardly less prickly General de Gaulle and his hostility to British membership

Left: *A.P. Herbert, by Cosmo Clark, c.1966.*

of the Common Market. Both Hayter and Reilly belonged, like Baring and Maud, to a generation that received early professional promotion in part because of the gaps left by their elders killed in the First World War.

Modern New College, except for one remarkable generation, never established a steady relationship with political power of the sort enjoyed by Christ Church or even Balliol. There has been a steady trickle of eminent and/or notorious cabinet ministers, as well as a few accidental politicians, such as A.P. Herbert (1890–1971), humorist, legal absurdist and independent MP *par excellence* (for Oxford University, 1935–50), or, in a different sense, H.A.L. Fisher, called from the vice-chancellorship of Sheffield to be Lloyd George's President of the Board of Education (1916–22) and an MP until 1926. Although New College could be said to have embodied a liberal tradition, at least with a small 'l', some of the most powerful figures were or became Conservatives. Apart from Milner, two stand out as pre-Second World War cabinet ministers of very different stamp. Sam Hoare (1880–1959) epitomized the career politician, ambitious, competitive, industrious. Prim and precise, keen on honours, few warmed to

him; one leading civil servant in 1940 thought he could have become Britain's Quisling. Yet through skilful administration and perseverance he scaled the political heights between the world wars as Secretary for Air, for India, First Lord of the Admiralty, Home Secretary and Lord Privy Seal. His brief tenure as Foreign Secretary in 1935 ended with the humiliation of the repudiated Hoare–Laval pact, an early essay in appeasement that did nothing to dampen his principled support for placating the continental dictators over the next few years. The advent of war in 1939 and Churchill in 1940 ended his hopes of further promotion, but by then he had spent the best part of two gruelling decades in high office.

Duff Cooper (1890–1954) could hardly have presented a greater contrast. A glamorous, energetic socialite and sybarite, he held high office only briefly, as Secretary of State for War (1935–7) and First Lord of the Admiralty (1937–8). Much of his serious political reputation rested on his resignation over the Munich agreement in 1938, as well as his spell as ambassador to Paris (1944–7), where his political and social skills merged seamlessly if occasionally exhaustingly. He shone,

Above: *Sam Hoare, (second from left in the front row), Boojums, 1902.*

Right: *Duff Cooper, photographed by Bassano, 1925.*

not always evanescently, in many parts, including that of a well-matched biographer of Talleyrand. The aura of dilettante never left him. On one occasion in his political life the New College connection served him well. His maiden speech in the House of Commons in 1924, after a by-election victory at Oldham over another New College man, Edward Grigg, was praised by the following speaker

as 'brilliant, perfect in form'. The encomium came from H.A.L. Fisher, his old history tutor.

Much more remarkable in their way, if only for coincidence, were the left-wing politicians nurtured at New College in the 1920s who rose to sit in Labour cabinets after the Second World War. They did not, however, form a coherent political or social group. Their general political allegiance reflected national change. Those of liberal inclinations, unlike in Fisher's day, increasingly looked beyond the Liberal Party to the Labour Party. Pre-First World War recruits to this new force were few, including the socialist political theorist Harold Laski (1893–1950), who got a first in history in 1914. A future Labour Chancellor of the Exchequer, Stafford Cripps had won the first ever New College scholarship in chemistry from Winchester in 1907 but had turned it down in favour of University College London.

Between 1927 and 1930 there graduated five New College men who went on to exert a significant influence on the Labour party and national politics: Frank Pakenham (1905–2001), Hugh Gaitskell (1906–63), Evan Durbin (1906–48), Douglas Jay (1907–96) and Richard Crossman (1907–74). Three of them, Gaitskell, Jay and Crossman, were Wykehamists. Jay and Crossman read Mods and Greats, the other three PPE. All but Pakenham won parliamentary seats as Labour candidates in 1945 or, in Jay's case, 1946; as a consolation, Pakenham was elevated by Attlee to the Lords. In the 1930s each held academic positions: Gaitskell at University College London, Durbin at the LSE, Pakenham at Christ Church, Jay became a fellow of All Souls, and Crossman a philosophy fellow at New College. Each served as wartime civil servants, not in the armed forces. All, bar Durbin, who drowned saving his daughter from the sea in 1948, became cabinet ministers. Durbin, however, was a major intellectual influence in forming the Labour party's postwar synthesis of Keynesianism and socialism. Gaitskell, having been Chancellor of the Exchequer (1950–51), led the Labour Party from 1955–63. A reformist egalitarian, with a desiccated public manner belying a relaxed social life, a brave, emotional but stubborn politician, his early death confirmed a career of heroic failure.

Pakenham, later 7th Earl of Longford, originally a Conservative before joining the Labour Party in 1936, served in Attlee's cabinet and was leader of the House of Lords from 1964 to 1968. In later life he was notorious for Roman Catholic apologia, prison visiting and loud campaigns against pornography. Jay, a major economic influence under Attlee, became President of the Board of Trade (1964–7) and later championed left-wing opposition to entry into the Common Market, a view he shared with Gaitskell. Crossman, who had to give up his fellowship on marrying the divorced wife of a New College colleague, sat on the left wing of the Labour Party, generally opposed to what he regarded as Gaitskell's revisionism. In the Wilson governments of 1964–70, he served in the cabinet as Minister of Housing, Lord President and Leader of the House of Commons and Secretary of State for Health and Social Security. More lasting than his political legacy, perhaps, were his detailed and indiscreet diaries of his years in cabinet, published following much controversy after his death.

The careers of these closely acquainted contemporaries encompass the accession of middle-class intellectuals and middle-class voters to the Labour Party after the First World War as well as the battles and compromises of the effort to make it a regular party of government from 1945. To them may be added Kenneth Younger (1908–76), another Wykehamist who read PPE, of Conservative stock but who became a Labour MP in 1945 and acted as the ailing Ernest Bevin's effective deputy at the Foreign Office in 1950–51. They also show how narrow and elitist certain aspects of the political world remained in the generation after full democracy. The role

of New College must remain speculative, perhaps less important than, in Gaitskell's case at least, the General Strike of 1926. It remains a remarkable conjunction for a college not noted for such political tradition. Perhaps the arrival of Fisher as warden in 1925 played a part, with his array of guests from the political world who were regularly paraded before the undergraduates and his habitual reminiscences of his days in the cabinet.

Another influential college figure who came with experience of public service was Alic Smith, who had served in the Scottish Office before returning to New College as a fellow after the First World War. The new PPE course, Modern Greats as it was then known, clearly exerted an influence on some of this group, but it does not explain the leftwards direction. Gaitskell and Durbin were both taught by Lionel Robbins, a lecturer (1924–5) and fellow in economics (1927–9), later famous as a professor at the LSE and for his seminal report on higher education (1963) that led to the great expansion of the university system. Individual oedipal rebellion and rejection of family orthodoxies or a search for independence from highly conventional backgrounds might seem a convenient psychological explanation for the radicalism of this group. This may be too glib. New College, at exactly the same time, continued to produce Tories, initially like the Etonian Pakenham and another Wykehamist, David Eccles (1904–99), who also read PPE and was taught by Robbins. Nicknamed 'Smarty Boots', Eccles, after wartime experience in the civil service, became a Conservative MP in 1943 and served as Minister of Works (1951–4), when, for a time, his parliamentary secretary was Hugh Molson, a New College contemporary and himself a future Minister of Works. Eccles was a highly innovatory and expansionist Minister of Education (1954–7, 1959–62), President of the Board of Trade (1957–9) and an effective *de facto* minister for the Arts (1970–73).

Top left: *Richard Crossman, photographed 1926.*

Bottom left: *Kenneth Younger, photographed 1927.*

R. Hamilton

81/100

Above: *Hugh Gaitskell as 'a famous monster of filmland,' by Richard Hamilton, a lithograph based on his painting of 1964.*

Interestingly, none of these future cabinet ministers came from political dynasties, unlike, later, Tony Benn (born 1925), whose grandfathers and father were all MPs. Whatever the personal reasons propelling these undergraduates of the 1920s towards politics, and admitting the importance of chance and luck, New College of the time was more open to the outside world than ever before, with non-Oxford or Oxbridge fellows and the legacy of the older undergraduates returning from war. In retrospect, it appears as a golden age, one that produced in addition to these public figures lawyers such as Richard Wilberforce and John Sparrow, and the legal philosopher Herbert Hart. Robbins, from the vantage point in the SCR, remembered of this period: 'We were not self-consciously on the crest of a wave. But unconsciously we knew it and this gave to much of what we said and did that kind of exhilaration.' Something of this cannot but have rubbed off on the undergraduates.

Despite easy caricature of a Wykehamist-dominated training ground for civil servants, dons and lawyers, arguably one of New College's chief characteristics in the twentieth century was its lack of prescriptive identity, its humane liberal ethos producing a relaxed diversity, an absence of a recognized or recognizable type. Perhaps two final examples help make the point. Just as the college produced two twentieth-century Lord Chancellors, so it educated two General Secretaries of the Trades Union Congress. George Woodcock (1904–79), for 12 years a weaver in a Lancashire cotton mill, came on a delegacy of extra-mural studies scholarship to New College via Ruskin College in 1931 to read PPE, falling under the influence of Crossman. After gaining a first in 1933, he joined the TUC research department, the first university-trained intellectual to do so. After a lifetime working for the TUC and establishing himself as, it has been described, 'the philosopher king of trade unionism', Woodcock was General Secretary from 1960 to 1969. Len Murray (1922–2004) arrived at New College in 1945 after a brief period at Queen Mary College, London, and being wounded in Normandy in 1944, to read for a shortened ex-serviceman degree in PPE, partly though the ministrations of the now ex-fellow and soon to be MP Crossman. Murray's background, an illegitimate son from rural labouring stock in Shropshire, was less propitious even than Woodcock's. Yet under Woodcock's patronage, after graduating in 1947, Murray joined the TUC and rose, like his patron, to the top, being General Secretary in the enormously demanding years for trade unionism of 1973–84.

In these two careers may be detected a faint echo of New College's earliest days: scholars from humble backgrounds being fitted to join the establishment of public service where they found help in their careers from fellow alumni but prospered through their own wits. Perhaps more than the modern gilded products of his other foundation, such men matched William of Wykeham's original educational intentions if not his political, social or religious tastes.

AUTHORS

WILLIAM POOLE

The earliest literary activities of the college are slight and hard to recapture. Rather in the manner of a monastic community, the New College fellows venerated the Founder in quasi-cultic fashion, and perhaps the earliest literary work here comprised appreciations of Wykeham's life and achievements. The most celebrated collection of such materials is the 'Chaundler manuscript', assembled by the mid-fifteenth century warden, Thomas Chaundler (1454–75). His collection contains verse and prose on Wykeham and his colleges and also four famous pictures by one anonymous artist. One is of New College, looking from the south to the north ranges of the original quadrangle, with a mass portrait of a warden and all the scholars in the foreground. It is the earliest depiction of the college. The other pertinent picture is an idealized group portrait of Wykeham and associated worthies. Wykeham sits in the centre, holding models of his two colleges. To his left is Henry Chichele, holding a model of All Souls chapel. To Wykeham's right is Thomas Cranley, the first warden of Winchester. The other major worthies are Thomas Beckington, bishop of Bath and Wells and college benefactor, and William Waynflete, bishop of Winchester and founder of Magdalen College. This iconography of Wykeham flanked by Chichele and Waynflete, symbolizing the dependence of All Souls and Magdalen on New College, has had a long subsequent history and is repeated, for instance, in the portrait of the Founder that still hangs today in Hall in the centre of the east wall above high table.

Biographical homage to Wykeham had three or more centuries of afterlife in the college, producing in 1597 the *Historica descriptio* of Thomas Martin (1520/1–1592/3, matriculated 1540), prominent civil lawyer and a statesman who achieved dubious eminence in his time. This effusive work was republished unrevised at the instigation of the warden in 1690, this time under the Sheldonian imprint. The college copy of the first edition is especially interesting, as it is covered in green velvet and boasts a hand-drawn frontispiece of Wykeham, Waynflete and Chichele. Its style suggests that it was drawn by Richard Haydocke (1569/70–c.1642, matriculated 1588), an important artistic figure. Finally, in 1758 Robert Lowth (1710–87, matriculated 1730) published his own documentary life of the Founder, based on extensive archival work in Winchester, New College and elsewhere, and it was Lowth who brought sensible standards of documentation to the previously rather uncritical genre of Wykeham-worship.

If the college had a literary heyday in its first four centuries, then it was in the late Elizabethan and Jacobean periods. Among the Elizabethans there were the Latin poets George Coryate (matriculated 1560, died 1609) and John Owen, known as 'Audoenus' (1563/4–1622?, matriculated 1582), the memorably named vernacular epigrammatist Thomas Bastard (1565/6–1618, matriculated 1586) and the lawyer and wit John Hoskins (1566–1638, matriculated 1585). Sir Henry Wotton (1568–1639), like Hoskins a friend of John Donne, also matriculated at New College in 1584, but soon moved on to Hart Hall and then the Queen's College.

Opposite: *The hand-drawn frontispiece in a copy of Thomas Martin's* Historica descriptio, *an early biography of Wykeham, showing the Founder flanked by Chichele and Wayneflete.*

The 1580s, indeed, were the most vigorous decades of the century for college writing. Among the younger generation there was the Latin poet John Reinolds (1584?–1614, matriculated 1602), the epigrammatist John Heath (*c.*1585–?, matriculated 1605) and the scribe and poet Thomas Master (1602/3–1643, matriculated 1622). Most of these men were primarily epigrammatists, and Owen and then Reinolds reached a national and even international audience. Owen remained a Latin staple for schoolboys and young students for almost two centuries and was translated into many different vernaculars, including English in Newfoundland. As Wood said of him, 'he had an ingenious liberty of joking', and so was placed on the Roman Catholic Index of prohibited books, on account of anti-Catholic couplets such as this:

An Petrus fuerit Romæ, sub judice lis est;
Simonem Romæ, nemo fuisse negat.

[Whether Peter were ever at Rome is the case under judgment; No one denies that Simon was there.]

But virtually all New College fellows, as was the fashion of the time, could turn out an epigram or two and occasionally longer poems. In 1587 New College issued *Peplus*, a volume of Latin poems lamenting the death of Sir Philip Sidney, and the 1605 New College volume of Latin and Greek verses on the death of Ralph Warcop was co-written by no fewer than 17 fellows of the college. An elegant 1636 presentation manuscript of verses to Lady Elizabeth Paulet was, with only one exception, again composed entirely by New College men. Poems by scholars, fellows and wardens of New College lie scattered throughout the university collections of the time.

Of all these men, perhaps Bastard and Hoskins are the most interesting (*see page 154*). Hoskins, however, has the great distinction of being the inventor of English nonsense verse. His gibberish starts thus:

Even as the waves of brainlesse butter'd fish,
With bugle horne writ in the Hebrew tongue,
Fuming up flounders like a chafing-dish,
That looks asquint upon a Three-mans song …

Although the college literati focused on poetry, at least one Elizabethan prose production deserves mention. This was the translation into English in 1597 of the contemporary Italian art theorist Gian Paulo Lomazzo, the first translation into English of any work of Italian art theory. It was undertaken by Haydocke the artist, who illustrated the translation with his own finely engraved portraits. Haydocke also took occasion in this important work to announce the intention of Sir Thomas Bodley, the dedicatee of the volume, to restore the university library.

Among the generation of Jacobean–Caroline writers, Thomas Master was perhaps the most versatile, known in his time for English, Latin and Greek poetry, as well

Far left: *A seventeenth-century miniature of an unknown man by Thomas Flatman (near left), 1682.*

GEORGE HUDDESFORD

George Huddesford (1749–1809), the satirical poet and painter, was briefly a fellow of New College in the late eighteenth century; he was elected in 1771, but resigned on his marriage a year later. His poems included the volumes *Topsy Turvy; with Anecdotes and Observations illustrative of the Present Government of France* (1793) and *Bubble and Squeak: a Gallimaufry of British Beef with the Chopp'd Cabbage of Gallic Philosophy and Radical Reform* (1799). A student of Joshua Reynolds, his paintings hung in the early showings at the Royal Academy, and he painted his self-portrait in an historical manner in 1780.

as eloquent preaching. In the 1630s he was employed as a scribe by the philosopher Edward Herbert of Cherbury. Master's work was read well into the Restoration, and Abraham Cowley translated his poem on the Passion from Greek into English. The Interregnum was notable for the presence of the competent poet and excellent miniaturist Thomas Flatman (1635–1688, matriculated 1654). Flatman published volumes of poetry, but he appears to have left the college by 1658, decades before his once-popular *Poems and Songs* (1674, four editions to 1686). Thereafter the writing of literature declined in college for a century and more, but the fragmentary fellows' borrowing register from the Restoration period shows

that fellows still read a good deal of vernacular, often immediately contemporary literature. If a fellow died in his chambers, at the time a list of his possessions was usually drawn up, and where books are itemized, a rather pleasing taste in English poetry is revealed, otherwise invisible from this historical distance. John Hutton, for instance, a young *artista* who died in 1652 at the age of 24 or 25, read in his rooms John Gower, Ben Jonson, John Donne and Abraham Cowley, as well as an array of works by New College writers, some of whom must have chambered just metres from his own room.

The late seventeenth and early eighteenth centuries did not witness much interesting literary work, but a large prose venture, edited in 1714 by John Ayliffe (1676–1732, matriculated 1696), *The Antient and Present State of the University of Oxford*, achieved notoriety. This work contains a valuable eye-witness description of New College of the time, but Ayliffe also attacked mismanagement in the university and was sued by the vice-chancellor and the warden of New College for injury and damage. The last major literary figure of the age was Joseph Spence (1699–1768, admitted 1720), Oxford Professor of Poetry and the friend of Alexander Pope. His *Anecdotes*, published only in 1820 in ever-expanding editions, remains the principal source for the literary biography of his age. But Spence spent most of his time among the literati, and not living in college.

Early-modern students put on and occasionally wrote plays too. There had probably always been a certain amount of drama or at least entertainment commissioned by New College for special occasions. The bursarial rolls and the accounts of the Seneschal of Hall record payments from the late-fifteenth to the mid-sixteenth centuries to *histriones*, *mimi* and *lusores*. We also know that a 'learnyd Tragedy' was acted at Christmas in New College in the reign of Mary I, using costumes supplied by Sir Thomas Cawarden, first Master of the Revels, but the play itself alas no longer survives. The cast list, however, included kings, dukes, councillors, a queen, gentlewomen and a

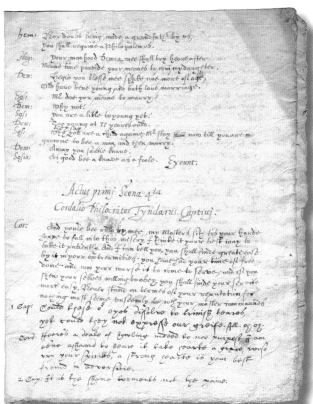

Left: *The anonymous seventeenth-century version of Plautus's play,* Captives.

Far left: *Richard Zouche, elected a scholar in 1607, then fellow in 1609, attributed to Cornelius Johnson, 1620.*

prince, so it will have been a substantial and luxuriant production, possibly in Latin.

It seems likely too, that the students wrote vernacular plays for their own pleasure. A few years ago, in a box marked 'Trash Papers' in the college archives, was found about half of a manuscript play that appears from internal evidence to have been written in the early seventeenth century. It is a lively and still slightly funny translation and adaptation of Plautus' *Captives*, but now featuring a Jacobean malcontent and love-plot entirely absent in the original. This script represents Jacobean humanistic education at its best – the skilful reworking of classical source material, modernized for a new environment. Another fascinating play was written not long afterwards by the jurist and academician Richard Zouche (1590–1661, matriculated 1607). Zouche became the Regius Professor of Civil Law and an MP and was one of the architects of the Laudian Code for Oxford. He wrote many legal textbooks and is regarded as one of the founders of international law. Yet in 1639 there appeared a more obviously entertaining work, *The Sophister*, also surviving in a variant manuscript text entitled *Fallacy*. Attributed to Zouche, the original play was written probably sometime in the second or third decades of the century, and, given Zouche's swift rise to academic and political eminence, it seem more likely to be an early work and hence from Zouche's days in New College. It is an academic allegory of the type popular among students, in which the various characters represent various bits and pieces of the undergraduate arts curriculum. So the play opens with 'Fallacy' appearing with his 'dark lanthorne', and his servant 'Ambiguity'. 'Demonstration' and 'Topicus', Fallacy's younger brothers (but better born), are preferred by their father 'Discourse', who intends them in marriage for 'Scientia' and 'Opinion'. Ambiguity therefore bears two vials of madness-inducing potion for 'Fallacy' … and so forth.

After this period, banished by the Interregnum authorities, drama fled from New College, and failed to return at the Restoration. It is only in modern times that student acting has been revived, much to the exasperation of some contemporary tutors.

JOHN GALSWORTHY

For all the distinction of its fellowship and the range and achievements of its old members, to date New College can boast only two Nobel Laureates. The Californian William Lamb (1913–2008; Wykeham Professor of Physics 1956–62) actually won his prize, for Physics, a year before becoming a fellow. A seemingly far less likely prospect was John Galsworthy (1867–1933), who received the Nobel Prize for Literature in 1932. From a respectable and conventional middle-class business and legal background, as a boy at Harrow, Galsworthy had been hardworking and hearty. Both attributes he decided to abandon when he arrived at New College in 1886 to read law. His biographer commented that at Oxford 'he proposed to apply his undoubted powers of concentration to having a good time'. His main interest was racing. Even though he managed the top law second of his year in 1889, his college friend and contemporary, H.A.L. Fisher recalled, with delicate irony, that at the time 'no one would have predicted that he would be prominent as an imaginative writer'.

His literary development was partly framed by new perspectives on British society gained through his international travels in pursuit of his family's business interests. On one of these trips he met a ship's first mate, Joseph Conrad, who remained a friend for life. The far from stuffy critical appraisal of contemporary middle-class values and habits that characterized his plays and novels also conformed to an increasingly prominent liberal reformist critique of late Victorian and Edwardian society and the effects of materialism, attitudes he shared with New College associates such as Fisher and Gilbert Murray. His hostility to stultifying convention and social propriety may have been encouraged by his decade-long affair with Ada Nemesis Pearson, the wife of his cousin, whom he finally married in 1905.

Galsworthy began publishing in 1897. His first popular success came in 1906, with the production of a play, *The Silver Box*, an attack on the law's unequal treatment of rich and poor, and the publication of a major novel, *The Man of Property*, which introduced the Forsyte family whose fortunes Galsworthy subsequently chronicled in a sequence of novels written over the following quarter of a century, collectively known as *The Forsyte Saga*. Many of the Forsyte novels in the 1920s proved immensely popular at the time and earned the respect of foreign commentators, for instance in Germany, for their sharp social observation, if only of a narrow propertied class – Galsworthy's own. They constitute a sustained critical analysis of the material values of the British ruling upper middle classes, which he also explored in his plays, which had initially proved more popular than his novels. Belying his very conservative appearance, Galsworthy was active in his support for anti-war movements, the suffragettes, animal rights, the reform of the penal code and the House of Lords. During the First World War he spent time as a hospital masseur for wounded soldiers.

Although earning the predictable disdain of writers such as D.H. Lawrence and soon falling out of fashion as the social world he had eviscerated itself soon vanished, his best work is well-constructed, far from bland and contains some memorable and not entirely stereotyped characters. If he never imaginatively escaped his own milieu, his plays and novels were merciless in exposing its moral and aesthetic flaws.

Christopher Tyerman

Below: *John Galsworthy, photographed by Olive Edis, 1929.*

CONTEMPORARY NEW COLLEGE WRITING

ZOË NORRIDGE AND OTHERS

Surveying the writing published by New College fellows and alumni since 1979, what is striking is both how enduringly international the college remains and how much its members have changed. While the memoirs published in the late 1970s and early 1980s still refer to an institution populated largely by Wykehamists and Etonians engaged in spirited high jinks in the Garden Quad, by the start of the next millennium the college boasted a Whitbread prize-winning female novelist, a world-renowned female biographer and a Zimbabwean writer who arguably changed the face of African literature.

In the mid-1970s Brian Johnston, having entertained BBC listeners for over 27 years with his cricket commentary, published his autobiography, *It's Been a Lot of Fun*, with a typically playful and punning chapter about his time at New College in the 1930s. Admitting that 'I doubt whether I really passed the rather cursory entrance examination, but in those days the family connection was all-important', he goes on to describe the 'delightful characters' of college. These included a chaplain (Lightfoot) who was reportedly 'crucified' with croquet hoops on the lawn by celebrating undergraduates and a 'rather earnest Wykehamist in spectacles', who turns out to be Richard Crossman. The sporting highlight of those student days is the account of the

race meeting he organized in Port Meadow one summer, where 'a local bookie shouted the odds' and an inexperienced rider was launched into the Thames by his horse.

One year his junior, William Gibson's account of New College in the mid-1930s, *No Time to Slow Down*, adds an American perspective. Dining with 'noisy students from all corners of the globe' and observing the arrival of undergraduates with trunks from 'New Zealand, San Francisco, Capetown and even Cambridge', Gibson provides an atmospheric account of a college lit by gas lamps and cloisters haunted by the names of those killed in the First World War.

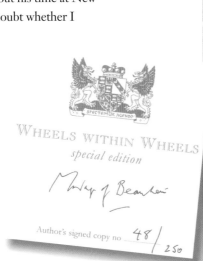

WHEELS WITHIN WHEELS
special edition

Author's signed copy no 48 / 250

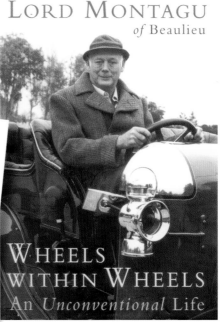

LORD MONTAGU
of Beaulieu

WHEELS WITHIN WHEELS
An *Unconventional* Life

Below: *Dambudzo Marechera, by Victor Mavedzenge, 2008.*

Writing after the war that follows, his compatriot Willie Morris echoes Gibson's complaints about Oxford's 'perpetual fogs and rains'. In an essay entitled 'My Two Oxfords' from the collection *Homecomings*, the former editor of *Harper's* explores his unusual privilege of having lived for some time in both Oxford, England, and Oxford, Mississippi. Explaining that he began by 'spending considerable time in the pubs with the Australians', Morris continues with an alcohol-laden tour of the college, from Sunday morning sherry to W.H. Auden downing red wine.

Similarly boisterous times are described by Lord Montagu of Beaulieu, also a student in postwar New College, in his memoir *Wheels Within Wheels*. Openly bisexual and engaged in relationships with both male undergraduates and 'girls', Montagu seems to have been most torn in his allegiances between the Bullingdon Club and the Oxford University Dramatic Society. These conflicting commitments resulted in a late-night clash of cultures, his bicycle being thrown out of the window and the inevitable interview with the dean.

A decanal summons is also the topic of Dambudzo Marechera's loosely autobiographical short story 'Oxford, Black Oxford', which appeared in *West Africa* in June 1981 and was later published posthumously as part of the collection *The Black Insider*. Marechera was accepted to New College in October 1974 after having been expelled from the University of Rhodesia for his part in student protests against racial discrimination. A slight and bespectacled Zimbabwean, now recognized as one of the most talented writers of his generation, Marechera proved to be mercurial, threatening, provocative and violent. He was sent down before he began work on his seminal text *The House of Hunger*, which won the Guardian Fiction Prize in 1979. There followed years of episodic brilliance, public drunkenness and ongoing eccentricity in London and Harare, where he died with AIDS in the late 1980s. His legacy included a fierce refusal to engage with expected representations of Africa.

CYRIL HARE

Cyril Hare was the psuedoynm of Henry Herbert Gordon Clark (1900–58), who was educated at Rugby, read history at New College (where he was reputed to have heard Warden Spooner utter the immortal 'now we see through a dark grassly' in a sermon). He had a distinguished career as a lawyer, starting with a call to the Bar with chambers in Middle Temple in 1924. But it was as a detective novelist, writing under the pen name of Cyril (after his home in Cyril Court, Battersea) Hare (after his chambers in Hare Court, Middle Temple) that he created his detectives, the mediocre barrister Francis Pettigrew, who dryly investigated a series of cases dealing with issues and settings which followed Clark's own career, and Inspector Mallet, a man with a vast appetite; they appear together in three of his novels, which include *Suicide Expected* (1939), *Tragedy at Law* (1942), *With a bare bodkin* (1946), *When the wind blows* (1949), and *He should have died hereafter* (1958).

Another young writer who caused controversy during his time at New College is the South African-born Richard Mason. His debut novel was bought by Penguin during his first year at Oxford, with a two-book contract for the princely sum of £100,000. Hyped as the next Martin Amis, when *The Drowning People* finally appeared in 1999 it was both praised and lambasted for its geographical and temporal ambition and went on to sell over 5 million copies in 120 countries. His second novel, *Us*, is set closer to home in Oxford, but his third, *The Lighted Rooms*, takes a transnational approach once more as Mason juxtaposes descriptions of a Boer War concentration camp with contemporary London. These days he balances writing fiction with running the Kay Mason Foundation, a South African charity that offers scholarships to high-school-aged children from disadvantaged backgrounds.

Reflecting its evolving demographics of college, another successful college novelist is Rachel Cusk, whose novel *Saving Agnes* won the Whitbread First Novel Award in 1993. Since then she has published eight further works to critical claim, won the Somerset Maugham Award for *The Country Life* in 1997 and was shortlisted by the Orange Prize for *Arlington Park* in 2007. So far she has mostly focused on fiction, with topics ranging from the uncertainties of young women beginning their careers in London to family entanglements in the country. Garan Holcombe has praised her work for the 'dark subtle comedy, the creeping sense of menace below its surface, and its exquisitely sensitive treatment of the failure of expectation'. Such features also characterize her segue into autobiographical writing in *A Life's Work: On Becoming a Mother*. In this she has much in common with another influential New College alumna, Naomi Wolf, best known for her feminist politics, who also explores the challenges of motherhood in her hybrid memoir *Misconceptions: Truth, Lies and the Unexpected Journey to Motherhood*, published in the same year, 2001.

In a different genre, the tradition of pointed comedies of manners is freshly represented by Charlotte Mendelson, winner of the John Llewellyn Rhys Prize (2003) and a Somerset Maugham Award (2004) for her second novel, *Daughters of Jerusalem*, some of the most memorable scenes in which are set in New College, notably a moment of lesbian epiphany in the cloisters. Another winner of a Somerset Maugham Award (2008) is Adam Thirlwell, pupil and protégé of Craig Raine (fellow in English 1991–2010). A Prize Fellow of All Soul's, Thirlwell's intensely intellectually self-conscious and showy novels owe much to the influence of Milan Kundera but seek to break new ground between elite literary referencing and popular explicit eroticism.

Right: *Richard Mason, photographed by Benjamin Morse, 2008.*

Some of the most notable literary writing by New College alumni over the past 30 years falls not into the category of autobiographical reflections on the college nor into fiction, but instead dwells in the realm of biography, a field mastered and defined by former New College fellow, practitioner and commentator Hermione Lee. A regular on Radio 4, CBE and now president of Wolfson, Lee's work includes *Willa Cather: A Life Saved Up*, *Edith Wharton* and *Virginia Woolf*, the last of which was described by the *Financial Times* as 'one of the most impressive biographies of the decade'.

Although Robin Lane Fox specifically claims the text is not a biography, it would also be tempting to slip his 'magnificent, compelling epic' (*Sunday Telegraph*), *Alexander the Great* into a brief survey of New College writing. Less controversial in terms of type if not content are Michael Crick's best-selling biographies of Jeffrey Archer, Michael Heseltine, Michael Howard and Alex Ferguson. Further towards the popular market are the biographies of women by Lisa Hilton, whose work has straddled various accessible genres.

Finally, even the briefest of surveys would not be complete without a mention of New College's many poets. Numbering among the ranks of those producing work in this period are John Holloway, whose poetic meditation on life in Cambridge, *Civitatula*, was published in 1994; John Fuller, appreciated for his critically acclaimed novels and also for his 15 collections of poetry (winning the Forward Prize for *Stones and Fires* in 1996); D.M. Thomas, another much-loved poet-novelist; Jonathan Griffin, the UK's most 'noteworthy green poet'; and the Japan-based Gavin Bantock.

However, the poet who has perhaps had the most impact on the generations of English students he has taught at New College is Craig Raine. *A Martian Sends a Postcard Home*, the collection that launched a movement, was published in 1979. Raine won the Sunday Times Writer of the Year Award in 1986 and founded the literary magazine *Areté*.

ENDWORD

CHRISTOPHER TYERMAN

During the preparation of this book, one former undergraduate recalled memories from her time at college. These are united by a feeling of belonging: at interview 'how genuinely welcome and accepted I was made to feel by people who had no inherent need or self-interest to ask me to join them'; as a student 'we were a real co-operative'. If one thread runs through this work, it is that of New College people: the medieval fellows who trod their own paths in manipulation of the Founder's wishes; the donors of books whose tastes and generosity were as crucial as the texts themselves; the battling theologians and ludic literati of the early modern college; the dispossessed royalists; the antiquarians, pedants and eccentrics; the comfortable yet far from intellectually inert fellows who sat out the Enlightenment; the reformers and reactionaries doing battle in the age of reform; the earnestly ambitious of the modern college; the pious and the pagan; the scholars, artists, musicians, swats, idlers and sporty of all generations; the staff who actually keep the college running; the women offering new perspectives while civilising the men. Such were – and are – not aggregates, but individuals with their own messy histories and unique destinies who, coming together, in Ernest Barker's words, 'entered into the inheritance of this place', and in doing so enriched both it and themselves. This is New College's *genius loci*, something of which we hope we have been able to capture.

Right: *The New College sundial medal, commemorating the millennium, and the restoration of the seventeenth-century sundial, designed by Rod Kelly and struck by Spink, 2000.*

WARDENS OF NEW COLLEGE

Nicholas Wykeham	1379–89	Martin Culpepper	1573–99	John Purnell	1740–64
Thomas Cranley	1389–96	George Ryves	1599–1613	Thomas Hayward	1764–8
Richard Malford	1396–1403	Arthur Lake	1613–17	John Oglander	1768–94
John Bowke	1403–29	Robert Pincke	1617–47	Samuel Gauntlett	1794–1822
William Escourt	1429–35	Henry Stringer	1647–8	Philip Shuttleworth	1822–40
Nicholas Ossulbury	1435–54	George Marshall 1649–58 *(intruded)*		David Williams	1840–60
Thomas Chaundler	1454–75	Michael Woodward	1658–75	James Sewell	1860–1903
Walter Hill	1475–94	John Nicholas	1675–9	William Spooner	1903–25
William Porter	1494–1520	Henry Beeston	1679–1701	Herbert Fisher	1925–40
John Rede	1520–1	Richard Traffles	1701–3	Alic Smith	1944–58
John Young	1521–6	Thomas Braithwaite	1703–12	William Hayter	1958–76
John London	1526–42	John Cobb	1712–20	Arthur Cooke	1976–85
Henry Cole	1542–51	John Dobson	1720–4	Harvey McGregor	1985–96
Ralph Skinner	1551–3	Henry Bigg	1725–30	Alan Ryan	1996–2009
Thomas Whyte	1553–73	John Coxed	1730–40	Curtis Price	2009–

LIST OF CONTRIBUTORS AND READING LIST

LIST OF CONTRIBUTORS

Michael Burden, Fellow of New College

Richard Compton Miller (Old Member 1963)

Sir Roger du Boulay (Old Member 1940)

Edward Higginbottom, Fellow of New College

Robin Lane Fox, Fellow of New College

Zoë Norridge, Lecturer, University of York, formerly Junior Research Fellow of New College

David Parrott, Fellow of New College

John Platts (Old Member 1949)

William Poole (Old Member 1995), Fellow of New College

Alan Ryan, Honorary Fellow of New College

Jennifer Thorp, Archivist of New College

Christopher Tyerman (Old Member 1971), Fellow of Hertford College, Lecturer of New College

Penry Williams (Old Member 1947), Honorary Fellow of New College

Sir Marcus Worsley (Old Member 1947)

READING LIST

The Archives of New College Oxford by F. Steer (Chichester, 1974)

The History of Oxford University, gen. ed. T.H. Aston et al (8 vols Oxford, 1984–94)

New College by H. Rashdall and R. Rait (London, 1901)

New College and its Buildings by A.H. Smith (Oxford, 1952)

New College, Oxford, 1379-1979, ed. J. Buxton & P. Williams (Oxford, 1979)

The Oxford Dictionary of National Biography: from the earliest times to the year 2000, ed. H.C.G. Matthew & B. Harrison (Oxford, 2004)

The Stained Glass of New College by C. Woodeforde (Oxford, 1951)

William Wykeham: A Life (London, 2007) by Virginia Davis

LIST OF SUBSCRIBERS

This book has been made possible through the generosity of the following:

Jack R. Aaron	1944	G.A. Barratt	1949	Charles Brereton	1942
Clio Adam	2008	Eur Ing Dr James R. Barron	1981	Emily J. Brettle	1986
Dr Neil Adams	1972	Dr T.H.K. Barron	1947	Luke Bridgeman	1990
Trevor John Adams	1965	Tony Baston-Hall	1989	Stephen Briggs	1975
Stephen W. Adcock	1975	S.J. Bates	1972	Kate Bristow	1981
Mr Mark Ager	1979	Mark Batten	1975	Peter Brook	1974
Mark David Agrast	1978	Dr Alan D. Baxter	1965	Jackie Brown	1980
Juliet Allan	1986	Jessica Baylis	2005	Michael Brown	2005
Dr Simon T.M. Allard	1993	Mark T. Beaudouin	1977	Richard Brown	2008
R.J. Alston	1958	Stephen Bechade	2004	Desmond Browne QC	1965
Alexander Americanos	2008	Robin Behar	1960	Donald G. Browne	
David Anderson	1975	Stephen Beke	1988	Professor Attila Brungs	1994
Alexander Ando	1974	Derek J. Benham	1972	Hugh Brunt	2004
Justine Andrew	1989	Fiona Bennett (née Dillon)	1987	Alistair Buchanan	1956
Dr Stuart Andrews	1961	Dr Nicholas Bennett	1966	Patrick K. Buckley	1993
Mathew Armstrong	1989	Andrew Bent	1967	Dr J.C. Buitelaar MA	1974
Siân Armstrong (née Jones)	1993	Mark Bentley	1986	Allan E. Bulley III	1990
Richard Ashdowne	1996	Helen Bessemer-Clark		Emeritus Professor Alan O. Bullock	
Hugh Ashton	1971	Derek von Bethmann-Hollweg	1957		1957
Peter Atkinson	1972	Professor Alan Bilsborough	1965	G.H. Bullock	1951
Katrina M. Atsinger	1996	John K. Birley	1955	A.R. Bullough	1951
D.P. Aughey	1987	John Birtill	1970	Camilla R. Bullough	2009
Dr T.B. Austin	1967	Andrew Boggis	1972	Michael Burden	Fellow
Walter Aylen	1957	Terence John Bollen		Brian V. Burdett	1953
John Edward Ayres	1965	Christopher Bond	2001	Professor Jeffery Burley CBE	1957
Jenny Ayres	1992	John Bonds	1955	Bishop Andrew Burnham	1966
Malcolm G. Bacchus	1972	His Hon. Judge Guy Boney QC	1963	Nick Butler	1987
John T. Bach	1956	Paul N Bongers de Rath	1962	C.N. Butters	1989
Dr Rachel Bailey-Williams	1980	Dr Didier C.L. Bonnet	1983	Robin Byatt	1950
T.C. Barker	1948	Peter Bosher	1979	Dr Mark Byford	1980
Charles Baker-Glenn	1996	Michael Ingram Bostock	1940	Paul R. Cahill	1976
Matthew Ball	2008	Lord Boswell of Aynho	1961	W. Richard Cantwell	1953
Catherine Barlen	1984	Chris Bosworth	1990	Reg Care	1950
James John Barnes	1954	Mr W.R. Boulter	1976	Sir Roderick Carnegie AC	1954
John Michael Barnes	1946	David R. Bowen	1954	Ian David Carr	1978
Luke Barnes	1987	James Bowman OBE	1960	Peter Carter	1975
Dr Phillip R.J. Barnes	1984	John D. Boyce	1954	Paul Cartledge	1965

John A. Cartwright	1953	John William Devine	2005	John P.H. Frearson	1966
Alexander Case	1995	Terence Diggory	1973	Tim Freegarde	1982
John D. Cashion	1966	Ian Dilks	1971	Douglas Frewer	1951
Jim Caterer	1963	Charles Dinwiddy	1960	Dr Peggy Frith	Fellow
Judith Catterall		Mr Denis Doble	1957	Dr Ian Kelsey Fry	1942
J.A.T. Caulfeild	1957	Brian Dolan	1997	Christopher C. Gabriel	1991
John Cavanagh	1979	Patrick Dolan	1950	Mags Gadsden	2004
Jonathan Cave	1972	Raymond Douse	1965	Francis Gale	1951
Hugh Cecil	1960	Brigadier A.L. Dowell	1943	Dr Ferdia Gallagher	1996
Prabal Chakrabarti	1995	Dominic Dowley	1977	John Galloway	1969
Charles Chan Kwai Chun	1992	Catherine Downie	1983	Christopher Garman	2000
W.E.W. StG. Charlton	1955	Alexander Dragonetti	2004	Graeme Gates	1967
John Chester	1981	Leslie Drain	1944	Jeremy Gauntlett SC	1974
Hazel E. Childs	2006	James P. Draper	1981	Mr Nick Georgano	1952
Philip Christison	1984	Paul C. Drury	1988	Paul Georgiou	1961
Winston J. Churchill	1962	Ian S. Duff	1969	George P. Giard, Jr	1960
Jessica Mary Clay	1999	Allan G. Duncan	1963	Daniel Gieve	1998
Alfred Clayton	1971	Geoffrey Durbin	1963	P.G. Giles	1973
Mr D.S.J. Clegg	1992	Alan Durden	1967	Allan Gillan	1942
Jonathan Clenshaw	1986	Stewart Dutfield	1972	Dr Barry Goalby	1944
Timothy E. Clifford	1976	Wade T. Dyke	1981	Stuart M. Golodetz	2003
Chris Clothier	1998	P.E.	1992	Anthony Goodenough	1960
Revd Dr Simon Cocksedge	1978	William Eason	1968	Dr C.L. Goodfellow	1982
R.E. Cockton	1971	Dr Douglas East	1946	Anthony Goodman	1982
Terence A. Coghlan	1964	Andy Eastwood	1997	Piers N.G. Goodman	1981
Charles Mortimer Coleman	1983	Sir Gerald Elliot	1946	Dr A.J. Gossage	1941
David Collins	2005	John C. Elliot	1970	Dr J.M.R. Goulding	1998
Peter J. Collman	1968	Robert J. Elliott	1958	Richard Graham	1996
Richard Compton Miller	1963	Sir Roger Elliott	1946	Joanne Grateley (née Boyd)	1989
John M. Cone	1963	Paul Ellis	1979	Dr Richard Grayson FRSA FRGS	
Oliver Cone	1992	Andrew Emery	1998		1972
Dr Christopher P. Conlon	1974	Sir Geoffrey Errington Bt OBE	1944	Emma Josephine Green	1987
R.O. Cook	1966	Mr Chris Esslin-Peard	1981	A.J. StG. Gribbon	1970
Cathy Cooper (née Taylor)	1982	Mr B. Evans	1964	R.C. Gridley	1956
J.K. Cordy	1940	David W. Evans	1957	Martin Griffiths QC and	
Luis Miguel Arez Romao		Helen Evans	1995	Sue Burden	1981
Brito Correia	1992	R.A. Evans	1970	Paul D. Grinke	1961
Wilson Cotton	1974	R.J. Evans	1987	Paul L. Gritz	1972
J.D. Cragg-James	1971	Samuel A. Evans	2002	Patrick Grundy	1941
Richard Craig	1991	Christopher H.D. Everett	1953	Ivor Guild	1942
John Crawshaw	1968	Mr Chris Eyre	1971	Robert Gullifer Headmaster	
Michael Crick	1976	Stephen Eyre	1976	New College School, 2008-	
Sophie Cross	2001	Malcolm J. Fair	1969	Campbell Gunn	1974
M. Cunningham	1959	Chris Fallows	1974	J.M.A. Gunn	1947
David Darby	1958	Andrew Farmer	1983	Brian, Anne and Lucas Gustason	1997
Peter Stormonth Darling	1953	Dr Ian D. Fawcett	1989	Martin Gwinnutt	1980
Francis Davey	1951	Michael Scott Feeley	1987	John Hagel III	1972
Sir David Davies	1959	Richard J.H. Fisher	1971	Nick Hale	1976
E.F. Day	1982	Dr Michael Flemming	1966	Mr Paul R. Hale	1971
Melissa Day (née Begg)	1993	Professor Michael R.D. Foot	1938	Gavin Hales and Sarah Metcalf	1995
Nick Day	1993	Graeme Forbes	1977	William Andrew Hallett	1981
Adrian De Froment	2001	Mrs John Fowles		Mr Andrew D. Halliwell	1989
The Revd Canon L.S. Deas	1971	Chris and Lesley Fox		Keith Halstead MA (Oxon) FCA	1975
Dr Christopher M. Dent	1976	Paul G. Fox	1974	Victoria Hamilton	1993
Nigel Denton	1966	T.J.W. Foy	1942	Mark Handley-Derry FRCPCH	1970
Xerxes Desai	1958	Graham Francis	1996	David Hannay	1956

J. Owen Hardwicke	1942	Richard J.M. Inman	1971	Michael Lester	1959
Robin Hargrave	1973	Michael M. Ismail	1990	Stanley Letchford	1949
Chris Harper	1971	Anthony George Ive	1948	Helen Hok-Sze Leung	1987
Derek Harraway	1954	Brian Iverson	1956	Ben Levy	1994
S.F. Harris-Huemmert	1985	Drs Andrew and Rosamond Jackson		Dr James J.C. Lewis	1999
Giles Harrison	1993	(née Gilbert)	1980 and 1982	Mengxue Mia Li	2005
Mary Harrison		Professor Ashley Jackson	1992	S.D.R. Liddle	2005
(née Garnons Williams)	1989	Graham Jackson	1953	Michael Likierman	1960
Christopher Harrold	1944	Glen W. James	1970	Earl of Limerick	1981
John R.S. Hart	1950	Robin Gareth James	1975	Dr David Lindgren	1993
Emeritus Professor G.F. Hartford	1955	Shelina Janmohamed	1992	Michael D. Lindsay	2008
Roger Hartley	1966	Karl Jansen	1990	Philip Ling	1965
Rowan Harwood	1982	Christopher Jaques	1980	G. Linnell	1951
Andrew Hayward	1983	Peter Jefferies	1998	Peter J.N. Linthwaite	1975
Mr Philip A.R. Hayward	1992	Matthew Jenkinson		Lesley Little (née Neal)	1982
Matthew Heath	1983	Dr Michael Jewess	1966	John Littlewood	1956
Dr Peter Heath	1970	Robert Johnson	2004	Sir Michael Llewellyn-Smith	1958
Paula Maria Heister	2005	Stephen Johnson	1957	Jean Lodge	Emeritus Fellow
Lesley-Ann Hellig	1984	Barbara Johnston	2006	Anthony Loehnis	1956
Dr A.A. Helm (née Cooley)	1985	Claire Johnston	2008	Daniel Long	1991
A.G. Hemingway		Alastair Jollans	1971	Kathryn Long (née Talbot)	1980
Dr Frances M.S. Henderson	1987	Terry Jones	1979	William Lord	2003
S.G. Henry	2000	Richard Anthony Joseph	1966	Peter Lovegrove	1980
Jim Heppell	1971	Russell Julius	1978	His Hon. Judge Andrew Lowcock	
Dr Annabel C. Hesford	1983	Georgy Kantor	2006		1969
Julia Heslop		Tim Kaye	2004	Peter Lowndes	1946
(née Woodham-Smith)	1979	Elizabeth Kelly	1980	Sir David and Lady Lumsden	1959
Dr Michael Heuchemer	1998	Laurence Kelly FRGS FRSL	1952	Dr J.T. Lynch	1962
Bruce W. Hickey	1995	James Kennedy	2008	Patrick Macartney	1968
Michael Hignett	1961	Richard Kennedy	1992	Mr and Mrs J. Mackison	
Geoffrey Hillier	1959	Valerie Kenny		Stephen Macklow-Smith	1982
John G.R. Hindley	1959	Ben Kent	1984	Guy R. MacLean	1953
Sebastian Hirsz	2008	Damian Keogh	1991	J.J. MacNamara	1975
Charles Hoare	1994	Adrian Kerr	1985	Professor Richard Macve	1964
Christopher Hobart	1946	William T. Kerr	1963	John Madden	1967
John Hobbs	1952	Lauren Kickham	2009	Brian Mahoney	1956
Brent Hoberman	1988	B.C. Kilkenny	1946	Andrew J. Mainz	1968
R.T.A. Hohler	1954	Robert Kimberly	1968	Philip Malkin	1990
A.S. Holliday	1969	N.G.A. King	1975	Anthony J. Malpas	1957
Richard Holloway	1984	Wilfrid Knapp	1942	Peter Malpas	1948
Michael Hope	1948	Dr Derek J. Knight	1997	Andrew Maltby	1969
Emily Hopson-Hill	2001	J. Koolmann		Charles V. Mann MA MChir FRCS	
Paul Horner	1980	Henry L'Estrange	1989		1945
Richard Horton	1971	T.F. La Dell	1964	R. David Mann	1956
Adrian Houghton	1969	Roger M.U. Lambert	1977	James Manning	2009
N.R. (Bob) Howard	1949	C. Seth Landefeld	1976	Peter Mantle	1984
John Hoyle	1958	R.R. Langley	1959	Paul N. Marks	1944
Valerie P. Hoyle	1983	Nick Lanyon	1963	Barnaby Marsh DPhil	1999
Maxwell Hudson	1973	Sophie Lavender	2003	David Marshall	2004
Chris Hughes	1958	Mr J.A.H. Lawden	1974	Niels Peter Q. Marstrand	1987
R.A. Humphreys	1971	Jim Lawley	1976	Hugh Martin	1989
Roy F. Hunnisett	1949	Diana L.P. Layfield	1989	Uwe Maskos	1987
Nathaniel Hutner	1975	Ross Lee	1966	G.C.S. Mather	1973
Chris Iley	1979	Mike Leigh	1971	Howard S.G. Mather	1976
Norman Illingworth	1949	Mr E.G. Leonard	1958	J.E.F. Mawer	1947
Dr R.M. Ingram	1949	J.E. Lester	1994	John F.M. Maxwell	1961

Nicholas May	1973
Dr David Mayers, Emeritus Fellow, and Stella Mayers	
Morris McCain	1964
Gordon McCallum	1978
Brian McCarter	1981
Samantha McCollum	1996
Lowell Richard McComb	2001
Elizabeth McDonagh	2006
Andrew Michael McDonald	1999
Eric J. McFadden	1977
John F. McGilp	1969
Stephen J.J. McGlynn	2007
Iain McIntosh	1982
Christopher McKane	1965
J.M. McKean	1952
Neil Simon Peter McLarnon	1998
Andrew McLennan	2002
Jack Meadows	1954
Clifton Melvin	1973
Rupert Merson	1982
Mark Meynell	1989
Greg Michael	1986
Dr William Michael	1956
Chelsea Hermes Michele	
Mr Michael Michell	1980
Revd Dr Romilly Micklem	1979
Richard Middleton	1958
Nicholas Midgley	2001
Andrew Pickens Miller	1954
William H. Miller	1933
Stewart I. Millman	1967
Dolly Mirchandani	1992
Bob Mitchell	1977
Graham Mitchell	1959
Rachel Moles	2005
Dr Shane Monks	2001
Revd Canon B.G. Moore	1944
Terry Moran	1962
Mr Denis Morgan	1943
Roger Morgan	1961
Stephen Morgan	1975
Susanna Morgan	1994
Thomas O. Morris	1969
Christopher Jeremy Morse	1949
S.J. Mortin	1972
Kate Moss (née Muir)	1986
Joseph B. Mounsey	1967
John Mowbray QC	1949
Dr Vladislav V. Mudrych	1999
James Muir	1989
Richard Murray-Bruce	1993
D.G. Neill	1942
Carl Newton	1953
Ian Newton	1970
I.D. Nisbet	1976

Joe Nixon	2006
Alan Noble	1975
P.C.K. O'Ferrall	1954
Chris O'Leary	1981
James Onions	1966
A.C.L. Orme	1967
Geoffrey Orriss	1959
P.A. Osmond	1947
Jonathan G. Ouvry	1957
I.S. Ouwehand	2008
Oxfordshire Studies, Central Library, Oxford	
Dr Stephen Page	1983
Andrew M. Palmer	1972
Major Peter H. Parker	1936
Beresford N. Parlett	1951
James Parry-Crooke	2009
Sarah Passey	1981
Dr Keith Paterson	1965
Frank Pattison	1964
David Pearson	1968
Canon John G. Pedlar	1968
Philip Percival	1965
Robert Allen Perkins	1938
Rajan Phakey	1995
Oliver Phillips	
Terence Phipps	1969
Mrs Linda Pike	1992
Charlotte Pincher	2008
Nigel Pitchford	1987
John Platts	1949
Michael Pointon	1983
James L. Pope	1967
Beatrice Potter	
Sasha E. Powell	1989
Peter W. Price	1952
M. Priestley	1971
Michael Pugh	1958
Rupert D. Pullan	1978
David Puttock	1964
C.F. Pygall	1968
Dick Pyle	1962
Lord Quinton	1955
Robert W. Radtke	1987
Michael Ratcliffe	1971
Professor R.G. Ratcliffe	Fellow
Robin Raw	1957
Mr Richard Rawlence	1957
Elisabeth Rees	
Mrs Anita Rendel	
Dr Andrew Rhodes	1987
Revd G.S. Rhys	1980
Nigel Rich CBE	1964
William Richardson	1979
Dr Barrie Ricketson	1948
David H. Ridgeon	1972

Penny Ridley (née Barr)	1982
Professor Brian Rigby	1963
Gregory Roberts	1986
Terry James Roberts	2008
David Robertson	1993
R.E. Robinson	1946
Neil Cormack Robson	1956
Alexander George Roche	1951
Ivan Rockey	1993
Graham Rogers	1965
Thomas Rogers	2002
Kirsty Ross	2002
Peter Roth	1971
Matt Rowland-Jones	
G. Elyot Rowland	1942
John Rowland	1998
W.N.K. (Jim) Rowley	1943
Emily C. Rudgard	1989
Jeffrey B. Rudman	1970
Daniel John Ruiz	1987
Piers Russell-Cobb	1972
Richard Rutnagur	1983
Tommaso Di Ruzza	2002
James Sabben-Clare	1960
Brian R. Salter	1959
Christopher Saunders	1944
Dr C.G. Scales	1965
Claire Schaefer	2005
Canon J.L. Schaefer	1967
Stephen Schlich	1952
Deryck and Paddy Schreuder	1964
Andrew Schuller	1963
G.D. Scott-Kerr	1954
R.G. Searle-Barnes	1951
D.R.K. Seddon	1957
Mike Seigel	1969
Dr Kate Selway	1989
Vishnu V. Shankar	2006
S.W. Shaw	1971
John Sherlock	1973
Kevin Sherman	1972
Rab Shiell	1959
Cherish S. Shirley	2008
David Shirt	1967
Mr and Mrs Shum	1998
Dr John H.S. Sichel FRCP	
Simon Simpson	1985
Alasdair M. Sinclair	1956
D.D. Singh	1957
Nikki Singla	1995
Professor Peter Skegg	1971
Michael G. Skelton	1972
Sir Christopher Slade	1946
Jennifer Louise Small	2004
Ian Smart	1951
Andrew Smith	1989

Darren S. Smith	1989	Keith Thompson	1952	Philip Watson	1955
Professor G.S. Smith		Kelly Anne Thompson	1995	Matthew D.S. Webster	2001
Emeritus Fellow		Peter Titchmarsh	1948	Antonia Weetman (née Kellaway)	1990
Richard Smith	1961	Alan Tonkyn	1970	Richard Welch	
Fiona Smout	1985	Farouk K. Toukan	1960	Peter Wellings	1975
Geoff Smout	1984	John Tregellas	1982	Gordon C. Wells	1959
Liam Laurence Smyth	1974	Professor Roger Trigg	1960	Harry M. Werksman, Jr	1988
Helen Elizabeth Snapp	1983	M.A. Trowbridge	1954	Adam Harold Colin West	2007
Antony Snow	1954	Linsay Hannah Trueman		R.A.B. West	1952
Mark Snowden	1976	(née Watt)	1994	Derek and Pat Westcott	
Murray Somerville	1967	Dr Edmund B. Tucker	1946	Gordon Wetherell	1966
Beverley Southgate	1957	G.R.W. Turbutt	1948	Andrew Whiffin	1969
Peter J.M. Southwell	1961	Dr A.F. Turner	1980	Ian White-Thomson	1956
Toby J. Spanier	1993	Andrew Tusa	1984	Simon Whiteley	1969
Stewart Spencer	1969	Miss R.S. Tweddle	2005	Phil and Emma Whiting	
The Hon. Richard Stanley	1951	Professor Nasir Tyabji	1967	David Whitter	1954
Mr Andrew J.F. Stebbings	1970	John O. Udal JP	1948	David L. Wigley	1952
Mr Mark Steers	1978	Sir Brian Unwin	1955	Stuart Wild	1978
Professor J. Stein	1959	Sir William B. Utting	1951	S.K. Wilkinson	1982
Hannah Steiner	2006	John Uttley	1964	Mr C.D.P. Williams	1959
Peter Stevens	1956	Toby Vacher	2007	Charles Williams	1981
Colin Stevenson	1981	Marcus R. Vale	1979	David M. Williams	2006
David J. Stevenson		Francois van der Spuy	1997	Donovan and Eunice Williams	
Nicolette Stickland	2008	Richard Varey	1966	and family	1959
S. Adfeldt Still	1996	Dr A.J. Varney	1985	Nigel Gavin Williams	1987
Dr Robin Stinchcombe		Mrs S. Varney (née Fowler)	1986	Dr Richard G. Williams	1964
Emeritus Fellow		Herbert Vaughan		Travis D. Williams	1996
Sandy Stirling	1948	Tim Vaughan	1978	Jan Willisch DPhil (Oxon)	1978
Adrian Stokes	1948	Michelle Anne Vickers	2006	Donald Wilson	1982
John Stone	1951	Catherine Vickery	1994	Graeme Wilson	1946
Jonathan Storey	2002	Rajesh Vidyasagar	1970	Michael J. Wilson	1953
Geoffrey Summerfield	1966	Ruxton Villet	1965	A.J.H. (John) Winder	1940
Jeremy Summerly	1979	Charles Villiers	1959	Professor Werner Wolf	1948
Wilson A. Sutherland	1967	P.J.C. Vincent	1951	Michael Wong	2008
T.M. de Swiet	1988	Tony Vincent	1955	R.P.H. Woods	1968
Jonathan Swift	1984	Sir Anthony Vineall	1952	Sir Marcus Worsley Bt	1947
Steven Swindells	1986	Jonathan Virden	1957	C.C. Wright	1958
Andrew Symes	2008	James Adam Mark		David J. Wright	1959
Nick Szczepanik	1972	von Moltke	1988	Norine Wright	
Jessica Tait	2008	Dr G. Walford		Robert Lionel Willis Wright	
Robert E. Tang	1971	Leslie Walford	1945	Laura Wu	2003
Norman Taralrud-Bay	1968	Mrs Daphne Wallace		Sarah Wyatt	1982
L.C. (Kim) Taylor	1946	Phil Wallace	1968	Mrs Mary Yeadon	
Olivia Tebbutt	1999	Phillip Ward-Green	1954	Corinne Yee	1987
Romain Thill		R.J.O. Ward	1949	Dr J.A. Yeoman	1999
Benjamin Thomas	2003	Dr Allen Warren	1964	John Young	1949
Caroline Thomas	Fellow	Mrs Isabel Wartho		Miles Young	1973
Mark Thomas	2000	(née Rawlence)	1987	Richard Young	1967
Andy Thompson	2002	Gordon Wasserman	1959-61;	Robin Zebaida	1982
Bruce Thompson	1979	Research Fellow 1964-7		Robert M. Zelenka	1974
Isabel Thompson		Chris Watson	1976		
(née de May)	1988	Hugh Watson			

INDEX OF NAMES

Italics denotes picture or image
Bold denotes contributor

Abbot, Charles 68
Aeschylus 123
Alcibiades 122
Allen, Sir Hugh 77, 78, 79, 81,
    116, 118, 120
Allnatt, Alfred 63
Amis, Martin 184
Andrews, H.K. ('HKA') 78, 79,
    80, 81
Anne, Queen 161
Anselm, Archbishop 90
Archer, Jeffrey 185
Ardizzone, Edward 138
Aristophanes 122
Aristotle 148
Armstrong Taylor, Tim 79
Arnold, Dr 109
Astor, J.J. *111*
Astor, John Jacob 110
Attlee, Clement 168, 173, 178
Aubrey, John 62, 154–5
Auden W.H. 183
Austen, Jane 163
Austin, David 85
Aycliffe, John 73, 179
Ayer, A.J. 68, *68*, 71
Ayres, Ralph 141
Ayrton, Michael 95, 96

Bach, J.S. 78, 80
Bachardy, Don 68
Baker, Ernest 116, 117, 188

Baker, John 92
Balfour, A.J. 170
Bandinel, Bulkeley 68
Bantock, Gavin 185
Bardsley, Cuthbert 165
Baring, Evelyn (later Lord Howick
    of Glendale) 171, 172
Barnard, Richard 92
Barton, Anne *51*, 53
Bassano 173
Bastard, Thomas 154, 155, 176,
    178
Bayly, Clifford 14
Baynes, Colin 79
Beales, Peter 83
Beaton, Cecil 73
Beckington, Thomas 36, 167, 176
Beckley, Serjeant 115
Beerbohm, Max 94, 169
Beeston, Henry 189
Bell, Harry (H.E.) 53, 106, 124,
    138
Bell, K.N. Rev. 107
Bell, Steve 94
Benn, Tony 175
Bennett, G.V. 63, 138
Berlin, Isaiah 20, 71, *71*, 151
Berenson, Bernard 135
Bevin, Ernest 174
Bigg, Henry 189
Bilson, Thomas 61–2, *160*, 161
Birkbeck 171
Birley, Oswald 164
Blair, A. 170
Blandy, William 65

Blockley, Rev. 80
Bodley, Sir Thomas 102, 178
Bohun, Ralph 67
Bonaparte, Napoleon 71, 97
Boniface IX, Pope 36
Booth, Frank 119
Bourget, Paul 116
Bourne, Gilbert, Professor 18, 111
Bourne, Robert 111
Bower, Sir John Dykes 78
Bowke, John 189
Bowra, Maurice 136, 150
Boyce, William 77
Boyle, Robert 66, 67, 103
Bradley, James 67
Bradley, Savile 155
Braithwaite, Thomas 45, 189
Bratby, John 95
Briggs, Asa 124
Browne, William 92
Brydges, James 166
Budd, William 130
Bullock, Alan 71, 106, 124, *125*
Burden, Michael **10–18**, 78, **94–7,**
    140–44
Burdon-Miller, Rowland 20
Burger, F.W., Dr 96, 97
Butcher, Keith **117**
Button, Sir John 92
Button, Sir William (of Alton
    Priors) 92
Button, Sir William 92
Buxton, John 20, 82, 138, 139
Byrd, William 14, 18, 44, 78, 80

Calvin, Jean 42, 66
Carrick, Serjeant 115
Casear, Julius 84, 89
Casson, Stanley 118
Cawarden, Sir Thomas 179
Cecil, Lord David 73, 120, 121,
    122, 151
Champneys, Basil 10, 13
Chapman, John 15
Charles I, King 114
Charles II, King 106, 161, 162
Charles, Duke of Burgundy 159
Charlett, Arthur 155, 156
Chaucer, Geoffrey 67, 102
Chaundler, Thomas 33, 36, 54,
    130, 135, 167, 176, 189
Chichele, Henry 36, 163, 167,
    167, 176, *177*
Churchill, Winston 169, 172
Clark, Cosmo 172
Cobb, John 189
Cole, Henry 133, 189
Collingridge, James 92
Colquhoun, Robert 96
Commandinus 74
Compton Miller, Richard 97, 136
Compton Miller, Sir John 97
Conrad, Joseph 181
Cook, Warden 83
Cooke Wilson, John 68
Cooke, Arthur 47, 135, 189
Cooper, Duff 172, *173*
Corby, Robert 92
Coryate, George 176
Cowley, Abraham 179

Cox, Sir Christopher 71, 107, 150–1, *150*, 156, 157, *157*, 171
Coxed, John 189
Cranley, Thomas 35, 130, 176, 189
Cranmer, Thomas, Archbishop 39
Crick, Michael 185
Cripps, Stafford 173
Croft, William 77
Cromer, Lord 171
Cromwell, Thomas 39, 102, 160
Crossman, Richard 71, 112, 149, 150, 173, 174, *174*, 175, 182
Culpepper, Martin 99, 133, 154, 189
Curtis, Lionel 169, 170
Cusk, Rachel 184
Cutbrush, Harold 80

Darrell, Thomas 65
David, Jacques-Louis 97
Dawkins, Richard 165
de Bése, Théodore 66
de Gaulle, General 171
de Sainte Croix, Geoffrey 83
Delamotte, William 143
Dobson, John 189
Donne, John 176, 179
Dorman, Thomas 65
Dove, John 169
du Bartasm G. 104
du Boulay, Sir Roger **120–23**
Durbin, Evan 149, 173, 174
Dymock, Abraham 92
Dymock, Joseph 92

Eccles, David 174
Edington, William 26
Edis, Olive 181
Edward II, King 26
Edward IV, King 33
Edward VI, King 39, 40, 41, 61
Egerton, John 105
Elgar, Edward 80
Elizabeth I, Queen 40, 41, 161
Elvey, Stephen 77
Epstein, Jacob 63, 94, 134
Escourt, William 189
Esdale, Captain *116*
Essex, R. 28
Evans, Powys 150
Evelyn, family 67
Eyre, Edward John 92

Fairfax, Thomas 43
Farley, John 36, 64, 65
Fawkes, Guy 152
Feetham, Rochard 169
Ferguson, Alex 185
Field, Head Butler 141
Fielding Dodd, R. 10, 19
Fiennes, Celia 105
Fiennes, family 41
Filmer, Edward 73
Firth, C.H. 106
Fischer, Bram 149
Fisher, family *132*
Fisher, Herbert (H.A.L.) 11, *48*, 54, 70, 71, 93, 118, 121, 135, 136, 146, 149, *150*, 151, 169, 170, *171*, 172, 173, 174, 181, 189
Fisher, John 152, 160
Fisher, Mary *132*
Fisher, Mrs 79, 121, 157
Flatman, Thomas, 178, 179
Forres, S.W. 97
Fowler, John 40
Foxe, John 131
Freeth, H.R. 168
Frogley, Richard 14
Froissart, Jean 26
Fuller, John 185

G.E.D. 133, 148
Gaitskell, Hugh 149, 173, 174, *175*
Galsworthy, John 181, *181*
Gardiner, Stephen 40
Gauntlett. Samuel 91, 99, 189
Gear, William 95
George, Hereford Brooke 48, 49, 68, 74, 105, 146, 148, *148*
Gibb, H.J. Laurie 118
Gibbons, Orlando 80
Gibson, William 182, 183
Gill, Eric 116, 118
Gillray, James 94, 96, 97
Gladstone, William 147, 148
Gore-Brown, Robert 116
Gormley, Anthony 95
Gorrod, David 87
Gotch, Bernard 18
Gower, John 179
Greco, El 63, 94
Green, Maurice 77

Green, Samuel 16
Greenbury, Richard 62, 94
Greenhurst, Ralph 36, 167
Greening, Dick 81
Grenville, Lord 96
Grey, Lord 164
Griffin, Jonathon 185
Griffiths, James 144
Grigg, Edward, 1st Baron Altrincham 171, 173
Grocyn, William 36, 64
Groser, Michael 14
Gross, Mr 105
Gwynn, Nell 162

Haakon of Norway, King 81
Haldane, John Burdon Sanderson 68, 149, *149*
Haldane, John Scott 68, *68*, 149
Halley, Edmond 67
Hamilton Mortimer, John 77
Hamilton, Richard 94, 175
Hampshire, Stuart 71
Handel, Frederick 74, 77, 80
Hankford, Richard 37, 114
Hardiman, Marius 89
Harding, Thomas 39, 40, 65
Hardy, G.H. 68, *68*, 149
Hare, Augustus 45, 146
Hare, Cyril 184
Harman, John 66
Harmar, John (nephew) 66
Harpsfield, John 39, 65
Harpsfield, Nicholas 39, 65
Harris, Sir William 78
Harris, Waler 67
Hart, Herbert (H.L.A.) 70, *70*, 71, 175
Hatton, Christopher 41
Haydocke, Richard 153, 155, 176, 178
Hayes, Philip 77, *77*
Hayter, Iris 136
Hayter, Sir William 135, 136–9, *137*, 166, 171, 172, 189
Hayward, Thomas 92, 189
Heath, John 178
Heathcote, Gilbert 77
Heete, Robert 64
Henry VI, King 36, 37, 167
Henry VII, King 159, 160, 167
Henry VIII, King 38, 39, 65, 131, 160, 167

Hepworth, Barbara 95
Herbert, A.P. 172, *172*
Herbert, Edward 179
Herland, Hugh 10, 34, 144
Herodotus 122, 123
Heron, Bill 82
Heseltine, Michael 185
Hide, Thomas 65
Higginbottom, Edward **76–81**
Hill, Walter 35, 93, 189
Hilton, Lisa 185
Hirst, Damien 95
Hitchins, Lionel 169
Hitler, Adolf 71, 80, 106
Hoare, Sam *111*, 172, *173*
Hobbes, Mr H.T. 66
Hockney, David 96
Hodges, William *143*, 144
Holcombe, Garan 184
Holes, Andrew 167
Holland, Henry, 3rd Baron 164
Holloway, John 185
Homer 116
Hooke, Robert 103
Hopkins, Thomas 152
Horman, William 64
Horton, Percy 106
Hoskins, John 154, 155, 176, 178
Howard, Michael 185
Howell, Henry 103
Howley, William 163
Huddesford, George 149, *179*
Hughes, Thomas 108
Humfrey, duke of Gloucester 64, 114
Humphrey, Hannah 96, 97
Humphrey, William 97
Hutton, John 179
Huxley, Julian 149

Ironside, C.C. 151

James I, King 155
James II, King 106, 162
James, Thomas 65, 102, 168
Jardine, Douglas 111
Jay, Douglas 149, 173, 174
Jennings, James 92
Johnson, Cornelius 180
Johnston, Brian 182
Jonson, Ben 179
Joseph, Horace W.B. 71, *74*, 117, 120, 150

Jowitt, William 168, *168*

Kapoor, Annish 96
Kelly, Rod 50
Ken, Thomas 161, *161*, 162, 166
Keynes, J.M. 151
Khrushchev, Nikita 171
Kingsley, Charles 108
Kingsmill, John 36, 167
Kipling, Rudyard 170
Knowles, Kenneth 74, 106
Knyght, John 99
Kundera, Milan 185

'le Longe', John (father of William of Wykeham) 26
'le Longe', Sybil (mother of William of Wykeham) 26
L.L. 143, 144
Lake, Arthur 62, *62*, 66, 73, 74, 104, 133, 134, 135, 189
Lamb, William 181
Lamb, Willis 70
Landseer, Edwin 94, 163
Lane Fox, Robin **82–90**, 185
Laski, Harold 173
Laud, William, Archbishop 4265, 133
Lawrence, D.H. 181
Lee, Hermione 185
Lewis, C.S. 104
Lewis, Wyndham 95, 96
Lightfood, Robert Henry, Rev. Dr 62, 80, 122, 182
Lloyd George 169, 172
Lloyd, Bishop 13
Lloyd, James 51
Loggan, David 13, 17, 42, 108, 143
Lomazzo, Gian Paulo 178
London, John 30, 37, 38, 39, 130–1, 133, 152, 189
Lord Montague of Beaulieu 183
Louch, John 141
Lowth, Robert 67, 68, *69*, 162, 163, 176
Lucar, Cyprian 66
Lumsden, David 78
Lydiat, Thomas 66

Machiavelli, Niccolo 134
Macmillan, Harold 139
Macmillan, Joshua 139

Malchair, William 131
Malford, Richard 189
Malke, Anthony 92
Malton, Thomas 16
Manningham, Thomas 161, 162
Marc 94
Marechera, Damdubzo 183, *183*
Maredzenge, Victor 183
Margaret of York 159
Margoliouth, David 70
Margoliouth, Moses 70
Marriott, Jim 89
Marriott, Sir John Arthur Ransome 70
Marshall, George 43, 128, 189
Martiall, John 65
Martin, Thomas 176
Mary I, Queen 39, 40, 61, 65, 161, 162, 179
Mason, Richard 184, *185*
Master, Thomas 178
Matthewson, Percy 116
Matthison, William 86
Maud, John (later Lord Radcliffe-Maud) 112, 171, 172
Mayhew, Richard 38, 159
McFarlane, Bruce 27
McGregor, Harvey 135, 189
Mendelson, Charlotte 185
Mendelssohn, Felix 80
Milner, Alfred, Viscount 100, 115, 169, *169*, 170, 172
Molson, Hugh 174
Montagna, Bartolomeo 151
Moore, Henry 96
Morant, Robert 170, 171
More, Thomas 103
Morris, Willie 183
Moyle, John, Dr 18
Murray, Gilbert 149, 181
Murray, Len 175
Musgrave, William 67
Myres, Sir John 120, 121, *121*, 122

Nash, John 84
Nash, Joseph 15
Neal, Thomas 65
New, Hort 17, 129
Newton, Isaac 103
Nicholas, John 18, 189
Nichols, Patteson 110
Nicholson, William 103, 128, 171
Noakes, Michael 150

Norridge, Zoë **182–5**
Nowell, Robert 161

Ogg, David 71, 106, *106*, 124
Oglander, Jane Mary 131
Oglander, John 131, *131*, 189
Oglander, William 134
Oldrid Scott, John 13
Ossulbury, Nicholas 189
Owen, John 176

Pace, G.G. 78
Packett, William 35
Pakenham, Frank 149, 173, 174
Palestrina 80, 81
Palmer, Edwin 147
Parkin, David 94
Parrott, David **38–45, 158–65**
Parry, C.H.H. 80
Passmore, Victor 96
Paulet, Lady Elizabeth 178
Payne, John 98, 99
Pearson, Ada Nemesis 181
Penn Warren, Robert 149
Percival, John 152
Pericles 122
Phillips, Thomas 45
Phillips, Tom 125
Philpot, John 65
Pilbrow, Giles
Pincke, Robert *41*, 42, 43, 93, 94, 114, 128, 133, 134, 189
Pine, Robert Edge 68
Piper, John 96
Pittis, William 67
Plato 123, 150
Platts, John **79–81**
Plautus 180
Pole, Reginald, Cardinal 103
Poole, William **60–3, 64–71, 72–5, 102–3, 128–39, 152–7, 176–80**
Pope, Alexander 179
Popper, Karl 150
Porter, William 189
Poyntz, Robert 65
Price, Curtis 135, *135*, 189
Price, H. 71
Prideaux, Vice-Chancellor 114
Proctor, Patrick 95
Ptolomey 65
Purcell, Henry 77, 80
Purnell, John 45, 189

Quinbey, John 37, 131

Radcliffe, George 151, *151*
Raine, Craig 185
Rainham, Lady Townshend of 104
Rait, R. 165
Ramanujan, Srinivasa 68
Randall, Richard 92
Rashdall, Hastings 49, 62, 70, 146, *148*, *164*, 165
Rastall, John 65
Rede, John 189
Rees, Goronwy 111
Reilly, Patrick 171, 172
Reinolds, John 178
Reynolds, Joshua 179
Richard II, King 28, 100
Richard III, King 38, 159, 167
Richardson, Sir Albert 19, 20
Richmond, William 146
Robbins, John 87
Robbins, Lionel 149, 174, 175
Roberts, Clarrie 80
Roberts, David 18, 49
Robinson, Alfred 48, 74, 105, 109, 146, 147, *147*, 148, 150
Robinson, Arthur 13
Robinson, George 110
Robinson, Thomas 13, 14
Rolfe, David 87
Rolles Driver, Samuel 70
Romney, George 94, 131
Roper, Paul 89
Rose 141
Rose, Kenneth 87
Rose, Saul 85, 89
Rotherham, Thomas 159
Round, J.H. 104
Russ, Charles Rupert 95
Russ, Mrs 95
Russ, Sydney, Dr 95
Russell, John 37, 38, 54, 158, 159, 167
Rutherson, Albert 121
Ryan, Alan **46–53**, 99, 135, **146–51**, 156, 189
Ryves, Bruno 133
Ryves, George 133, 189
Ryves, John 133
Ryves, William 129

Sackville West, Vita 85

Sackville West, Vita 85
Salisbury, Lord 170
Saunders, Nicholas 40, 65
Saye and Sele, Lord 42
Sayers, Dorothy 17
Schoen, Ervine 89, 141
Schwabe, Randolph 11
Schweitzer, Albert 78
Scott, Sir George Gilbert 12, 13, 15, 17, 48, 62
Scotus, Duns 103
Sewell, James (J.E.) 13, 99, 110, 115, 128, *133*, 134, 135, 189
Shakespeare, William 103, 116
Sharrock, Robert 67
Sheppard, John 76
Shuttleworth, Philip 45, *45*, 68, 74, 105, 134, 189
Sibelius, Jean 78
Simonds, Gavin 168, *168*, 169
Singer Sargent, John 77
Skelton, Kevin *79*
Skinner, Ralph 39, 40, 189
Smart, Christopher 67
Smith, Alic (A.H.) 19–21, 42, 55, 79, 118, 119, 120, *120*, 121, 124, 134, *134*, 135, 136, 141, 174, 189
Smith, Geoffrey 149
Smith, Lionel Abel 116
Smith, Miles 160
Smith, Sydney 100, 156, *163*, 164, 165
Smith, William 68
Snow, Sasha 79
Sparrow, John 112, 175
Spence, Joseph 179
Spooner, William (W.A.) *46*, 48, 99, 116, 117, 122, 133, 135, 146, 148, 149, *152*, *155*, 156, 184, 189
Spradbery, Walter 116
Spy 94
Stanbridge, John 64
Stanford C.V. 80, 81
Stapleton, Thomas 40, 65
Steer, Francis 100
Steptoe, John 87
Stokowski, Leopold 78
Streaks, Cuthbert 144
Stringer, Robert 43
Strong, Samson 28
Sturgeon, Richard 167

Sutherland, Dame Lucy 53
Sydney, Sir Philip 178

Talbot, Robert 65
Taverner, John 76
Taylor, A.J.P. 124
Taylor, John 166
Temple, Lord 96
Tennel, David 133
Themistocles 122
Thirlwell, Adam 185
Thomas, Dean Merlin 136, 185
Thomas, Rachel 63
Thompson, Bob 82
Thorne, William 66
Thorp, Jennifer **90–93**, **98–101**, **114–19**
Thucidydes 123
Thurban, Robert 55
Tilney, Henry 163
Tonworth, Richard 35
Topolski, Dan 113
Townesend, William 18
Townshend, Robert 104
Traffles, Richard 189
Trapier, William 154, 146
Trevor-Roper, Hugh 135
Trimnel, Charles 45
Turges, Edward 76
Turner, Francis 67
Turner, J.M.W. 15
Turner, William 83
Twisse, William 65, 66
Tyerman, Christopher **26–8**, **30–7**, **108–13**, **117**, **116–75**, **181**, **188**

Upton, Nicholas 37, 64, 114
Urquhart, F.F. 157

Van Oss, Tom 68
Vaughan, Keith 96
Vickers, Butler 141
Virgil 103, 116
Von Herkomer, Hubert 94, 147
von Sell, Freiherr Wilhelm 117
von Speyer, Erwin Beit 117

Walker, John 68
Wallis, John, Rev. 67, 73, 74, 99
Walter, John 64
Warcop, Ralph 178
Ward, Leslie 133

Wardle, Peter 70
Warham, William 15, 36, 38, 39, 38, 158, 159, *159*, 160, 163, 167
Warner, John 92
Watson, Sydney, Dr 78, 79, 81
Waynflete, William 38, 159, 176, *177*
Weelkes, Thomas 77
Weldon, John 77
Wesleys, the 80
Weston, Garry 18
Weston, Robert 92
Whitaker, Serjeant 115
White, John 161
White, Richard 65
Whyte, Thomas 40, 152, 189
Wickham, Edward (E.C.) 48, 74, 105, 146, *146*, 147, 148
Wilberforce, Richard 175
Willes, Richard 65
William III (of Orange), King 161, 162
Williams, David 74, 189
Williams, Martin 55, *55*
Williams, Penry **19–21**, **104–7**, **134**, 138
Williams, Ralph Vaughan 78, 81
Williams, William 83
Wilson, Harold 174
Wilson, Herbert 110
Wodehouse, P.G. 134
Wolf, Naomi 184
Wolsey, Cardinal Thomas 38, 160
Wood 80, 81
Wood, Anthony 64, 66, 114, 154, 155, 178
Woodcock, George 175
Woodforde, James 74, 75, 100, 105, *105*, 108, 113, 158, *162*, 163, 164
Woodforde, Samuel 162
Woodward, Michael *43*, 44, 91, 99, 103, 130, 134, 189
Woolf, Virginia 85
Worcester, bishop of 42
Worsley, Sir Marcus **124**
Worthington, Sir Hubert 17, 19, 118
Wotton, Sir Henry 176
Wyatt, Samuel 15, 16, 17, 77
Wyclif, John *27*
Wykeham, Nicholas 30, 35, 130,

189
Wykeham, William of 10, 17, 26, 27, 28, *29*, 30, 33, 34, 35, 36, 37, 41, 60, 63, 64, 65, 72, 74, 76, 79, 90, 102, 103, 104, 128, 129, 130, 158, 167, 176, *177*
Wynford, William 10, 13, 33, 34

Yevele, Henry 10
Yorke, Eric (E.C.) *106*, 107, 151
Young, John 100, 189
Younger, Kenneth 174, *174*

Zouche, Richard 66, 180, *180*
zu Waldeck-Pyrmont, Prince Wolrad-Friedrich 117

ILLUSTRATION ACKNOWLEDGEMENTS

While every effort has been made to locate holders of copyright material used in this book, further claimants should get in touch with the publishers as soon as possible.

The captions for the illustrations were written by Michael Burden.

GENERAL ACKNOWLEDGEMENTS
Roger Ainsworth, Kathleen Anderson, Martin Brayne, Eric Christiansen, Kirsty Clarke, Maggie Davies, Colin Dunn, Suzanne Foster, Adrian Gibbs, Robin Ilbert, Richard Mason, Victor Mavedzenge, Jeremy Moran, Jennifer Thorp, Selwyn Tillett, Naomi Van Loo, Martin Williams, Penry Williams.

PHOTOGRAPHS
Most of the photography in this book is the work of Jeremy Moran, with extra photography by Roy Fox and Colin Dunn. All images, apart from those listed below, are reproduced with the permission of, and are copyright to, the Warden and Scholars of New College, Oxford, and the Bridgeman Art Library. The following images or objects appear in alphabetical order and also have copyright interest as follows: **(34, 50, 113, lower, 115, upper)** Julian Andrews; **(138)** Edward Ardizzone; **(95, lower)** Michael Ayrton; **(68, far right)** Don Bachardy; **(14)** Clifford Bayly; **(73)** Cecil Beaton; **(172)** Cosmo Clark; **(10)** R. Fielding Dodd; **(94, 135)** Jacob Epstein; **(168)** H.R. Freeth; **(120)** Gillmans; **(175)** Richard Hamilton; **(106, left)** Percy Horton; **(151)** C.C. Ironside; **(2, 7, 12, 186)** Cambridge Jones; **(50)** Rod Kelly; **(106, right)** Kenneth Knowles; **(51)** James Lloyd; **(150)** Michael Noakes; **(137)** *Oxford Mail and Times*; **(142, lower)** Giles Pilbrow; **(121)** Albert Rutherston; **(11)** Randolph Schwarbe; **(70)** Peter Wardle.

The following images are copyright as follows: **(145)** English Heritage, NMR; **(183)** Victor Mavedzenge; **(185)** Benjamin Morse; **(173, 180)** The National Portrait Gallery, London; **(79)** New Chamber Opera, and Sasha Snow; **(125)** Tom Phillips, and the Master and Fellows of St Catherine's College, Oxford; **(162)** The Rector and Parochial Church Council, All Saints Church, Weston Longville, and Martin Brayne; **(16)** Tate Britain; **(160)** The Warden and Fellows of Winchester College.

INVENTORY, LIBRARY AND ARCHIVE REFERENCES FOR NEW COLLEGE ITEMS
(Endpapers) NCI 99; **(4)** NCI 4199; **(5, and after)** NCI 605; **(10)** NCA PA/SMA 10/4; **(11)** NCI 101; **(12, lower)** NCA 5601/1; **(14)** NCI 1850; **(15, upper)** NCI 103; **(15, lower)** NCA 14951/5; **(16, upper)** NCI 1179; **(17)** NCA 10271; **(18)** NCI 98; **(20)** NCA PA/SMA addl 3; **(21)** NCA PA/SMA addl 1; **(26)** NCI 1753; **(27, left)** NCI 2748; **(27, right)** NCI 1752; **(28)** NCI 114; **(29)** NCI 446; **(30)** NCI 1738; **(31)** NCA 9431 f. 1ʳ; **(32)** NCL MSS 288 f. 4ʳ; **(33)** NCI 1732; **(34, upper)** NCA LIB/J 24; **(35)** NCI 1571; **(36)** NCA 9839; **(37)** NCI 1743; **(38)** NCI 1755; **(39)** NCI 1741; **(41)** NCI 631; **(42)** NCA PPP2; **(43)** NCI 1457; **(44)** NCA 1171; **(45)** NCI 521; **(46)** NCA SCR/A3; **(47)** NCA SCR/A3; **(48)** NCA JCR/L1/2, p. 20; **(49)** NCA LIB/J 28/6; **(50)** NCI 111; **(51)** NCI 1229; **(60)** NCI 1745; **(61)** NCI 3123; **(62)** NCI 219; **(63)** NCI 2751; **(64)** NCL MS 281, f.49ᵛ; **(65)** NCL MS27, f.140ʳ; **(66, left)** NCL BT3.170A 6; **(66, right)** NCL BT3.240.14 (1); **(68, left)** NCA 14543; **(68, centre)** NCA SCR/A4; **(68, right)** NCI 71; **(69)** NCI 217; **(69, inset)** NCL BT3.281.1-2; **(70, upper)** NCI 69; **(70, lower)** NCI 770; **(71, upper)** NCL NC/FIS v.3; **(71, lower)** NCA PA/COX 8/3; **(72)** NCI 1548; **(73)** NCI 1220; **(74)** NCI 456; **(76)** NCL MSS 368/1/38; **(77, left)** NCI 634; **(77, right)** NCI 74; **(78)** NCL MS Organ Book, verso end, pp.68-69; **(83, upper)** NCA 14433; **(83, lower)** NCI 469; **(84)** NCI 3960; **(85)** NCI 279; **(86)** NCI 2956; **(90)** NCA 13152; **(91, left)** NCA 1822; **(91, right)** NCA 2434; **(92)** NCA 5641; **(93)** NCA 5617; **(94)** NCI 1469; **(95, upper)** NCI 1002; **(95, lower)** NCI 3908; **(96)** NCI 2482; **(97)** NCI 3253; **(99)** NCA 11402/1; **(100, left)** NCA 5361; **(100, right)** NCA 9747, p. 195; **(101, upper)** NCA JCR/R/Mallett; JCR/K3/7,8; **(101, lower)** NCA JCR/L2/5; **(102)** NCA 14607/6; **(103)** NCL MS 369, f.29ʳ; **(105, upper left)** NCA 9506; **(105, upper right)** NCA 9574/4; **(105, lower)** NCI 105; **(106, left)** NCI 65; **(106, right)** NCI 462; **(107)** NCA PA/COX 3/1; **(108, detail)** NCI 97; **(110)** NCA JCR/P5/10, f. 2; **(110, inset)** NCI 3651; **(111, top)** NCA JCR/R/Congleton, p. 34; **(111, inset)** NCA JCR/R/Loraine, p. 5; **(111, lower)** NCA JCR/R/Congleton, p. 9; **(112, upper)** NCA JCR/L2/11; **(112, lower left)** NCA JCR/R/Parker, p. 38; **(112, lower right)** NCI 774; **(113, upper)** NCA JCR/R/Parker, p. 34; **(114)** NCI 280; **(115, upper)** NCI 1318; **(115, lower)** NCA 11403/1; **(116, upper)** NCI 1225; **(116, centre)** NCA 11716; **(116, lower)** NCI 1975; **(117)** NCI 1456; **(118)** NCI 2344; **(119)** NCA 9216; **(120)** NCA JCR/L1/4; **(121)** NCI 247; **(122)** NCA JCR/E27; **(123)** NCA LIB/J6; **(128)** NCI 3036; **(129, left)** NCA 10271; **(129, right)** NCI 632; **(130)** NCI 1856; **(131, upper)** NCI 409; **(131, lower)** NCI 952; **(133, left)** NCI 102; **(133, right)** NCI 3127; **(134)** NCI 213; **(137)** NCA PA/HAY 7/1; **(138)** NCI 2959; **(140)** NCI 3110; **(141, upper)** NCI 3539; **(141, lower)** NCA 962; **(142, upper)** NCA 3584 f. 11ᵛ; **(142, lower)** NCI 3590; **(143, left)** NCI 494; **(143, right)** NCI 645; **(144)** NCA DB/R/Streaks; **(146)** NCI 2; **(147)** NCI 349; **(148, left)** NCA 11716, p. 16; **(148, right)** NCI 3136; **(149)** NCA JCR/P5/5, f. 21; **(150, left)** NCI 68; **(150, right)** NCI 1599; **(151)** NCI 454; **(152)** NCI 1485; **(153)** NCI 95; **(154, upper)** NCI 1949; **(154, lower)** NCI 778; **(155)** NCA 11755; **(156-57)** NCA PA/COX 8/3; **(157)** NCA PA/COX 8/3; **(158)** NCI 1747; **(159)** NCI 303; **(161)** NCI 216; **(163)** NCI 1216; **(164)** NCI 2755; **(166)** NCI 215; **(168, upper)** NCI 873; **(168, lower)** NCA JCR/R/Loraine, p. 22; **(169, lower)** NCI 327; **(170)** NCA Milner addl; **(171)** NCI 2933; **(172)** NCI 1060; **(173, upper)** NCA JCR/R/Loraine, p. 36; **(174, upper)** NCA JCR/L1/2, p.36; **(174, lower)** NCA JCR/L1/2, p.36; **(175)** NCI 1221; **(177)** NCL BT1 .132.17; **(178, left)** NCI 62; **(178, right)** NCI 3029; **(179)** NCI 1223; **(180, right)** NCA 14999; **(181)** NCA PA/GAL 1; **(182)** NCL NC/MON; **(188)** NCI 2938; **(Back jacket):** NCI 97. **(Back jacket, inset):** NCI 1751.